EUROPE AND RUSSIA

Prentice Hall

Needham, Massachusetts
Upper Saddle River, New Jersey
Glenview, Illinois

Program Consultants

Heidi Hayes Jacobs

Heidi Hayes Jacobs has served as an educational consultant to more than 1,000 schools across the nation and abroad. Dr. Jacobs served as an adjunct professor in the Department of Curriculum on Teaching at Teachers College, Columbia University. She has written a best-selling book and numerous articles on curriculum reform. She completed her undergraduate studies at the University of Utah in her hometown of Salt Lake City. She received an M.A. from the University of Massachusetts, Amherst, and completed her doctoral work at Columbia University's Teachers College in 1981.

The backbone of Dr. Jacobs' experience comes from her years as a teacher of high school, middle school, and elementary school students. As an educational consultant, she works with K–12 schools and districts on curriculum reform and strategic planning.

Brenda Randolph

Brenda Randolph is the former Director of the Outreach Resource Center at the African Studies Program at Howard University, Washington, D.C. She is the Founder and Director of Africa Access, a bibliographic service on Africa for schools. She received her B.A. in history with high honors from North Carolina Central University, Durham, and her M.A. in African studies with honors from Howard University. She completed further graduate studies at the University of Maryland, College Park, where she was awarded a Graduate Fellowship.

Brenda Randolph has published numerous articles in professional journals and bulletins. She currently serves as library media specialist in Montgomery County Public Schools, Maryland.

Michal L. LeVasseur

Michal LeVasseur is an educational consultant in the field of geography. She is an adjunct professor of geography at the University of Alabama, Birmingham, and serves with the Alabama Geographic Alliance. Her undergraduate and graduate work is in the fields of anthropology (B.A.), geography (M.A.), and science education (Ph.D.).

Dr. LeVasseur's specialization has moved increasingly into the area of geography education. In 1996, she served as Director of the National Geographic Society's Summer Geography Workshop. As an educational consultant, she has worked with the National Geographic Society as well as with schools to develop programs and curricula for geography.

Special Program Consultant
Yvonne S. Gentzler, Ph.D.
Iowa State University
College of Family and Consumer Sciences
Ames, Iowa

Content Consultant on Russia, Eastern Europe, Central Asia
Janet Vaillant
Davis Center for Russian Studies
Harvard University
Cambridge, Massachusetts

Content Consultant on Western Europe
Ruth Mitchell-Pitts
Center for West European Studies
University of North Carolina
Chapel Hill, North Carolina

ISBN 0-13-062981-2

1 2 3 4 5 6 7 8 9 10   06 05 04 03 02

On the Cover
❶ Three Russian babushka nesting dolls

❷ Miniature wooden shoes from the Netherlands

❸ Model of an English double-decker bus

❹ Model of the Eiffel Tower

❺ Miniature Ukrainian bandura (a stringed instrument)

❻ Five-pound note from Great Britain

Content Consultants for the World Explorer Program

Teacher Advisory Board

TABLE OF CONTENTS

EUROPE AND RUSSIA 1

OF SPECIAL INTEREST

Maps and charts providing a closer look at countries and regions

ACTIVITY SHOP

Step-by-step activities for exploring important topics in Europe and Russia

CITIZEN HEROES

Profiles of people who made a difference in their country

Maps and statistics for Russia and every nation in Europe

SKILLS ACTIVITY

A hands-on approach to learning and applying social studies skills

LITERATURE

Literature selections by European authors

Detailed drawings show how the use of technology makes a country unique

A view of a country through the eyes of a student artist

MAPS

CHARTS, GRAPHS, AND TABLES

READ ACTIVELY

How can I get the most out of my social studies book? How does my reading relate to my world? Answering questions like these means that you are an active reader, an involved reader. As an active reader, you are in charge of the reading situation!

The following strategies tell how to think and read as an active reader. You don't need to use all of these strategies all the time. Feel free to choose the ones that work best in each reading situation. You might use several at a time, or you might go back and forth among them. They can be used in any order.

BEFORE YOU READ

Give yourself a purpose

The sections in this book begin with a list called "Questions to Explore." These questions focus on key ideas presented in the section. They give you a purpose for reading. You can create your own purpose by asking questions like these: How does the topic relate to my life? How might I use what I learn at school or at home?

Preview

To preview a reading selection, first read its title. Then look at the pictures and read the captions. Also read any headings in the selection. Then ask yourself: What is the reading selection about? What do the pictures and headings tell about the selection?

Reach into your background

What do you already know about the topic of the selection? How can you use what you know to help you understand what you are going to read?

WHILE YOU READ

Ask questions

Suppose you are reading about the continent of South America. Some questions you might ask are: Where is South America? What countries are found there? Why are some of the countries large and others small? Asking questions like these can help you gather evidence and gain knowledge.

Predict

As you read, make a prediction about what will happen and why. Or predict how one fact might affect another fact. Suppose you are reading about South America's climate. You might make a prediction about how the climate affects where people live. You can change your mind as you gain new information.

Connect

Connect your reading to your own life. Are the people discussed in the selection like you or someone you know? What would you do in similar situations? Connect your reading to something you have already read. Suppose you have already read about the ancient Greeks. Now you are reading about the ancient Romans. How are they alike? How are they different?

Visualize

What would places, people, and events look like in a movie or a picture? As you read about India, you could visualize the country's heavy rains. What do they look like? How do they sound? As you read about geography, you could visualize a volcanic eruption.

AFTER YOU READ

Respond

Talk about what you have read. What did you think? Share your ideas with your classmates.

Assess yourself

What did you find out? Were your predictions on target? Did you find answers to your questions?

Follow up

Show what you know. Use what you have learned to do a project. When you do projects, you continue to learn.

EUROPE AND RUSSIA

Europe is a continent filled with countries. Russia is one country that actually lies on two continents— Europe and Asia. Together, Europe and Russia form a gigantic landmass. Together, they also form a rich pattern of different cultures, histories, and languages that stretch back hundreds of years.

GUIDING QUESTIONS

The readings and activities in this book will help you discover answers to these Guiding Questions.

1 GEOGRAPHY How has physical geography affected the environment and cultures of Europe and Russia?

2 HISTORY How have the people of Europe and Russia been shaped by historical experiences?

3 CULTURE What values and traditions do the people of Europe and Russia have in common?

4 GOVERNMENT How have changes in government affected Russia and some European nations?

5 ECONOMICS How have Russian and European economies developed into what they are today?

PROJECT PREVIEW

You can also discover answers to the Guiding Questions by working on projects. You can find several project possibilities on pages 174–175 at the back of this book.

1 How has physical geography affected the environment and cultures of Europe and Russia?

2 How have the people of Europe and Russia been shaped by historical experiences?

3 What values and traditions do the people of Europe and Russia have in common?

5 How have Russian and European economies developed into what they are today?

4 How have changes in government affected Russia and some European nations?

A journal can be your personal book of discovery. As you explore Europe and Russia, you can use your journal to keep track of things you learn and do. You can also record your thoughts about your explorations. For your first entry, write your thoughts on where in Europe or Russia you would like to go and what you would want to see there.

EXPLORER'S JOURNAL

ACTIVITY ATLAS

DISCOVERY ACTIVITIES ABOUT

Europe and Russia

Learning about Europe and Russia means being an explorer and a geographer. No explorer would start out without first checking some facts. Begin by exploring the maps of Europe and Russia on the following pages.

Relative Location

LOCATION

1. Explore Europe and Russia's Location

A geographer must know where a place is located in order to study it. Use the map at left to describe Europe and Russia's location relative to the United States. Which ocean separates Europe and Russia from the United States? Which is closer to the Equator, Europe and Russia or the United States? Which is closer to the Arctic Circle? Many people think the climates of Europe and the United States are similar. Look at the map. Then list three reasons why this might be so.

PLACE

2. Explore Europe and Russia's Size

Are Europe and Russia together larger or smaller than the United States? How does the size of Europe alone compare to that of the continental United States? Based on what you know, estimate the number of countries in Europe.

Relative Size

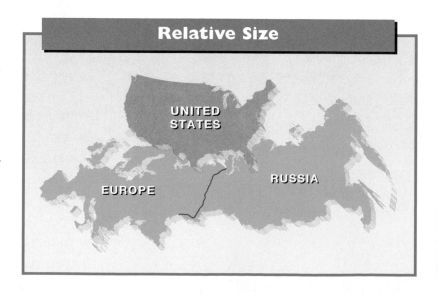

PLACE

3. Explore Europe and Russia Russia is not only the largest country on Eurasia, the large landmass upon which Europe and Asia are located, but it is also the largest country in the world. Some of the smallest countries in the world are also located in Europe. Which European countries are the smallest? Europe is surrounded by several important seas. What are the names of the seas that surround Europe?

REGIONS

4. Predict Climate and Its Effects Find the Arctic Circle on the map. In regions north of the circle, there is a day when the sun never sets and a day when it never rises! Regions this far north are also very cold. Which countries have areas that lie north of the Arctic Circle? How do you think the cold climate affects the way people in these areas live?

Europe and Russia: Political

Europe and Russia: Political KEY

— National boundary
⊛ National capital
• Other city

Two-Point Equidistant Projection

LOCATION

5. Identify the Mountains of Europe and Russia The Alpine mountain chain stretches through much of central and southern Europe. It includes the Pyrenees, the Alps, the Carpathians, the Balkans, and the Caucasus. Find these mountains on the map. Locate the Ural Mountains. They form the border between the western part of Russia that is in Europe and the eastern part that is in Asia.

LOCATION

6. Locate Europe's Peninsulas Europe has several major peninsulas. A peninsula is a piece of land that is almost completely surrounded by water. Which peninsula is farthest north? What bodies of water border this peninsula? Name Europe's other peninsulas. Notice that even the continent of Europe itself is one big peninsula!

Europe and Russia: Physical

MOVEMENT

7. Plan Geo Leo's Trip on the Rails Geo Leo wants to explore Europe and Russia by train. Read the goals he has set for his trip. Then, use the map below to help him plan generally which routes he should take. Estimate the distance of each route.

A. *"After my plane lands in Paris, I want to travel to Warsaw by the shortest route."*

B. *"From Warsaw, I want to go as far north as possible on my way to Moscow."*

C. *"From Moscow, I want to travel to Rome. I want to pass through as many major cities as I can on the way."*

D. *"From Rome, I will need to head straight back to Paris. What's the shortest route I can take?"*

BONUS

Using the physical map on the previous page and the map below, describe the physical features over which Geo Leo will travel during his train trip.

GEO LEO

Europe and Russia: Major Railroad Lines

KEY
- — Railroads
- ⊛ National capital
- • Other city

Robinson Projection

Oslo • Helsinki • • St. Petersburg
Stockholm •
Glasgow • North Sea • Baltic Sea • Moscow
London • Berlin • Warsaw •
Brussels • Frankfurt • Kiev • Volgograd
Paris • Vienna •
ATLANTIC OCEAN • Lyon • Milan • Bucharest •
Rome • Black Sea • Caspian Sea
Madrid •
Athens •
Mediterranean Sea

0   300   600 mi
0   300   600 km

PLACE

8. Compare Population Densities Population density is the average number of people living within a certain area. Compare the parts of Europe that have many people to the parts that have only a few people. Do the same for Russia. How would you describe the population densities of the two regions? What geographic features might explain the low population density of countries like Finland and Norway? What other factors might affect population?

INTERACTION

9. Analyzing Population Charts Find the five largest cities in Europe on the map. Which cities are located on the coast? Which cities are located far inland? How do you think life in these cities is different due to their inland or coastal locations? Study the chart on the next page. Which two cities are located in Russia? How would you describe the rest of the country's population density?

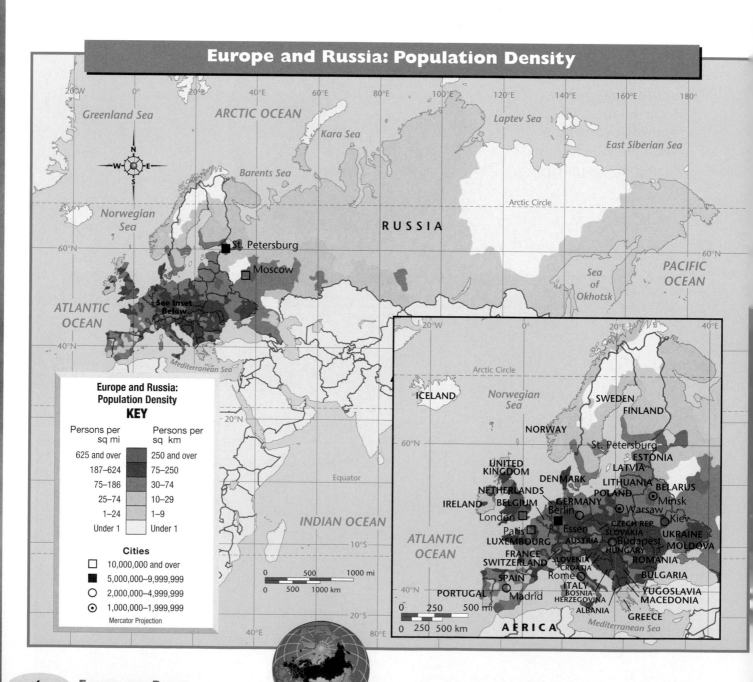

Europe and Russia: Population Density

Europe and Russia: Population Density
KEY

Persons per sq mi	Persons per sq km
625 and over	250 and over
187–624	75–250
75–186	30–74
25–74	10–29
1–24	1–9
Under 1	Under 1

Cities
- ☐ 10,000,000 and over
- ■ 5,000,000–9,999,999
- ○ 2,000,000–4,999,999
- ◉ 1,000,000–1,999,999

Mercator Projection

REGIONS

10. Compare Climates in Europe and Russia

As you can see on the map below, Europe and Russia have a wide variety of climates. Compare Russia's climates to those in Europe. Does Europe have a greater or lesser variety of climates? Look at the Five Most Populated Cities chart. In which climate regions are the two most populated cities in Europe and Russia located?

Europe and Russia: Climate Regions

KEY
- Semiarid
- Arid
- Mediterranean
- Humid subtropical
- Marine west coast
- Humid continental
- Subarctic
- Tundra
- Highlands

Mercator Projection

The Five Most Populated Cities in Europe and Russia

City	Country	Population (in millions)
1. Moscow	Russia	13.2
2. London	United Kingdom	11.8
3. Paris	France	10.2
4. Essen	Germany	6.1
5. St. Petersburg	Russia	5.6

Source: Information Please Internet Almanac

EUROPE AND RUSSIA

Physical Geography

PICTURE ACTIVITIES

Water and land have affected where and how people live in Europe and Russia. The picture shows a freighter traveling the Rhine (ryn) River in Germany. To get yourself thinking about the ways in which geography affects people's lives, complete the following activities.

Study the picture
How do you think water is being used? What is the land used for? How can these uses of water and land help certain areas of Europe to grow?

Make a comparison
Compare the area shown in the picture to the area where you live. Consider the features of the land, the plant life, and what you can tell about the climate. How is the area similar to the area where you live? How is it different? Make a list of the similarities and differences.

Land and Water

BEFORE YOU READ

Reach Into Your Background

How are land and water used where you live? Do you live near fertile plains, forested mountains, or an ocean coast? Do you live in a farming region or an industrial city? Think of the physical features of your area. Then list two ways in which these features have affected your way of life.

Questions to Explore

1. What are the main physical features of Europe and Russia?
2. How have the physical features of Europe and Russia affected where and how people live?

Key Terms

polder
population density
peninsula
plateau
tributary
navigable

Key Places

Europe
Russia
Eurasia
Ural Mountains
Alps
Siberia

If you cross a farm field in the Netherlands (NETH ur luhndz), you might well be walking where sea waves once roared. Water once covered more than two fifths of the country. Centuries ago, the people of the Netherlands began an endless battle to make land where there was water. They built long walls called dikes to hold back the water. They pumped the water into canals that empty into the North Sea. They also created patches of new land called **polders** (POHL durz).

The polders that lie below sea level are always filling with water. Netherlanders must continually pump them out. In early times, they set whirling windmills to do this work. Now they use pumps with powerful motors. Keeping the polders dry has always been important because the richest farmlands and the largest cities in the Netherlands are located on polders.

▼ Polders, like the ones shown on either side of this canal, make up about 3,000 square miles (7,770 sq km) of the Netherlands.

Why have the Netherlanders worked so hard to make new land? Consider the country's **population density,** or average number of people living in an area. The Netherlands has about 1,002 people per square mile (466 people per sq km). By comparison, the world average is about 116 people per square mile (46 people per sq km). The Netherlanders need all the land they can get.

Europe, in general, has a much higher population density than most of the world. By comparison, Russia has a much lower population density—only about 22 people per square mile (9 people per sq km). Few people live in the vast plains and mountains of eastern Russia. The poor soil and cold climate make it a difficult place to live.

Size and Location

Europe and Russia are parts of Eurasia, the world's largest landmass. This landmass is made up of two continents, Europe and Asia. The country of Russia stretches over both continents. About one fourth of Russia is in Europe; the rest is in Asia. Find the Ural (YOOR ul) Mountains on the physical map of Asia in the Atlas at the back of the book. These mountains mark the dividing line between Europe and Asia.

A Small Continent and a Large Country Europe is a small continent. Only Australia is smaller. While Europe lacks size, it has many different countries. Some 47 countries are located on the continent. As you might guess, most of the countries are small. Many are the size of an average state in the United States. Russia, on the other hand, is the largest country in the world. It is almost twice the size of Canada or the United States.

Farther North Than You Might Expect How far north do you think Europe and Russia are? As far north as the United States? You can figure this out by comparing latitudes. First, find the World Political Map in the Atlas. Second, follow one of the lines of latitude across the map from the United States to Eurasia. You will see that a lot of Europe, and nearly all of Russia, is farther north than the United States. Berlin, the German capital, lies at about the same latitude as the southern tip of Canada's Hudson Bay.

Far to the North

This small church is located in the Highlands area of Scotland. Part of Europe's Northwestern Highlands region, the Scottish Highlands lie north of the 55°N line of latitude. In contrast, all of the United States, except for Alaska, is located south of 50°N.

Major Landforms of Europe and Russia

Look again at the physical map of Europe in the Atlas and study the shape of Europe. The continent of Europe forms a **peninsula** (puh NIN suh luh), a body of land nearly surrounded by water. The European peninsula juts out into the Atlantic Ocean. Look closely, and you will see that Europe has many smaller peninsulas with bays. These bays include many harbors, or sheltered bodies of water, where ships can dock. Good harbors have enabled Western European countries to become world leaders in the shipping industry.

Now find Russia on the political map of Asia in the Atlas. Notice that Russia lies on the Arctic Ocean. This body of water is frozen for most of the year and cannot be used for shipping. Between Russia and the countries of Europe, however, there are no physical features that form travel barriers. Movement between these two regions has always been easy.

Plains and Uplands of Europe Within the peninsula of Europe are four major land regions: the Northwestern Highlands, the North European Plain, the Central Uplands, and the Alpine Mountain System. Find these regions on the map on the next page.

The Northwestern Highlands stretch across the far north of Europe. These old mountains have been worn by wind and

READ ACTIVELY

Visualize If you flew in a plane over Europe and Russia, what physical features would you see?

▼ The Swiss Alps are popular with hikers and climbers in winter and summer.

weather. Because they have steep slopes and thin soil, they are not good for farming, and few people live here. Large parts of this region have fewer than 25 people per square mile (10 people per sq km). But the forests here support a successful timber industry.

Notice on the map below that more than half of Europe is covered by the North European Plain. Can you see where this plain begins and ends? It includes most of the European part of Russia and reaches all the way to France. This region has the most productive farmland and the largest cities in Europe.

In the center of southern Europe are the Central Uplands. What do you think uplands are? You probably guessed that this is a region of highlands. In fact, it is made up of mountains and **plateaus** (pla TOHZ), or large raised areas of mostly level land. Most of the land in this region is rocky and not good for farming. But the uplands have other uses. In Spain, people raise goats and sheep here. In Portugal, people mine the uplands for minerals.

Europe: Land Regions

KEY
Elevation

Feet	Meters
Over 13,000	Over 3,960
6,500–13,000	1,980–3,960
1,600–6,500	480–1,980
650–1,600	200–480
0–650	0–200
Below sea level	Below sea level

Lambert Azimuthal Equal-Area Projection

0   300   600 mi
0   300   600 km

Map Study This map shows Europe's four major land regions. **Regions** Which of the four land regions covers the greatest area? Some parts of Europe have land areas that are below sea level, but are not covered with water, like the polders of the Netherlands. Where else in Europe can you find land that is below sea level?

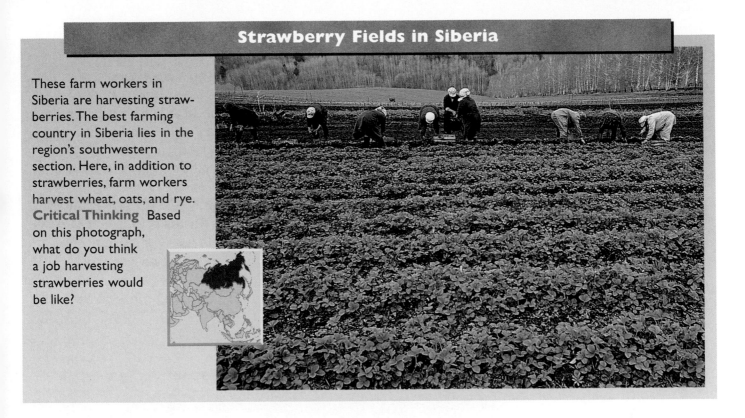

Strawberry Fields in Siberia

These farm workers in Siberia are harvesting straw-berries. The best farming country in Siberia lies in the region's southwestern section. Here, in addition to strawberries, farm workers harvest wheat, oats, and rye. **Critical Thinking** Based on this photograph, what do you think a job harvesting strawberries would be like?

Are you ready to see a spectacular landform? Look for the Alpine Mountain System. These mountains stretch from France to the Balkan Peninsula. The Alps are the highest and most beautiful mountains in this system. They are also a popular vacation place. Some families make a living from small-scale farming in the mountain valleys and meadows of the Alps.

Russian Plains and Uplands Europe and the western part of Russia share the North European Plain. Russia's largest cities, Moscow (MAHS kow) and St. Petersburg, are in this region. Most of Russia's industries are here, too. There are more people living in this region than in any other part of Russia.

Where the plains end, the uplands begin. On the eastern border of the European Plain you will find the Ural Mountains. To the east of the Urals is the Asian part of Russia—a region known as Siberia (sy BIHR ee uh). This region makes up about 75 percent of Russian territory, but it has only about 20 percent of Russia's people. The region's harsh climate has limited settlement there.

If you continue east into Siberia from the Ural Mountains, you will cross the largest plain in the world—the West Siberian Plain. This low, marshy plain covers more than one million square miles (2.58 million sq km), but it rises only 328 feet (100 m) above sea level. Farther east is the Central Siberian Plateau, which slopes upward from the West Siberian Plain. If you travel still farther east, you will need to watch your step. The East Siberian Uplands include more than 20 active volcanoes among the rugged mountains and plateaus.

Ask Questions What questions would you like to ask a person who lives in a cold, harsh climate?

Legends of the Rhine The cliffs, castles, and gorges of the Rhine River have inspired many stories. On the Lorelei Cliff, it is believed that a beautiful maiden named Lorelei would sing. The power and beauty of her songs would echo through the cliffs. According to this legend, her songs would attract boatmen, and bring them to their death.

The Rivers of Europe and Russia

The highlands of Europe and Russia are the source for many important rivers. High in the Alps in Switzerland (SWIT sur lund), melting glaciers create two streams that combine to form the Rhine River. Winding through forests and plains, the Rhine makes a journey of 865 miles (1,391 km), from Switzerland to the Netherlands and the North Sea. Along its course through Germany, the river flows past old castles on cliffs and smoky mills and factories.

The Rhine River serves as a major highway. Canals and tributaries (TRIB yoo tehr eez) connect it to the furthest reaches of Western Europe. A **tributary** is a river or stream that flows into a larger river.

The longest river on the continent of Europe is Russia's Volga (VAHL guh) River. It flows 2,291 miles (3,687 km) through western Russia and empties into the Caspian (KAS pih un) Sea. The Volga has many tributaries and canals. They link the Volga to the Arctic Ocean and the Baltic

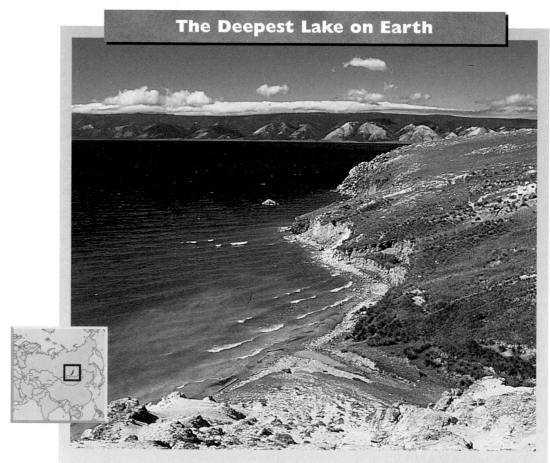

The Deepest Lake on Earth

Lake Baikal, Russia, holds about one fifth of Earth's fresh water. More than 300 rivers and streams flow into Lake Baikal from the surrounding mountains. Because Lake Baikal holds so much water, it affects the weather in the area around it. The land near the lake is cooler in the summer and warmer in the winter than land that lies farther away. **Critical Thinking** What other bodies of water can change the weather?

The Danube River

The Danube River flows from the mountains of Germany through eight countries before it empties into the Black Sea in Romania. It is the second longest river in Europe—only Russia's Volga River is longer. Because it is both navigable and long, the Danube is an important trade route. Ships from the Mediterranean can travel as far as this port in Braila, Romania, before their cargo is transferred to smaller vessels. **Critical Thinking** At one time, composers wrote music celebrating the beauty of the Danube River. Today, that beauty has been dimmed by air and water pollution from factories. What parts of this photograph are hard to see because of smog?

Sea. Unfortunately, the Volga freezes for most of its length for three months of each year. During the winter months, it is not **navigable** (NAV ih guh bul), or clear enough for ships to travel.

Other Russian rivers freeze, too. Some of them are frozen for five or more months of the year. And many flow north to the frozen Arctic Ocean, which is also not navigable. These rivers do not serve as dependable trade routes.

SECTION 1 REVIEW

1. **Define** (a) polder, (b) population density, (c) peninsula, (d) plateau, (e) tributary, (f) navigable.
2. **Identify** (a) Europe, (b) Russia, (c) Eurasia, (d) Ural Mountains, (e) Alps, (f) Siberia.
3. What are the major physical features of Europe and Russia?
4. Give two examples of ways in which physical features have affected life in Europe and Russia.

Critical Thinking
5. **Drawing Conclusions** Think about the areas of Europe and Russia that are the most densely populated. What physical features attract people to settle in those areas?

Activity
6. **Writing to Learn** Which physical feature described in this section are you most interested in learning more about? Why? In your journal, make a list of the things you would like to learn about this physical feature.

SECTION 2

Climate and Vegetation

BEFORE YOU READ

Reach Into Your Background

Do you live where it is warm year round? Or do you live in an area with warm summers and cold winters? Think of the climate in your area. Identify three ways in which it affects your way of life.

Questions to Explore

1. How do oceans and mountains affect climate in Europe and Russia?
2. What different climates and kinds of vegetation do Europe and Russia have?

Key Terms

rain shadow
prairie
tundra
permafrost
taiga
steppe

Key Places

Barcelona
Irkutsk

I t is February in Barcelona (bar suh LOH nuh), Spain. Twelve-year-old Nicholas wakes up to the sun streaming through his bedroom window. It's another warm day, and the temperature is already 65°F (18°C). Nicholas dresses quickly in shorts and a T-shirt and eats a breakfast of thick hot chocolate and *churros,* twisted loops of fried dough. He wants to get out and play soccer with his friends on this sunny Saturday morning.

At the very same moment, it is late afternoon in Irkutsk (ihr KOOTSK), a city in southern Siberia. Vasily (VAS uh lee) returns home from a day of cross-country skiing. He takes off his fur hat, gloves, boots, ski pants, and coat. The day has been sunny but cold, with an average temperature of −15°F (−11°C). Now Vasily warms up with a dinner of *pelmeny* (PEL muh nee), chicken broth with meat-filled dumplings.

▼ In the snowy Siberian winter, skiing is a good way to get from place to place.

A Wide Range of Climates

Nicholas and Vasily live in vastly different climates. Barcelona, where Nicholas lives, lies on the Mediterranean Sea. Here, the summers are hot and dry, and the winters are mild and rainy. In Irkutsk, Vasily's home in Siberia, summers are short, and the winters are long and very cold. Temperatures in winter can drop to −50°F (−45°C). Snow covers the ground for about six months of the year.

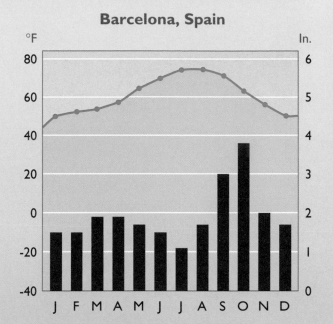

Irkutsk, Russia

Barcelona, Spain

Curved lines show temperatures in Fahrenheit degrees. Bars show precipitation in inches.

Graph Study Siberia, where the city of Irkutsk is located, endures the coldest winters of any place in the world except Antarctica. In contrast, Spain, where Barcelona is located, enjoys mild weather throughout the year. Critical Thinking Find Irkutsk and Barcelona on the climate regions map in the Activity Atlas. How do you think location influences the climates of these two cities?

Oceans Affect Climate You can partly explain the difference between the climates of Barcelona and Irkutsk by looking at the two cities' distances from an ocean or a sea. Areas that are near an ocean or a sea have fairly mild weather year round. Areas that are far from the ocean often have extreme weather.

Look at the map on the next page and find the Gulf Stream. Notice how it becomes the North Atlantic Current as it crosses the Atlantic Ocean. This ocean current carries warm water from the tropical waters of the Gulf of Mexico to northwestern Europe. Also, winds blowing from the west across the Atlantic Ocean are warmed by this powerful ocean current. The warm waters and winds bring mild weather to much of northwestern Europe.

London is farther north than any city in the continental United States, but it has mild weather. How is this possible? The North Atlantic Current is the reason. But the most dramatic effect of the North Atlantic Current can be seen in northern Norway. Snow and ice cover most of this area in winter. Yet Norway's western coast is free of ice and snow all year. Snow melts almost as soon as it falls. Norway's ice-free ports have helped to make it a great fishing country.

The ocean affects climate in other ways. Winds blowing across the ocean pick up a great deal of moisture. When these winds blow over land,

READ ACTIVELY

Predict How do you think the ocean affects the climate in some parts of Europe?

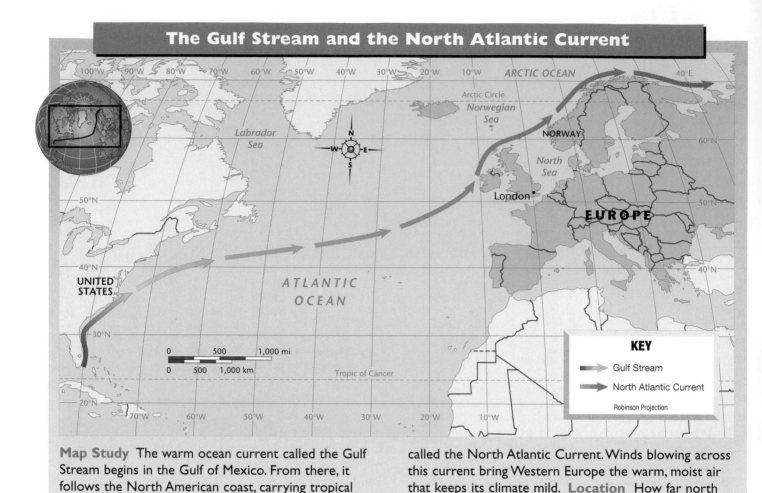

KEY

→ Gulf Stream

→ North Atlantic Current

Robinson Projection

Map Study The warm ocean current called the Gulf Stream begins in the Gulf of Mexico. From there, it follows the North American coast, carrying tropical waters from the Caribbean Sea. In the Atlantic, the Gulf Stream joins a large northeastward flowing current called the North Atlantic Current. Winds blowing across this current bring Western Europe the warm, moist air that keeps its climate mild. **Location** How far north does the North Atlantic Current flow?

they drop the moisture in the form of rain. Winds blowing from the west across the Atlantic bring a fairly wet climate to much of Western Europe.

Mountains Affect Rainfall Mountains also affect the amount of rainfall in an area. In Europe, areas west of mountains receive heavy rainfall. These areas include parts of Great Britain, France, Germany, and Norway. Areas east of mountains have much lighter rainfall.

Why is this so? As winds rise up a mountain, they cool and drop their moisture. The air is dry by the time it reaches the other side of the mountain. Areas on the leeward side of a mountain, or away from the wind, are in a rain shadow. A **rain shadow** is an area on the dry, sheltered side of a mountain that receives little rainfall.

Major Climate Zones of Europe and Russia

Earlier, you read that oceans affect climate. Look at the climate regions map in the Activity Atlas to see a good illustration of this. Notice that much of northwestern Europe has a marine west coast climate. The

North Atlantic Current helps make the climate mild all year. Moisture-carrying winds from the Atlantic Ocean make these areas rainy through all the seasons. In London, the capital of Great Britain, rain is a part of life. Many people who live here are in the habit of carrying an umbrella every day.

Look again at the map. Notice the climate region that surrounds the Mediterranean Sea. It is easy to remember the name of this type of climate—Mediterranean, just like the sea. Remember that Barcelona, where Nicholas lives, is on the Mediterranean. In this kind of climate, summers are hot and dry. Winters are mild and rainy. Look at the climate graph earlier in the section to see the average monthly temperatures and rainfall for Barcelona.

Some inland areas far away from the ocean have a humid continental climate. In these areas, winters are long and cold. But summers can be blazing hot!

Now find Irkutsk, Russia, on the map. Notice that it is located in a huge subarctic climate zone. Here summers are short, and winters are long and cold. You can see how cold it is all year by looking at the climate graph for Irkutsk. The northernmost areas of Europe and Russia have a tundra climate. In these areas it is just plain cold! On the warmest days, temperatures rarely get above 40°F (5°C).

LINKS TO SCIENCE

Hot and Cold Iceland's Loki volcano lies beneath Vatnjokul, Europe's largest glacier. In the fall of 1996, Loki erupted. This created a deep crack in the glacier some 6 miles (10 km) long. Melting ice and eruptions of water from a huge "underground lake" beneath the glacier flooded the surrounding area.

My Family in Winter

STUDENT ART

Helin Tikerpuu
13 years old
Estonia

This student has painted her family on a skiing trip. **Critical Thinking** Based on this picture, do you think Helin's family skis just for fun? Or do you think their ski trip has a more practical purpose? Explain your answer.

The Vegetation of Europe and Russia

The natural vegetation, or plant life, of Europe and Russia is as varied as the climate. And vegetation regions are related to climate regions. Compare the climate map with the natural vegetation maps below and on the next page to see how the climate and vegetation bands overlap.

Forests and Grasslands of Europe The natural vegetation of much of Europe is forest. However, most of these forests have been cleared to make way for farms, factories, and cities. In northern Europe, you can still find large coniferous (koh NIF ur us) forests, which have trees with cones that carry and protect the seeds.

The central and southern parts of the North European Plain were once covered by grasslands, called **prairies.** Like the forests, most of the prairies have also been cleared. Today, the land is used for farming.

The Russian Tundra, Forests, and Grasslands Russia has three great vegetation zones: the tundra, the forests, and the grasslands. The tundra and forest zones extend across Siberia. Grasslands cover southwestern Russia.

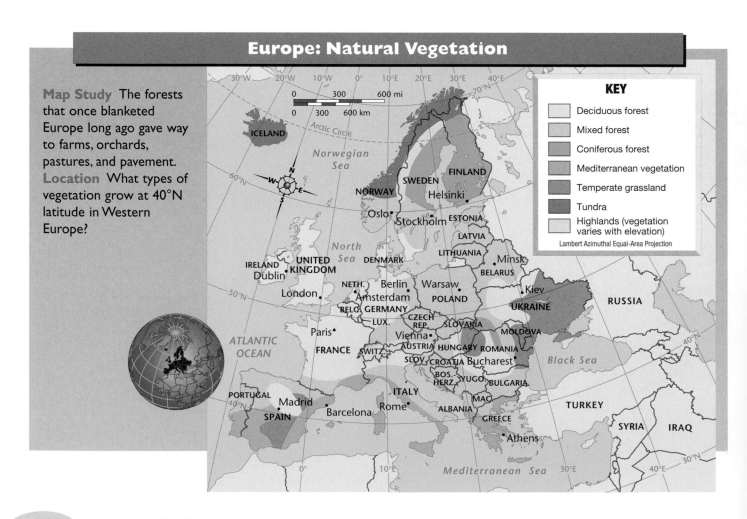

Europe: Natural Vegetation

Map Study The forests that once blanketed Europe long ago gave way to farms, orchards, pastures, and pavement. **Location** What types of vegetation grow at 40°N latitude in Western Europe?

KEY
- Deciduous forest
- Mixed forest
- Coniferous forest
- Mediterranean vegetation
- Temperate grassland
- Tundra
- Highlands (vegetation varies with elevation)

Lambert Azimuthal Equal-Area Projection

Russia: Natural Vegetation

KEY

- Deciduous forest
- Mixed forest
- Coniferous forest
- Temperate grassland
- Desert scrub
- Tundra
- Ice cap

Two-Point Equidistant Projection

Map Study Far from the Equator and from warm ocean currents, Russia's cool climate supports three types of vegetation. **Regions** Which type of vegetation covers the largest area? In the far north, what type of vegetation grows? Which region provides Russia's rich farmland?

The **tundra** is a treeless plain where grasses and mosses grow. Here, winters last up to nine months and the ground is **permafrost,** or permanently frozen soil. When the top surface of the permafrost thaws, fantastic growth spurts take place.

Russia also has more than its share of forests. One, called the **taiga** (TY guh), covers more than 4 million square miles (6.4 million sq km). It is the largest forest in the world.

The Russian grasslands are called **steppes.** The soil of this region is fertile and black and good for farming. The steppes are similar to the Great Plains of the United States.

SECTION 2 REVIEW

1. **Define** (a) rain shadow, (b) prairie, (c) tundra, (d) permafrost, (e) taiga, (f) steppe.

2. **Identify** (a) Barcelona, (b) Irkutsk.

3. How does the North Atlantic Current affect the climate of northwestern Europe?

4. What are the major climate and vegetation regions of Europe and Russia?

Critical Thinking

5. **Recognizing Cause and Effect** How do oceans and mountains affect climate?

Activity

6. **Writing to Learn** Plan a trip to one of the cities mentioned in this section. Decide what time of year you want to go. Based on the climate of the city you have chosen, make a list of the clothes you will pack.

SKILLS ACTIVITY

Using Regional Maps

Do you dream of someday traveling around the world? Just by crossing Russia, you can travel halfway around the world.

Russia is the largest country on the planet. It reaches across Europe and Asia. When it is noon at one end of the country, it is close to midnight at the other. How can this be?

Get Ready

There is such a big time difference because Russia stretches across 10 of the world's 24 time zones. Why do we have time zones?

Suppose every clock in the world showed the same time at once. At noon, the sun would be rising in some places and setting in others. It would be very confusing.

The Earth has 24 time zones—one for each hour of the day. Noon everywhere is always about when the sun is at its highest point.

You may someday be talking on the phone with people in Russia. If you understand time zones, you can avoid calling someone at 3:00 A.M. The best way to understand time zones is by learning how to read a time zone map.

Try It Out

The map on the next page shows time zones across the globe. Compare the number of time zones in the United States and in Russia. Use the time zone map to complete the following steps:

A. Find the time zone boundaries. The boundaries are shown by solid lines. Notice that they are mostly straight, but sometimes bend to follow political boundaries. Why do you think this is so?

B. Understand the difference between time zones. The difference in time between one time zone and the next is one hour. (Each time zone represents the distance the Earth rotates in one hour.) As you travel west of the Prime Meridian, the time becomes one hour earlier for every time zone you cross. As you travel east of the Prime Meridian, it becomes one hour later for every time zone you cross. Note the two sets of labels on the map on the next page. At the top are hours labeled A.M. and P.M.

The Prime Meridian is labeled 12 noon. The numbers below the map show the time difference in hours from 12 noon.

C. Follow a three-step process to use the map.

Step 1. The United States covers 6 of the 24 time zones. Find your location on the map. Check what time it is now.

Step 2. Locate the place for which you wish to know the time. Notice its time zone.

Step 3. If the place is in the same time zone as your location, the time is the same as your time. If it is in a different time zone, look at the times in the key below the map to see how many hours away it is. Then add or subtract the hours from your current time. Remember, if the place is east of where you are, add to your time. If it is west of where you are, subtract from your time.

Write down your current time. Now calculate the current time for the five United States cities shown on the time zone map.

Apply the Skill

Russia is the widest country on the Earth. In other words, it stretches across more time zones than any other country does.

1 Consider the differences in time. Study the map. In Russia, how many hours' difference is there between the time zone farthest east and the time zone farthest west? When it is 3 P.M. in Moscow, what time is it in Perm? What time is it in Novosibirsk? What time is it in Vladivostok? When it is lunch time in St. Petersburg, what part of the day is it in Anadyr?

2 Think about the challenges posed by these great differences. Write a paragraph to answer this question: What challenges might the Russian government and businesses face by having to work with so many different time zones?

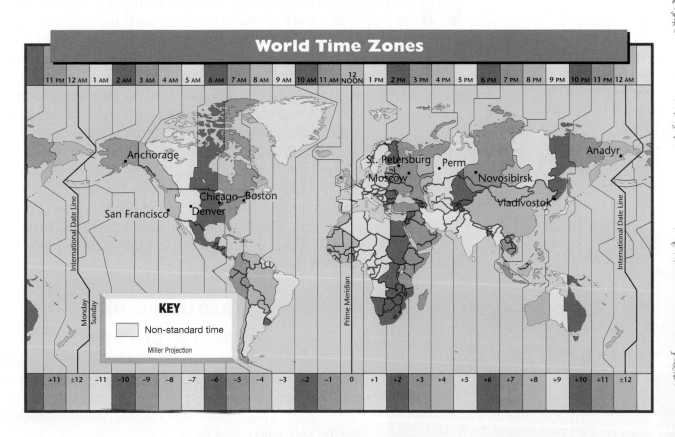

World Time Zones

| 11 PM | 12 AM | 1 AM | 2 AM | 3 AM | 4 AM | 5 AM | 6 AM | 7 AM | 8 AM | 9 AM | 10 AM | 11 AM | 12 NOON | 1 PM | 2 PM | 3 PM | 4 PM | 5 PM | 6 PM | 7 PM | 8 PM | 9 PM | 10 PM | 11 PM | 12 AM |

KEY

Non-standard time

Miller Projection

| +11 | ±12 | −11 | −10 | −9 | −8 | −7 | −6 | −5 | −4 | −3 | −2 | −1 | 0 | +1 | +2 | +3 | +4 | +5 | +6 | +7 | +8 | +9 | +10 | +11 | ±12 |

Natural Resources

BEFORE YOU READ

Reach Into Your Background

The United States has many natural resources. Which resources do you think are most important? Why?

Consider these questions as you read about the natural resources of Europe and Russia.

Questions to Explore

1. What are the major natural resources of Europe and Russia?

2. How do Europe and Russia differ in their use of natural resources?

Key Terms

loess
hydroelectric power
fossil fuel
reserves

Key Places

North Sea
Ruhr
Silesia

How would you like to live and work on an ocean? Oil workers on the North Sea work to pump oil from deep beneath the ocean floor. They anchor a tower called an oil rig over an oil field. In such a rig, oil workers live and work as if they were on a ship. But oil workers cannot sail for the safety of a harbor when a big storm is stirring. And the North Sea, located between Great Britain and mainland northwestern Europe, sometimes has violent weather. Severe storms with winds of up to 100 miles (160 km) an hour are common. Waves as high as 90 feet (27 m) batter oil rig platforms. Crews work around the clock to operate, inspect, and repair the rigs.

Making sure a rig operates properly is a very important job. Great Britain and other nations around the North Sea depend on oil and natural gas from the rigs. Without this fuel, Europe's industries would be in serious trouble.

Resources of Western Europe

Europe is a wealthy region and a world leader in economic development. Part of this wealth and success comes from Europe's rich supply of natural resources. This region's most important natural resources include fertile soil, water, and fuels.

▼ On a North Sea oil rig, workers brave icy seas and foul weather to drill for underwater petroleum deposits.

Europe: Natural Resources

KEY

⛏ Hydroelectric power
🕷 Iron
🛢 Copper
👜 Bauxite
👜 Phosphates

⚛ Uranium
C Coal
🛢 Petroleum
▭ Lead
🔥 Natural gas

Lambert Azimuthal Equal-Area Projection

ARCTIC OCEAN
Norwegian Sea
North Sea
ATLANTIC OCEAN
Black Sea
Mediterranean Sea

0   250   500 mi
0   250   500 km

Map Study Europe boasts fertile soil, fast rivers, and abundant petroleum and coal deposits. Trace the belt of coal fields that extends east from Great Britain. **Place** In addition to the United Kingdom, which other countries also have coal deposits? What mineral resources does Sweden possess? Name the natural resources that have enriched the countries that border the North Sea.

Fertile Soil   Why do you think soil is one of the most important natural resources? You have probably guessed that it is important because it is needed to grow food. Much of Western Europe is covered with rich, fertile soil, especially the region's broad river valleys.

Wind helps create the fertile soil of the North European Plain. Over thousands of years, winds have deposited a type of rich, dustlike soil known as **loess** (LOH es). This soil, combined with plentiful rain and a long growing season, enables European farmers to produce abundant crops.

An Excellent Supply of Water   Western Europe's water is another important resource. People need water to drink. Water nourishes crops. Water can also be used to produce electricity, an important source of energy for industries. To be used as a source of energy, water must flow very quickly. The force of water from a waterfall or a dam can be used to spin machines called turbines (TUR bynz). Spinning turbines generate, or create, electric power. Power generated by water-driven turbines is called **hydroelectric** (hy droh ee LEK trik) **power.**

Many countries in Europe have good locations for the development of hydroelectric power. Some rivers that flow down through the mountains have been dammed to create hydroelectric power. Norway

LINKS ACROSS THE WORLD

Loess in China Winds blowing from Mongolia and the Gobi carry loess to the Huang He valley. The river carries the soil downstream and, during floods, deposits it across the North China Plain. This fertile soil makes the plain one of China's most important farming areas.

From Plankton to Oil

1. Drifting throughout the oceans and fresh water of the Earth are tiny marine plants and animals called **plankton**. Plankton that died millions of years ago settled on the ocean floor.

2. Over the years, the plankton was covered with mud and sand. The weight of this material gradually changed the plankton into oil. The oil remained trapped inside **porous rock** that also formed.

3. With huge machinery people dig through the rock and remove the trapped oil, called **crude oil**.

4. Crude oil must then be cleaned, or refined. **Refined oil** is used to make many important products, including home heating oil.

From Plants to Coal

1. **Peat** is made of decayed plant material.

2. Over millions of years, material built up over ancient peat deposits. The pressure of this material gradually changed the peat into **brown coal**.

3. Continuing pressure gradually turned brown coal into soft coal. **Soft coal** is the most common coal found on the Earth. It is often used in industry.

Chart Study The fossil fuels coal and oil formed over millions of years. Oil formed when plankton died and was covered with mud. The plankton decayed and the mud turned to rock, filled with pockets of oil. Coal started with swamp-growing plants whose decayed remains formed a substance called peat. **Critical Thinking** What is the difference between crude oil and refined oil?

Connect What kinds of natural resources have you used so far today?

gets almost all of its electric power from water. Hydroelectric power also keeps factories in Sweden, Switzerland, Austria, Spain, and Portugal humming.

Fuels Like flowing water, fossil fuels provide a source of energy for industries. **Fossil fuels** include coal, oil, and natural gas. They are so named because they developed from fossils, or the remains of ancient plants and animals.

You already know that Great Britain has large deposits of oil and natural gas. Norway does as well. Great Britain also has large coal fields, as does Germany. The largest coal deposits in Germany are located in the Ruhr (roor), a region named for the Ruhr River. Because of its fuel resources, the Ruhr has long been one of Western Europe's most important industrial regions.

An abundance of coal, along with another mineral, iron ore, gave Western Europe a head start in the 1800s, when industries grew rapidly. Today, Europe remains a leading world industrial power.

Resources of Eastern Europe

Now, shift your view from Western to Eastern Europe. Turn back to the map showing Europe's natural resources. Notice that Eastern Europe has similar resources to those of Western Europe. Place a finger on the area around 50°N and 15°E. This is where Poland, the Czech (chek) Republic, and Germany come together. This area is called Silesia (sy LEE shuh). Large deposits of coal here have made Silesia a major industrial center.

Ukraine (yoo KRAYN), a large country in Eastern Europe, has coal deposits, too. It also has several other fuel resources—oil and natural gas. However, its most important resource is probably its soil. This black earth, or *chernozem* (CHEHR nuh zem), is very fertile. Not surprisingly, farming is an extremely important activity in Ukraine.

Resources of Russia

Russia has developed its natural resources far less than Western Europe. Russia has a huge variety of resources—even more than the United States. Our country has used its resources to become the richest nation on earth. You might wonder why Russia has not done the same. The answer is that Russia's harsh climate, huge size, and few navigable rivers have made it difficult to turn resources into wealth.

A Slovakian Steel Factory

Slovakia has large deposits of iron ore. However, it does not have enough iron to supply all its factories, so it imports some. This photograph shows steel being made out of iron at the steelworks in the Slovakian town of Podbrezova. **Critical Thinking** Steel is very strong and can be molded into many different shapes. What products do you know of that are made out of steel?

Russia: Natural Resources

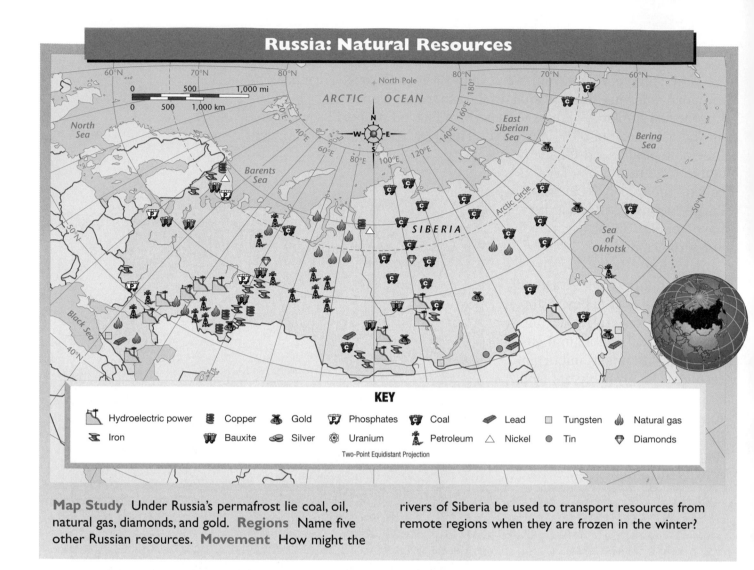

KEY

Hydroelectric power	Copper	Gold	Phosphates
Iron	Bauxite	Silver	Uranium

Coal	Lead	Tungsten	Natural gas
Petroleum	Nickel	Tin	Diamonds

Two-Point Equidistant Projection

Map Study Under Russia's permafrost lie coal, oil, natural gas, diamonds, and gold. **Regions** Name five other Russian resources. **Movement** How might the rivers of Siberia be used to transport resources from remote regions when they are frozen in the winter?

Predict How is the direction of a river's flow important for transporting resources?

Russia's Fossil Fuels and Iron Ore Russia can proudly claim the title of the world's largest oil producer. It also has the largest **reserves,** or available supply, of natural gas in the world. And scientists estimate that the country has about one third of the world's coal reserves.

In addition, Russia has the world's greatest reserves of iron ore, which is used to make steel. Many of these deposits are in the part of Russia that is on the continent of Europe. That is one reason why most of Russia's industry is west of the Ural Mountains.

The Special Case of Siberia Look at the map above. Notice that most of Russia's deposits of oil, natural gas, and coal are located in Siberia. Three fourths of the Russian forest lies here, too. This forest holds half of the world's reserves of softwood timber. Siberia is far from the population and industrial centers of the country, however. Retrieving these resources is not easy.

Russia's huge size presents a major challenge. Transporting Siberian resources to areas where they are needed can be a struggle.

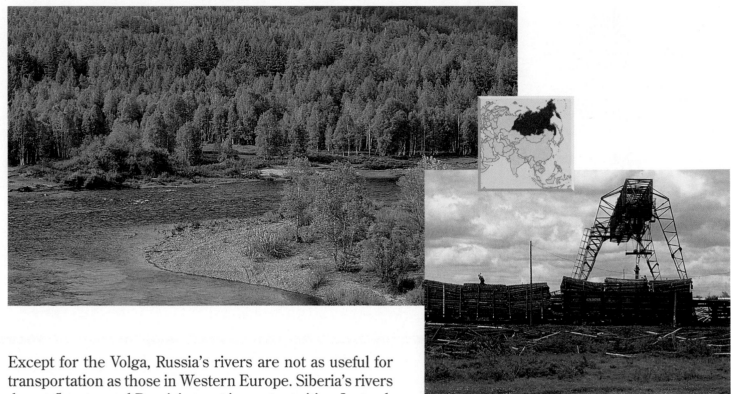

Except for the Volga, Russia's rivers are not as useful for transportation as those in Western Europe. Siberia's rivers do not flow toward Russia's most important cities. Instead, they flow north into the Arctic Ocean. In spite of these problems and the very cold weather, Russia is continually finding ways to move the resources from Siberia. Pipelines carry oil and natural gas, and railroads transport coal to European Russia.

The efforts to get to the resources and use them have created a new challenge—protecting the environment. Some of the world's worst cases of pollution are found in Siberia. Nuclear waste has been dumped into rivers for 40 years. Air pollution from factories is very high. Scientists not only have to find ways to develop Russia's valuable resources, they must also consider how to restore polluted areas.

▲ Siberia's forests (above left) are one of Russia's most important resources. Loggers transport wood from these forests to other parts of Russia by train (above). Unlike coal and oil, forests are a renewable resource if they are managed carefully.

SECTION 3 REVIEW

1. **Define** (a) loess, (b) hydro-electric power, (c) fossil fuel, (d) reserves.

2. **Identify** (a) North Sea, (b) Ruhr, (c) Silesia.

3. Describe the main natural resources of Western Europe, Eastern Europe, and Russia.

4. Explain how Western Europe and Russia differ in their development of natural resources.

Critical Thinking

5. **Drawing Conclusions** Russia is richer in natural resources than Western Europe. Yet Russians are generally not as wealthy as Western Europeans. How does geography help explain this?

Activity

6. **Writing to Learn** What do you think is Europe and Russia's most important natural resource? What makes that resource so important? Write a paragraph explaining your choice.

Review and Activities

Reviewing Main Ideas

1. Describe the land and rivers of Europe and Russia.
2. How have physical features aided Europe's growth and hurt Russia's growth?
3. Describe the climates of Europe and Russia.
4. Describe the vegetation of Europe and Russia.
5. What effect do large bodies of water have on climate in Europe and Russia?
6. Identify the main natural resources of Western Europe, Eastern Europe, and Russia.
7. Compare the development of natural resources in Western Europe and Russia.

Reviewing Key Terms

Use each key term below in a sentence that shows the meaning of the term.

1. polder
2. peninsula
3. plateau
4. tributary
5. rain shadow
6. prairie
7. tundra
8. permafrost
9. steppe
10. hydroelectric power
11. fossil fuel
12. reserves

Critical Thinking

1. **Making Comparisons** Choose one of the land regions of Europe or Russia. Compare it with the area where you live. Consider the landscape, climate, and vegetation.
2. **Recognizing Cause and Effect** Think about what you have learned about the rivers of Europe and Russia. Explain why the direction in which rivers flow is important.

Graphic Organizer

Copy the chart onto a separate sheet of paper. Then, using information from the chapter, fill in the empty boxes.

	Physical Features	Climate	Vegetation	Natural Resources
Europe				
Russia				

Map Activity

Europe and Russia

For each place listed below, write the letter from the map that shows its location. Use the maps in the Atlas at the back of the book to help you.

1. Europe
2. Ural Mountains
3. Alps
4. Siberia
5. Rhine River
6. Volga River
7. North Sea

Writing Activity

Writing a Travel Brochure

Write a travel brochure for Americans who want to visit Siberia. Provide descriptions of the land, climate, and plant life. Suggest clothing for the trip.

Take It to the NET

Activity Use the Internet to learn more about the climates and landforms of Europe and Russia. Make a map showing what you have learned. For help in completing this activity, visit **www.phschool.com**.

Chapter 1 Self-Test To review what you have learned, take the Chapter 1 Self-Test and get instant feedback on your answers. Go to **www.phschool.com** to take the test.

Skills Review

Turn to the Skills Activity.

Review the steps for using a time zone map. Then, use the U.S. time zone map to find the current time for the following places:

a) where you are
b) Boston, Massachusetts
c) Anchorage, Alaska

How Am I Doing?

Answer these questions to help you check your progress.

1. Can I identify and describe the main physical features of Europe and Russia?

2. Can I give some examples of how physical features, climate, and vegetation affect life in Europe and Russia?

3. Can I identify important natural resources of Europe and Russia?

4. What information from this chapter can I include in my journal?

Shaped by History

PICTURE ACTIVITIES

This is the Colosseum in Rome. It is an example of the ancient Romans' great skill in building. To help you understand the importance of this building, complete the following activities.

Write a caption
Identify the main features of this building. Then write a caption describing these features.

Sketch an American landmark
Sketch a building you think is a symbol of the United States. You might choose the United States Capitol or the Empire State Building in New York City. How is this building important to Americans? What do you think of when you see a picture of it?

From Ancient Greece to Feudal Europe

SECTION 1

BEFORE YOU READ

Reach Into Your Background

The accomplishments of ancient Europe still have an impact on our world. What U.S. accomplishments do you know about? Think of some great things Americans have done. Explain why people remember these achievements today.

Questions to Explore

1. What were the main accomplishments of the ancient Greeks and Romans?
2. What was the impact of Christianity and feudalism on life during the Middle Ages?

Key Terms

Middle Ages
democracy
city-state
policy
empire

Pax Romana
feudalism
manor
serf

Key People and Places

Alexander the Great
Augustus
Constantine
Athens
Rome

For many years now, on a special morning in April, thousands of people from around the world have come together in a small Massachusetts town. At noon, they begin a marathon race that requires great strength and willpower. The race ends in the city of Boston, some 26 miles (42 km) away.

But what does the Boston Marathon have to do with European history? To find out, you need to go back 2,500 years to a story about the ancient Greek city of Athens. In 490 B.C., the people of Athens were at war with the Persians. The Athenians finally won at the Battle of Marathon. To announce their victory, an Athenian soldier named Pheidippides (fuh DIP uh deez) ran all the way to Athens, about 25 miles (40 km) away. Pheidippides reached Athens and shouted, "Rejoice, we conquer!" as he entered the city. Then he died.

The story of Pheidippides may or may not be true. But the Greeks loved the story, and people all over the world still run long races called marathons. In repeating this race, people show how history lives on. This

▼ The glory of ancient Greece inspires each running of the Boston Marathon. Shown here is Moses Tanui of Kenya, the winner in the 1996 men's race.

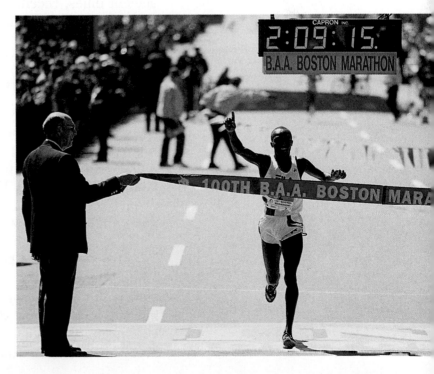

Greece's Accomplishments Live On

Chart Study Greece, whose ideas influence us to this day, borrowed ideas from older civilizations in Mesopotamia and Egypt. But the Greeks sometimes failed to give much credit to these other societies. In fact, the famous Greek thinker Plato bragged, "Whatever the Greeks have acquired from foreigners, they have, in the end, turned into something finer." **Critical Thinking** Which of Greece's achievements do you think has had the most important influence on our lives today? Why?

Area of Achievement	Influence on Modern Society
Drama	Aristotle created the rules for drama known as *The Poetics*. These rules are still used in plays and movie scripts.
Architecture	Many modern building designs reflect the common Greek styles known as Ionic, Doric, and Corinthian.
Science	The ancient Greeks introduced many principles of modern medicine, physics, biology, and mathematics.
Politics	The democratic ideals of government by the people, trial by jury, and equality under the law were formed in Athens around 500 B.C.
History	Herodotus collected information from people who remembered the events of the Persian wars. This method of research set the standard for the way history is recorded today.

chapter discusses three periods in the history of Europe and Russia—ancient times; recent times; and the time between the two, called the **Middle Ages.** We will see how the past affects the present in Europe and Russia.

The Greek Heritage

The Athenians and other ancient Greeks were Europe's first great philosophers, historians, poets, and writers. They did not accept old ways and old thinking. Instead, they observed plants, animals, and the human body. In the process, they invented today's scientific way of gathering knowledge. The Greeks also invented ideas about how people should live. One idea was **democracy** (dih MAHK ruh see), a kind of government that citizens run themselves.

The Power of Democracy In ancient times, there were over a hundred **city-states** in Greece. Each was both a city and an independent nation. This gave the Greeks plenty of chances to try different kinds of government. Many of their city-states were democracies.

The most famous Greek city-state was Athens. In this city-state, every male citizen voted on laws and government **policies,** or the

Connect How was democracy in Athens different from today's democracy in the United States?

methods and plans a government uses to do its work. Citizens were either elected or chosen at random for government positions.

Democracy was a fresh idea for the Greeks, but it was not the same as what we call democracy today. Citizens in Greece owned slaves. Non-Greeks, women, and slaves were not citizens. They could not vote. Still, the Greek idea that citizens should have a voice in their own government had a strong impact on people in later times.

Greek Ideas Spread Greek ideas might have stayed within their city-states if not for a young man named Alexander, later called Alexander the Great. At age 20, he became king of Macedonia (mas uh DOH nee uh), in northern Greece. But he was not satisfied with this small kingdom. In 334 B.C., Alexander set out to conquer the world. In only 10 years, he conquered an empire almost as big as the United States. An **empire** is a collection of lands ruled by a single government.

In all his new lands, Alexander established Greek cities, the Greek language, and Greek ideas. At the time of his death, in 323 B.C., Greek culture linked the entire Mediterranean world. The people who next ruled the region, the Romans, borrowed much from the Greeks.

▲ The Greek thinker Aristotle, shown here in this marble sculpture, was Alexander the Great's teacher. Later, Alexander spread Aristotle's ideas across an empire.

The Empire of Alexander the Great

KEY

- Alexander's empire at its height, 323 B.C.
- Route of Alexander, 334 B.C.–323 B.C.
- Towns founded by Alexander and his followers

Mercator Projection

Map Study Alexander moved from one military victory to the next without losing a single battle.
Movement How many towns did Alexander and his followers establish?

Critical Thinking After Alexander's death, his empire split into pieces. Why do you think Alexander's empire was difficult to keep united?

Even during the Pax Romana, Roman citizens continued to serve in the military. They kept the peace by stopping revolts in Egypt, Germany, and Britain. This carving showing Roman soldiers is on a column honoring Antoninus Pius, the emperor of Rome from A.D. 138–161. Antoninus Pius ruled Rome during the calmest period of the Pax Romana.

READ ACTIVELY

Visualize Visualize the building of roads and aqueducts without modern equipment.

The Glory of Ancient Rome

Have you ever heard the saying "All roads lead to Rome" or "Rome was not built in a day"? These expressions come from a glorious time—when the Roman Empire ruled a huge area and built magnificent cities and structures.

The cities of the Roman Empire were linked by roads—about 50,000 miles of hard-surfaced highways. The Roman system of roads was one of the most outstanding transportation networks ever built. Constructed over 2,000 years ago, some of these roads are still used today.

The Romans also built aqueducts, or canals that carried water to the cities from distant sources. Like Roman roads, some of these aqueducts are still in use.

The Pax Romana The Romans began building their empire soon after the death of Alexander the Great. The first emperor of Rome, Augustus, took command in 27 B.C. This began the **Pax Romana** (pahks roh MAH nah), or Roman peace. It lasted for about 200 years. During the Pax Romana, Rome was the most powerful state in Europe and in the Mediterranean. With Rome in charge, these regions remained stable.

Roman Law One of Rome's greatest gifts to the world was a system of laws. Roman lawmakers were careful and organized. They did not pass their laws on by word of mouth. Instead, they wrote them down. When a judge made a decision, he based it on written law. His decision was also put in writing to guide other judges. After a while, the law became so complex that the Romans organized it. Today, the legal system of almost every European country reflects the organization of ancient Roman law.

Roman laws protected all citizens. At first, citizens included only people who lived in Rome, except slaves. In time, however, the term came to include people all over the empire. The idea thus protected the rights of all citizens, not just the powerful and wealthy. Modern ideas about law and citizenship are based on this idea.

The Decline of Rome Hundreds of years of warfare followed the Pax Romana. People outside the empire grew strong and broke through Roman lines of defense. Sometimes they even entered Rome itself. There they terrorized, looted, and destroyed. The empire needed more and more soldiers. To pay for the wars, the government raised taxes. This hurt the empire's economy. The empire had grown too big for one person to govern, so it was divided into two empires, one in the eastern Mediterranean and one in the west. The eastern empire remained healthy. But the western one continued to weaken.

The Volcano and the City of Pompeii The city of Pompeii stood at the foot of a volcano called Mt. Vesuvius. In A.D. 79, the volcano erupted. Smoke, ash, and cinders rained on the city. In two days, the eruption covered the city with about 20 feet (6.6 m) of ash. It sealed the city like a volcanic "time capsule." Archaeologists have uncovered Pompeii's buildings, almost perfectly intact. They have even found loaves of bread in ovens!

◄This statue shows Augustus, who ruled Rome from 27 B.C. to A.D. 14. He declared that he had "found Rome brick and left it marble." Indeed, during the reign of Augustus, Rome's first emperor, the Romans constructed many buildings and built roads, bridges, and aqueducts.

The weakening of the Roman Empire in Western Europe led to a time of uncertainty. The powerful laws of the great Roman government no longer protected people. People had to look elsewhere for something to protect them.

Europe in the Middle Ages

Picture a building like a hollow mountain of stones. Each stone has been cut and set in place by careful workers. The building's graceful arches sweep to the sky. This building is a cathedral—a great church. Many cathedrals were built in Europe during the Middle Ages.

Today, a building can be raised in a few months. But in the Middle Ages, it took as long as 100 years to build a cathedral. People devoted so much time and energy to building cathedrals because they believed that the work was God's wish. Such strong religious faith was a key part of life in Europe during the Middle Ages.

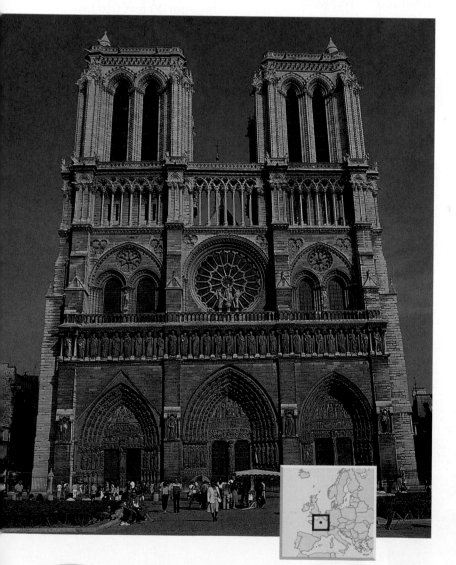

▼ Paris's Notre Dame Cathedral took about 150 years to complete. It was one of the first buildings constructed with flying buttresses, which are supporting arches on the outside of the building.

Christian Faith The religion of Christianity arose from the life and teachings of Jesus, who lived in a region called Palestine. After Jesus' death, his followers began spreading his teachings. These followers taught that Jesus was the Son of God.

One person who became a Christian, or follower of Jesus Christ, was a Roman emperor named Constantine. Christianity spread quickly throughout the Roman Empire. Later, the empire collapsed. Government, law and order, and trade broke down. But Christianity remained. The people of Europe, living in a period of difficulty and danger, drew strength from Christianity. In such dark times, faith was like a welcoming light.

Feudalism Christianity was one important part of people's lives during the Middle Ages. Another was **feudalism** (FYOOD ul iz um), which is a way to organize society when there is no central government. In feudalism, leaders called lords ruled the local areas. Lords swore oaths of loyalty to a more powerful leader, such as a king. In return, the king allowed the lord to own a piece of land called a **manor.** The lord owned all the crops and received all income from the land. He collected taxes, maintained order, enforced laws, and protected the **serfs,**

Feudal Society

Chart Study
European society in the Middle Ages was shaped like a pyramid. At the bottom were serfs, who made up 90 percent of the population. Above the serfs were the nobles, made up of knights, lords, and the king. Though there were many fewer nobles than serfs, the nobles had nearly all the wealth and power.

Critical Thinking
How did the feudal system tie different social groups together?

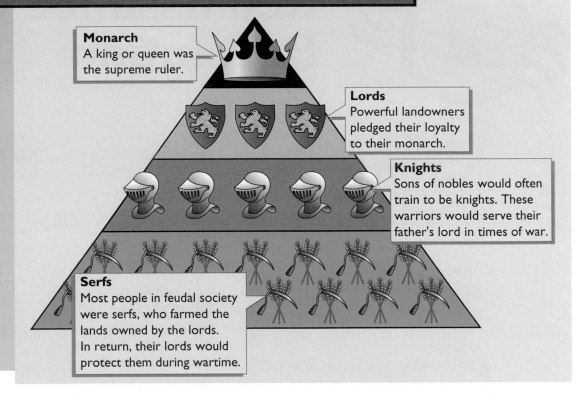

Monarch
A king or queen was the supreme ruler.

Lords
Powerful landowners pledged their loyalty to their monarch.

Knights
Sons of nobles would often train to be knights. These warriors would serve their father's lord in times of war.

Serfs
Most people in feudal society were serfs, who farmed the lands owned by the lords. In return, their lords would protect them during wartime.

the people who lived on the land and farmed it. Serfs were not slaves, but they could not leave without the lord's permission. They owned no land and depended on the lord for protection in times of war.

As centuries passed, life in Europe changed. Trade increased. Many serfs bought their freedom from the lords and moved to towns, which offered excitement and opportunity. Towns grew into cities. By the 1400s, a new way of life had begun to develop in Europe.

SECTION 1 REVIEW

1. **Define** (a) Middle Ages, (b) democracy, (c) city-state, (d) policy, (e) empire, (f) Pax Romana, (g) feudalism, (h) manor, (i) serf.

2. **Identify** (a) Alexander the Great, (b) Augustus, (c) Constantine, (d) Athens, (e) Rome.

3. What were the most important ideas given to us by (a) the ancient Greeks and (b) the ancient Romans?

4. What role did Christianity play during the Middle Ages?

5. What did feudalism provide during the Middle Ages?

Critical Thinking

6. **Making Comparisons** Describe some ways in which Europe under the Pax Romana was different from Europe in the Middle Ages.

Activity

7. **Writing to Learn** You are a Roman governor in Britain, far from your home and family in Rome. Write a journal entry describing the things you miss about Rome. Be as specific as you can.

Renaissance and Revolution

BEFORE YOU READ

Reach Into Your Background

Tales of rich and wondrous lands to the east inspired European explorers. Have you ever read or seen stories that made you want to travel to distant lands? Think of a list of places that you would like to visit. Write a few sentences telling how you learned about them and why you want to visit them.

Questions to Explore

1. Why did Europeans begin to look outward to other continents?
2. How did the Age of Revolution change science and government?

Key Terms

Renaissance
humanism
monarch
middle class
absolute monarch
revolution
colony
Scientific Revolution

Key People

Marco Polo
Michelangelo
Louis XIV

▼ More than 100 years after Marco Polo's departure from Venice in 1271, illustrations like this celebrated his adventures.

The time is about A.D. 1295. The place is a prison in an Italian city called Genoa (JEN uh wuh). An explorer named Marco Polo lies on a cot, telling stories to a fellow prisoner. The tales are amazing because Marco Polo has had quite a life! For a time, he was a messenger of the great Mongol (MAHN gul) emperor Kublai Khan (KOO bly kahn), ruler of China. Polo also traveled across burning deserts and sailed south of the Equator. He visited the Spice Islands, sources of cinnamon, nutmeg, and cloves—spices that Europeans loved. He earned great riches, only to be robbed on his way home to Italy.

These stories were published in a book we know today as *The Travels of Marco Polo.* From the very beginning, the book was a great success. Two hundred years later, Marco Polo's book inspired Christopher Columbus, another explorer. When Columbus sailed west from Europe, he was searching for a new route to the rich lands Marco Polo had described: China, Japan, and India.

Leonardo da Vinci (above), one of the best-known artists of the Renaissance, is famous for his painting, *Mona Lisa* (left). But he also excelled as a scientist, an engineer, and an inventor.

Glories of the Renaissance

Columbus's search for a new route to wealth was only one example of the energy sweeping Europe. The changes began in Italy in the 1300s and spread over the continent. Traders were busy buying and selling again. The rich were becoming even richer. They had the time to enjoy art and learning—and the money to support artists and scholars. This period is called the **Renaissance** (REN uh sahns), which refers to a "rebirth" of interest in learning and art. The Renaissance reached its peak in the 1500s.

Renaissance scholars and artists rediscovered the ancient world. Once again, people learned about its great poetry, plays, ideas, buildings, and sculpture. What they learned changed them. They began writing fresh, powerful poetry. They built glorious new buildings and filled them with breathtaking paintings. People began to focus on improving this world rather than hoping for a better life after death. In trying to understand the world around them, they looked at the ideas of Greek and Roman thinkers. This new approach to knowledge was called **humanism.**

Humanism affected every part of the Renaissance. For example, in the early Middle Ages, statues had been carved as stiff symbols. But during the Renaissance period, statues carved by artists such as Michelangelo (my kul AN juh loh), an Italian sculptor, were lifelike. In fact, some people say that no better sculptor than Michelangelo has ever lived.

READ ACTIVELY

Ask Questions What would you like to ask a Renaissance artist about the influence of humanism?

More Trade, Stronger Rulers

In the Renaissance, people also began to travel outside of Europe more often. In the 1400s, Portuguese explorers traveled along the western coast of Africa. There they traded in gold, ivory, and slaves. This trade was very profitable. Finally, the Portuguese reached the Indian Ocean. They set up new trade routes for the most profitable goods of all—spices. Rulers of other European countries envied the Portuguese. Spain, France, England, and the Netherlands all wanted a share of the trading wealth. Then, in 1492, Christopher Columbus found even more possibilities for wealth. Far to the west were two vast continents: the Americas.

The Effects of Trade   Europeans raced to the Americas in search of wealth. Precious minerals, such as gold and silver, and trade goods, such as fur and tobacco, poured into Europe. Most of the wealth went to European **monarchs** (MAHN urks), rulers such as kings and queens. Some of it went to traders and merchants. These people formed a group between the poor and the very rich. They became the **middle class.** The taxes paid by the middle class made monarchs even wealthier. Soon, kings no longer needed the support of feudal lords. Feudalism declined, local lords grew weaker, and kings gained power.

More Gold, More Knowledge

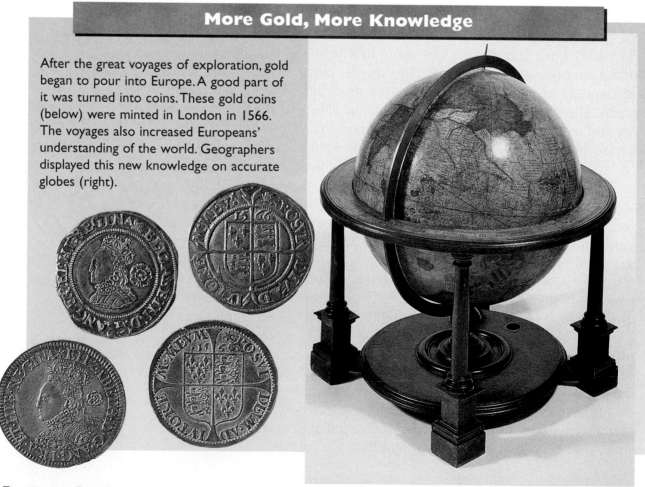

After the great voyages of exploration, gold began to pour into Europe. A good part of it was turned into coins. These gold coins (below) were minted in London in 1566. The voyages also increased Europeans' understanding of the world. Geographers displayed this new knowledge on accurate globes (right).

The Age of Monarchs

From 1643 to 1715, the king of France was Louis XIV. One of Europe's most powerful kings, Louis XIV ruled at a time when France was a leading world power. Like other kings of his time, Louis was an **absolute monarch**; that is, he exercised complete power over his subjects. As he said, "I am the state." His wishes were law, and no one dared to disagree with him. Like other European monarchs, Louis believed that his power to rule came from God. To oppose him was the same as opposing God.

Louis used his power to make people pay heavy taxes. These taxes, in part, paid for his very expensive lifestyle. But Louis also wanted to make France strong. Other rulers wanted the same thing for their countries. Over time, these monarchs made their countries stronger and more unified. As these changes took place, people began thinking again about government. What should it be? What should it do for them?

Hall of Mirrors

Twelve miles from Paris, the palace at Versailles with its glittering Hall of Mirrors advertised the French king's wealth. Paintings on the ceiling illustrate the royal family's accomplishments.

Revolutions in Government and Science

The 1600s and 1700s are often called the Age of Revolution. A **revolution** is a far-reaching change. European thought, beliefs, and ways of life all changed. This period was the beginning of the modern age of science and democracy that we know today.

Revolutions in Government   One sign of revolution was that people began questioning their governments. For instance, people wondered if kings should have all the power. In the 1600s, when England's king refused to share power with Parliament (PAHR luh munt), the elected legislature, he was overthrown. England had no monarch for several years. This change in power failed, and the monarchy returned. But this event showed that the people, not the monarch, should decide which type of government is best for them.

This idea of government spread to North America, where Great Britain had 13 colonies. A **colony** is a territory ruled by another nation,

LINKS ACROSS THE WORLD

A Share in Two Revolutions In 1776, Thomas Paine wrote *Common Sense*, a pamphlet urging the American colonies to fight for independence. The pamphlet sold more than 500,000 copies and greatly influenced the American Revolution. Later, Paine wrote *The Rights of Man,* in which he defended the French Revolution of 1789.

On July 14, 1789, an angry French mob seized control of the Bastille, a prison (below). The people were angry at King Louis XVI and the queen, Marie Antoinette (right), because the monarchs were spending money on clothes and building projects at a time when the poor in Paris were starving. Eventually, the king and queen were both executed.

Predict How might humanism have affected science?

usually one far away. In 1776, the colonies rebelled against the British king. The colonists defeated the British and formed the independent nation of the United States. And in 1789, 13 years after the Americans declared their independence, there was a revolution in France. The French Revolution overthrew the French monarchy once and for all.

The Scientific Revolution   There was also a revolution in science. For centuries, European scientists had studied nature to explain how the world fit with their religious beliefs. During the Age of Revolution, that approach changed. Scientists began to watch carefully to see what really happened in the world. They would base their theories on facts. They would not try to make the facts fit their religious beliefs. This change is called the **Scientific Revolution.**

The Scientific Revolution required new procedures. These procedures make up what is called the scientific method, in which ideas are tested with experiments and observations. Scientists do not accept an idea as correct unless several tests prove that it is.

Using the scientific method, scientists made dramatic advances. For example, in the Middle Ages, Europeans believed that the Earth was at the center of the universe. Later, Renaissance scientists challenged this belief. Then, during the Scientific Revolution, scientists used a new form

The Scientific Method

Chart Study A revolution in thinking paved the way for the scientific method, which today's scientists still use. Employing this method, scientists began to record what they could actually observe instead of what they merely believed to be true. Followers of the scientific method usually repeat their work many times, in order to make sure that their conclusions are accurate. **Critical Thinking** Why do you think scientists should repeat their work before coming to a conclusion?

STEP ONE

State the problem.

STEP TWO

Gather information about the problem.

STEP THREE

Form a hypothesis, or educated guess.

STEP FOUR

Experiment to test the hypothesis.

STEP FIVE

Record and analyze data.

STEP SIX

State a conclusion.

of mathematics called calculus (KAL kyoo lus). It helped them learn how the moon and planets move. Their work led to better ideas about such things as gravity.

By the end of the Age of Revolution, Europe was a continent of powerful nations. They were bustling with trade and bursting with new scientific ideas. Europe was about to begin a new kind of revolution. This time it would be an economic one—the rise of industry.

SECTION 2 REVIEW

1. **Define** (a) Renaissance, (b) humanism, (c) monarch, (d) middle class, (e) absolute monarch, (f) revolution, (g) colony, (h) Scientific Revolution.

2. **Identify** (a) Marco Polo, (b) Michelangelo, (c) Louis XIV.

3. How did Europeans' desire for wealth lead to voyages of exploration?

4. How did the art of the Renaissance differ from the art of the Middle Ages?

5. How did government and science in Europe change during the Age of Revolution?

Critical Thinking

6. **Identifying Central Issues** Explain how trade affected the power of kings during the 1500s and 1600s.

Activity

7. **Writing to Learn** Marco Polo's writings excited readers and made them want to explore the world just like he had. Think about a place that you have visited. What makes it special? What details make you like it—or dislike it? Then write about the place in a way that would make a reader want to go there, too.

Interpreting Diagrams and Illustrations

Sandra bolted through the front door of her grandmother's house.

"Hey, Grandma! Dad just told me that you went to France once, before I was born."

"Yes, I did," said her grandmother. "I went to visit my mother's family. But I was much younger then."

"What was it like? What did you do there?" Sandra wanted to know all about it.

"Well, that little town looked a lot different than it does now—that was 40 years ago."

"Did they have knights and castles then?" Sandra asked eagerly.

Her grandmother laughed. "Oh, no, it wasn't *that* long ago. But you can see for yourself. I think I still have my pictures from that trip. Shall we get them out?"

Sandra nodded.

"There's just one problem," her grandmother warned. "You'll understand the pictures, but all the writing is in French!"

Get Ready

There are many kinds of illustrations— maps, photographs, paintings, drawings, and diagrams, to name a few. Often, diagrams and illustrations are explained by captions and annotations. Annotations are labels that include extra information. They help you understand diagrams and illustrations.

To get the most out of any illustration, you need to study carefully both the illustration itself and all of the annotations. You may find this even more useful when you look at illustrations of life long ago. These illustrations can bring history alive for you. They can help you picture life in other times and other places.

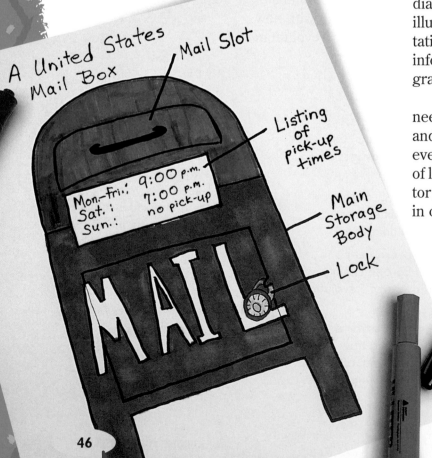

◀ You can learn how to interpret diagrams and illustrations by making one of your own. In addition to the labels shown on this mailbox, the student might have added a caption such as "The post office collects the mail and delivers it to the recipients."

Try It Out

Of course, the world today is much different than the world young people lived in hundreds of years ago. Far in the future, the world will be much different than it is now. Students many years from now will read in their history books about the way *you* live. You can help them out by creating an illustration to help them picture "life long ago"—your life today.

A. Choose your subject. Draw an illustration of something that is common today but might not be common in the future. Perhaps chalkboards will be replaced by computers, or automobiles by personal jets. Be sure to draw something you know well.

B. Illustrate your subject. Using a pencil and unlined paper, draw your subject. Try to be as accurate as possible. Imagine that the students of the future will never have seen the real thing.

C. Add annotations to your illustration. Write brief notes explaining the main features of what you have drawn. Try to have your annotations explain the object's parts. Tell how they are used or how they relate to each other.

Apply the Skill

Now that you have made your own illustration and annotations, you can read one by someone else. Complete the following steps.

1. **Study the illustration.** Look it over in a general way. What is the subject of this illustration? From what time period is it? Does it show something as it really looked, or does it show how something might have looked?

2. **Read the annotations.** The annotations provide key information about the illustration. What are the main parts of a manor? Who lived in the manor house? How were the fields divided? What was the demesne (dih MAYN)? How were the meadows used? Where did the serfs live?

3. **Think about the illustration.** After you have studied the illustration and read the annotations, take another look. This time, imagine yourself as the lord of the manor, or as a serf who worked there. What was life like for you? Write a journal entry from this point of view. Try to capture the sights, sounds, and smells of life on the manor.

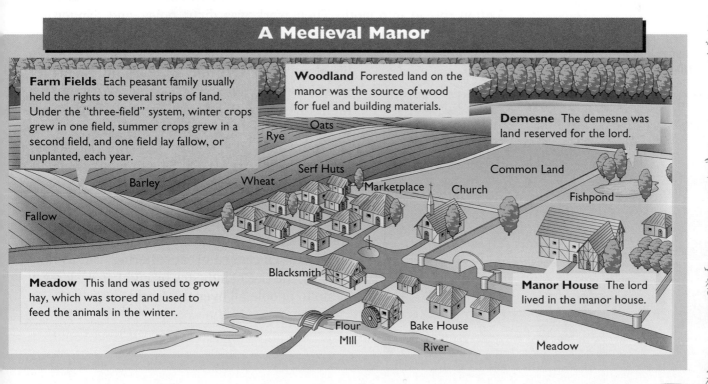

A Medieval Manor

Farm Fields Each peasant family usually held the rights to several strips of land. Under the "three-field" system, winter crops grew in one field, summer crops grew in a second field, and one field lay fallow, or unplanted, each year.

Woodland Forested land on the manor was the source of wood for fuel and building materials.

Demesne The demesne was land reserved for the lord.

Meadow This land was used to grow hay, which was stored and used to feed the animals in the winter.

Manor House The lord lived in the manor house.

Oats

Rye

Barley

Wheat

Serf Huts

Marketplace

Church

Common Land

Fishpond

Fallow

Blacksmith

Flour Mill

Bake House

River

Meadow

Industrial Revolution and Nationalism

BEFORE YOU READ

Reach Into Your Background

Have you ever spent a whole day working very hard? Perhaps you helped with spring housecleaning or took part in a car wash. Do you remember how tired you were at the end of the day? During the Industrial Revolution, many people your age worked in factories 12 hours a day, 6 days a week.

Questions to Explore

1. How did the Industrial Revolution change life in Europe?

2. How did nationalism change Europe?

Key Terms

Industrial Revolution
textile
imperialism
nationalism
alliance

I t was dawn. Thick, black smoke rose from the tall smokestack of the factory. Dust blew through the air and settled over the crowded rows of houses. The smoke and the roar of machines showed that the factory workday had begun.

Inside, women and children worked at rows of machines that wove cotton thread into cloth. Their work was dirty, noisy, and dangerous. The day before, a worker had caught his hand in a machine and was severely injured. Today, another worker stood in his place. Both were only 13 years old. No matter what, the machines kept going. Workers fed them thread for 12 hours every day—6 days out of every 7. Vacations did not exist.

You could see scenes like this all across Europe in the early 1800s. The great age of factories had begun. Products that once had been made by people in homes or in small shops were now made by machines in huge factories. This change is called the **Industrial Revolution.** The new factories caused great suffering. But as time went by, the rise of industry brought an easier way of life to people all over the world.

▼ This late 1800s picture shows smoke belching from factories beside the Don River in Sheffield, an industrial city in northern England.

From Spinning Wheel to Spinning Mule

During the Industrial Revolution, spinning wheels (below) were replaced by spinning mules (left) that could spin up to 1,300 times as much thread in the same amount of time. Special buildings, called factories, were built to house the spinning mules. **Critical Thinking** How do you think the shift from spinning wheel to spinning mule affected the average worker?

The Industrial Revolution

Did you ever wonder what life would be like without factories? You would have to make everything you need at home or buy it from a small shop nearby. People produced goods this way until about the late 1700s. Then, inventors began to create machines that could make goods quickly and cheaply. Huge factories housed the machines. People left their homes to work in the factories and keep the machines running. This was a revolution in the way goods were made. It was also a revolution in the ways people lived and worked.

Changes in Production   The Industrial Revolution began in Great Britain. The first machines were invented to speed up the spinning of thread and the weaving of **textiles,** or cloth products. The new factories made their owners very wealthy. Businesspeople in other countries saw this and decided to try the same thing. Factories sprouted up all over Europe and in the United States. By 1900, factories produced almost all goods made in the United States and most of Western Europe.

Changes in Society   The Industrial Revolution changed life across Europe. For hundreds of years, families had farmed the land. Now they moved to industrial centers to work in factories. Cities grew rapidly. People were packed into cramped, dirty housing. Because of unclean and crowded conditions, diseases spread rapidly.

Urbanization When industrialization took hold in Europe, people moved from the country to the cities in huge numbers. In 100 years, the population of London grew from 831,000 to 4.5 million. The population of Paris grew from 547,000 to 2.9 million.

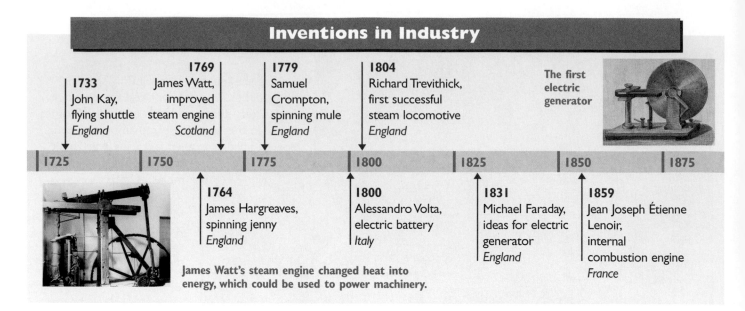

Inventions in Industry

1733
John Kay,
flying shuttle
England

1769
James Watt,
improved
steam engine
Scotland

1779
Samuel
Crompton,
spinning mule
England

1804
Richard Trevithick,
first successful
steam locomotive
England

The first
electric
generator

1725	1750	1775	1800	1825	1850	1875

1764
James Hargreaves,
spinning jenny
England

1800
Alessandro Volta,
electric battery
Italy

1831
Michael Faraday,
ideas for electric
generator
England

1859
Jean Joseph Étienne
Lenoir,
internal
combustion engine
France

James Watt's steam engine changed heat into
energy, which could be used to power machinery.

▲ As you read the time line, find the inventions that could be used to produce power. These inventions paved the way for machines that required more energy than humans or animals could provide.

READ ACTIVELY

Predict How did the Industrial Revolution promote democracy?

The changes were difficult for many people. For a long time, factory owners took advantage of workers. Wages were low. Factory conditions were not safe. However, workers slowly began to form labor unions and to demand better working conditions. In the early 1900s, governments began passing laws to protect workers. Conditions improved and wages rose.

Changes in Government

Government had to respond to workers' complaints. Making and selling goods was a big part of a country's economy. This meant that workers had become very important. As a result, the Industrial Revolution helped give working people a bigger voice in government. Many European nations became more democratic.

At the same time, though, European governments were becoming more aggressive abroad. During the 1800s, many European nations took over other countries and turned them into colonies. This is called **imperialism.** European nations were making more goods than their people could buy. They needed more customers. Colonies could supply those buyers. Colonies also provided raw materials, such things as cotton, wood, and metals, that industry needed.

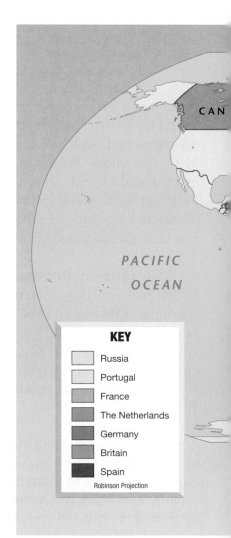

CAN

PACIFIC
OCEAN

KEY

Russia
Portugal
France
The Netherlands
Germany
Britain
Spain

Robinson Projection

The late 1800s are called the Age of Imperialism. Most of Africa was divided up by the European nations of Belgium, France, Italy, Spain, Portugal, Germany, and Great Britain. These countries also took over much of Southeast Asia and many South Pacific islands. In time, struggles among the colonial powers would bring disaster to Europe.

A Century of War and Nationalism

At the start of the 1900s, the people of Europe were filled with **nationalism,** or pride in one's country. Nationalism can either be a destructive or creative force, depending on how people express it.

Destructive Nationalism   Nationalism can be very destructive. It can make one nation harm another in an effort to get ahead. It can also prevent nations from working with one another. Then anger and hatred can erupt between countries. Between 1900 and 1950, destructive nationalism played a part in causing two world wars and the deaths of millions of people.

Ask Questions What would you like to know about the impact of nationalism on world history?

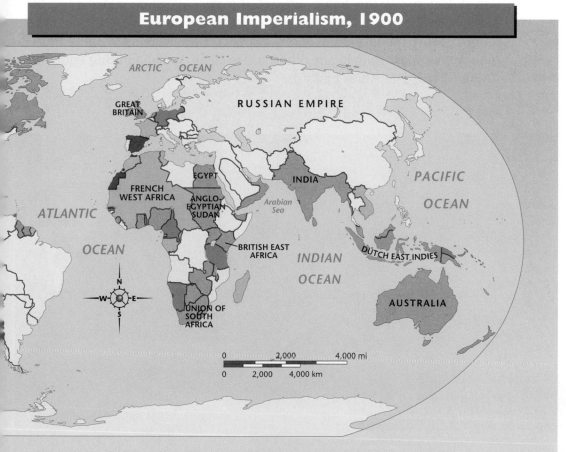

European Imperialism, 1900

Map Study Europe's history of colonizing other parts of the world did not begin in 1900. European countries began colonizing the Americas in the 1500s. Most of the Americas had become independent by 1900. **Regions** What three European countries had the largest empires in 1900?

CITIZEN HEROES

Working Together
Jeannine Picabia was 18 in 1941. She worked with a French medical group that traveled to places where prisoners were questioned by German soldiers. She listened carefully to the conversations. One day she decided to go to an American government building in France to tell what she had heard. Secretly, for the rest of World War II, she gathered information for the forces that were trying to defeat Germany.

▼ One of the most frightening weapons of World War I was poison gas. These Russian soldiers are caught in a German gas attack.

During the early 1900s, European nations feared one another. Each nation was afraid another would invade or try to take over its territory. To protect themselves, nations made **alliances** (uh LY un sez), or agreements with one another. In such alliances, a nation promises to protect its friends if someone attacks them. Soon, Europe was divided into two alliances. On one side were Germany, Austria-Hungary, and Turkey. On the other side were Great Britain, France, and Russia.

In 1914, fighting between the alliances broke out into what is now called World War I. By the end of the war, in 1918, over 9 million soldiers had been killed. About 13 million civilians, or nonsoldiers, had also died. Europe had lost almost a whole generation of young men.

But nationalism still burned like a flame. In 1939, another war broke out. This war was called World War II. Again there were two alliances. On one side were the Axis Powers—Germany and Italy, which were joined by Japan. These countries wanted to increase their national wealth and power. Therefore, they took control of other countries. They quickly captured most of Europe and parts of China and the South Pacific. Germany also attacked the Soviet Union, a nation made up of Russia and several smaller regions.

In time, the United States joined the Allies—Great Britain and the Soviet Union—in the battle against the Axis Powers. More than 50 nations took part in this war, which was the most destructive ever fought. More people died, more property was damaged, and more money was spent than in any other war in history. The fighting ended in August 1945. The Allies had won.

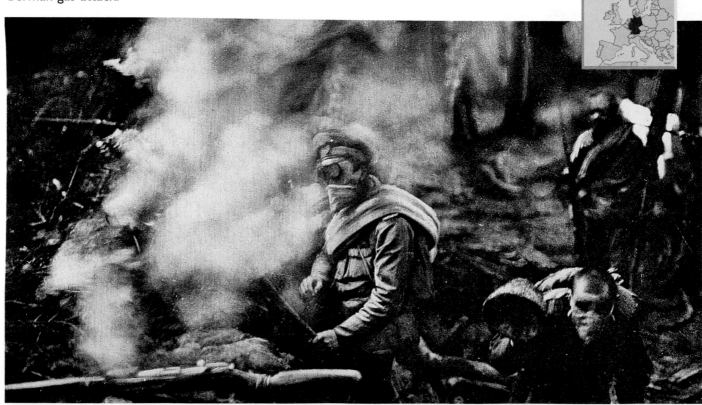

A Tunnel Connecting Britain to France

During the Ice Age, France and Great Britain were connected by a low plain. Later, the English Channel separated Britain and France—but not forever. In 1987, France and Great Britain began working together to dig a tunnel under the English Channel. In 1994, these men dug the breakthrough hole linking Britain and France. They exchanged flags and shook hands. Today trains carry passengers and freight through the Channel Tunnel, which many people call the Chunnel. **Critical Thinking** What do you think kept Great Britain and France from building the Chunnel earlier?

Creative Nationalism After the war, all of Europe was in ruins. It was time to rebuild. The European nations were sick of imperialism and war. After hundreds of years, they were no longer world leaders. Now the world looked on the United States and the Soviet Union as leading nations.

Europeans began learning to work together. They became trading partners, not competitors. A new type of nationalism began, a European nationalism. People have not forgotten that they are French, or British, or German. At the end of the 1900s, however, Europeans were working hard to build a common European community. It helped carry them into the new century in peace.

SECTION 3 REVIEW

1. **Define** (a) Industrial Revolution, (b) textile, (c) imperialism, (d) nationalism, (e) alliance.

2. What changes occurred in the lives of ordinary people during the Industrial Revolution?

3. What changes in government occurred in industrialized nations during the Industrial Revolution?

4. Give an example of creative nationalism.

Critical Thinking

5. **Identifying Central Issues** The Industrial Revolution caused many changes. Name two changes that helped bring about imperialism.

Activity

6. **Writing to Learn** After World War II, colonies in Africa and Asia demanded their freedom from the European colonial powers. Suppose you were a citizen of a colony. Write a paragraph explaining why you would want to be free from European rulers.

SECTION

4

Imperial Russia

BEFORE YOU READ

Reach Into Your Background

The rulers of Russia could do almost anything they wanted. They could make any laws and carry out any plans they chose. Imagine being able to make any changes you wanted in the United States. What would you change? What would you keep the same?

Questions to Explore

1. How did Russia develop into a huge empire by 1900?
2. How did the serfs' living conditions lead to opposition to the czars?

Key Terms
westernization
czar

Key People
Catherine the Great
Golden Horde
Peter the Great
Nicholas II

▼ This picture shows Catherine the Great wearing the crown of the empress of Russia.

At dawn on June 28, 1762, a maid awakened Catherine in her rooms at a small palace outside St. Petersburg, Russia. Catherine's supporter, Aleksei Orlov (ul yik SEEAY ur LAHF), was waiting for her. "Time to rise," he told her. "Everything is prepared." Catherine hurried to a coach waiting to whisk her to St. Petersburg.

As the coach hurried along, Catherine may have remembered how she had first come to Russia, 17 years before. At age 16, she had been brought here from Germany to marry Peter, who later became emperor. Peter was a weak and foolish ruler. Now Catherine was hoping to remove him from the throne and become empress herself. Would the Russian people support her?

As Catherine's coach rattled down St. Petersburg's main street toward the Winter Palace, crowds streamed out to cheer her on. When she arrived at the palace, she was greeted by government, military, and church leaders. Their support helped make Catherine the new Empress of Russia.

Catherine was witty and charming. She loved the arts, literature, philosophy, and French culture. Under her rule, the court at St. Petersburg glittered with French actors and dancers, German teachers and craftspeople, and artistic treasures from foreign lands. Her court attracted the greatest minds of Europe. She dreamed of creating a great nation, as glorious as France under Louis XIV. Little wonder that she was called Catherine the Great.

Catherine cared about Russia. She built schools and hospitals and gave people more religious freedom. Early in her rule, she became interested in ideas about liberty. She even thought about freeing the serfs, the peasant farmers who worked on the estates of wealthy landowners. Then there was a violent serf revolt, and Catherine changed her mind. She strengthened control over the serfs and crushed their attempts to gain freedom.

Though Catherine did not make Russia a land of freedom, she did make Russia a grand empire. By her death in 1796, she had expanded her nation's borders southward to the edge of the Black Sea. She had also taken over parts of Poland in the west. Her expansion followed a pattern of empire-building that had been taking place in Russia for many centuries.

As Catherine's rule shows, the history of Russia is a story with three themes: (1) expansion; (2) harsh treatment of the common people; and (3) slow **westernization,** a process of becoming more like Western Europe. As you read Russia's story, notice how these three themes show up again and again.

Predict What changes do you think took place because of Mongol rule?

Building a Vast Empire

Russia began as a small country called Muscovy (MUHS kuh vee), or Moscow. In the early 1100s, Kiev (KEE ev) was the most important city in the region. It was home to the grand prince. Other, lesser princes ruled their own lands. They continually fought among themselves. Each hoped to gain enough power to become the grand prince. In 1238, Mongol conquerors, who were called the Golden Horde, swept into the region from Asia. Weakened by the struggles among themselves, the princes were defeated quickly. In 1240, the Mongols conquered Kiev and the whole territory became part of the Mongol empire.

Life Under the Golden Horde
The Golden Horde dominated Russia for almost 250 years. The Mongols mostly wanted two things: to collect heavy taxes and to force the Russians to serve in the Mongol army. The conquerors appointed a Russian prince to handle the day-to-day

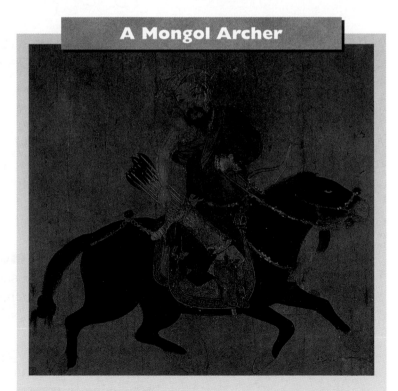

A Mongol Archer

Russians called Mongol warriors like this archer the Golden Horde after the color of their tents. The Mongols plundered and burned Kiev and other Russian towns. They killed so many Russians that a historian claimed "no eye remained to weep for the dead."

Russian Expansion, 1300–1955

KEY

- Principality of Russia, 1300
- Territory added, 1300–1462
- Territory added, 1462–1505
- Territory added, 1505–1584
- Territory added, 1613–1800
- Territory added, 1800–1855
- Territory added, 1855–1955

Two-Point Equidistant Projection

Barents Sea · Kara Sea · Baltic Sea · Bering Sea · Sea of Okhotsk · Sea of Japan · Black Sea · Caspian Sea · Aral Sea · Lake Balkash · Lake Baikal

Leningrad · Moscow · Kiev · Perm · Baku · Tashkent · Vladivostok

URAL MOUNTAINS · Dnieper River · Volga River · Lena River

0   500   1,000 mi
0   500   1,000 km

Map Study Between 1300 and 1584, Russia was a small area around Moscow. Then, during the 1600s and 1700s, the country pushed its borders both to the east and to the west. In the 1900s, Russia became part of the Soviet Union. **Regions** Locate the Ural Mountains, the natural feature that mapmakers consider to be the boundary between Europe and Asia. In 1584, was Russia mostly in Europe or mostly in Asia? In 1955?

affairs of the country. To make sure that the people did not rebel, the Mongols attacked the country from time to time. Because Russia was cut off from the West by the Mongols, Russia did not take part in the Renaissance of art and learning that was changing Western Europe.

The Rise of Moscow During the early 1330s, the Mongols selected Ivan I of Muscovy to be grand prince. Ivan collected taxes for the Mongols. In return, they let him keep some of the money. Ivan the Moneybag, as he was soon called, began to buy land and expand the size of Muscovy.

As Muscovy grew stronger, the Mongol empire began to fall apart. In 1480, Ivan III, Grand Prince of Muscovy, challenged Mongol control by refusing to pay taxes. The Golden Horde was too weak to force its wishes on Ivan and take back control of Russia.

Rise of the Czars As Muscovy became more powerful and spread its control over Russia, its grand prince became known as a **czar** (zar), or emperor. The first czar, Ivan IV, was crowned in 1547. He was also known as Ivan the Terrible. He was cruel and distrusted others. But he increased Russia's size by conquering Mongol lands in the southeast and by conquering western Siberia.

After Ivan IV's death, Russia lived through nearly 30 years of war. Finally, in 1613, Michael Romanov (ROH muh nawf) became czar. He was the first in a long line of Romanovs who ruled Russia until 1917. The Romanovs expanded Russian territory through the 1600s.

In 1689, Peter the Great came to power. A strong leader, Peter started to bring Western European ideas and culture to Russia. In 1697, he sent a group of Russian officials to visit Western Europe. His goals were to find out about western culture and methods and to meet with European officials. Peter went along, dressed as a minor official. On his return to Russia, he started new schools and reorganized his government and the army. He hired foreign professors, scientists, and advisors. He encouraged Russians to adopt western customs.

READ ACTIVELY

Visualize Visualize Peter the Great in disguise in meetings with European officials.

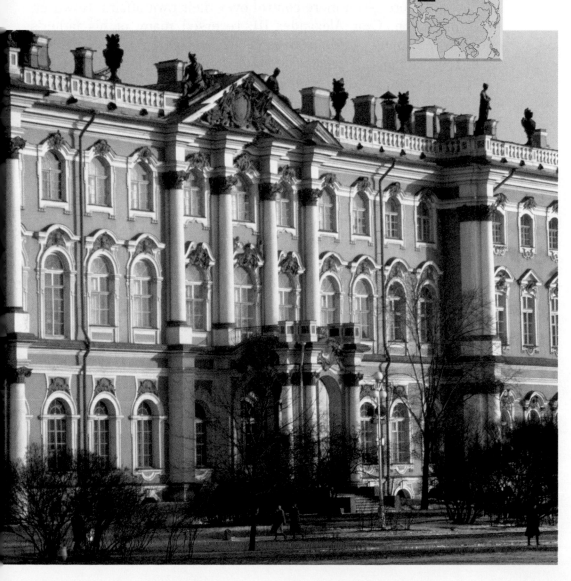

◀ The Winter Palace at St. Petersburg, completed in 1762, was the world's largest royal palace. It was the winter home of the czars until 1917.

Peter also enlarged Russia. He believed that Russia must have good seaports to become a world power, so he conquered land on the Baltic (BAWL tik) and Black seas. Czars who followed Peter, including Catherine the Great, continued to expand Russia's borders, gaining territories in Poland, Turkey, China, and Sweden. With many lands under its rule, Russia truly became an empire.

The Fall of the Czars

Russia was becoming powerful, but the lives of its serfs had not improved. For hundreds of years, Russia had been divided into two groups—the very rich and the very poor. Tension between the two groups began to rise.

In 1855, a new czar, Alexander II, came to the throne. He, too, wanted Russia to be more like European nations. One way to do that, he believed, was to have the czars and the wealthy give up some of their powers. In 1861, a few years before Abraham Lincoln ended slavery in the United States, Alexander freed the serfs and gave them their own land. Towns were given more control over their own affairs. However, Alexander's son, Czar Alexander III, reversed many of his father's reforms. The country again came under harsh rule.

In 1894, Nicholas II became czar. He would be the last. After Russia was badly beaten in a war with Japan in 1904 and 1905, unrest grew among serfs and workers. On January 22, 1905, thousands of workers in

LINKS
ACROSS THE WORLD

Peace Between Russia and Japan Between 1904 and 1905, Japan and Russia fought over control of Manchuria, in northeastern Asia, and Korea, a peninsula in East Asia. Finally, U.S. President Theodore Roosevelt arranged a peace conference in Portsmouth, New Hampshire. For his role in the settlement, Roosevelt was awarded the Nobel Peace Prize in 1906.

The Russian Famine of 1892

Even after Alexander II freed them from serfdom, the lives of Russian peasants did not improve much. In the 1890s, there were several bad harvests, and many peasants starved to death. This etching shows peasants begging in the streets of Kazan, Russia. The famine was one of many problems that eventually helped to incite the people of Russia to revolution. **Critical Thinking** How can you tell that the people in the sleigh were wealthy?

The Czar and the Czarevitch

Czar Nicholas II (right) and his son Alexis posed for a photograph shortly before the Russian Revolution of 1917. Alexis was the czarevitch, which means that he was the next in line to the throne. If the Russian Revolution had not taken place, he would have become the next czar. **Critical Thinking** Czars, like all monarchs, must learn to be strong leaders. What skills do you think the young czarevitch needed to learn in order to become czar?

St. Petersburg marched on the Winter Palace to ask the czar for reforms. They were met by troops, who fired into the crowd, killing hundreds.

After this mass killing, known as Bloody Sunday, Czar Nicholas was forced to agree to establish the Duma (DOO mah), a kind of congress. Members were elected by the people. The Duma held power, along with the czar, until 1917. Progress toward reform had been made. Some people wanted more, however, as you will read in the next section.

SECTION 4 REVIEW

1. Define (a) westernization, (b) czar.

2. Identify (a) Catherine the Great, (b) Golden Horde, (c) Peter the Great, (d) Nicholas II.

3. What territories did the princes of Muscovy and the czars take to expand Russian territory?

4. How did Russian czars treat the serfs?

5. Which rulers did the most to westernize Russia?

Critical Thinking

6. Identifying Central Issues At the beginning of the section, you learned about three themes in Russian history. How do the reigns of Ivan I, Ivan IV, and Peter the Great express those themes?

Activity

7. Writing to Learn You are Peter the Great. Write a journal entry about the ways in which you would like to make Russia a better and stronger country.

SECTION 5

The Rise and Fall of the Soviet Union

BEFORE YOU READ

Reach Into Your Background

Imagine going shopping and finding only one style of shoes or one type of shirt. What if the grocery store had row after row of empty shelves? How would your life be different?

Questions to Explore

1. What is communism and why did it fail in the Soviet Union?
2. What happened in the Soviet Union under Lenin and Stalin?

Key Terms

revolutionary
communism
civil war
dictator
Cold War
consumer goods

Key People

Vladimir Lenin
Josef Stalin
Mikhail Gorbachev

▼ A rival said that the fiery Lenin—shown here making a speech in Red Square, Moscow—was so determined that "even when he sleeps, he dreams of nothing but the revolution."

On the afternoon of April 16, 1917, a small group of Russians gathered at a railroad station in a German town. Among them was a man named Vladimir Lenin. Earlier, Lenin had been exiled to Siberia. He had been spreading ideas that the government thought were **revolutionary**—ideas that could cause a revolution, or the overthrow of a government. Then the government gave him permission to leave Russia.

Now the Germans were supplying a train to take Lenin back to Russia. The Germans made two rules. No member of Lenin's group could leave the train or talk to any Germans during their journey. The Germans, too, knew that ideas can be more powerful than any army. Germany was at war with Russia and hoped that Lenin would cause changes in Russia. And he did. Lenin led one of the most important revolutions in history.

Grigory Rasputin—The Czar's Adviser

Grigory Rasputin, an adviser to the czar's family, is often accused of having helped to bring about the Russian Revolution. Rasputin had some success treating the czar's son, Alexis, who suffered from a serious illness. As a result, Rasputin had a great deal of influence with the czar and the czarina, the czar's wife. Some people think Rasputin convinced the czar and czarina to make bad decisions in the years leading up to the revolution. Supporters of the czar feared Rasputin's growing power. A group of them murdered him in 1916.

The Russian Revolution

To understand why the Germans helped Lenin, you need to go back to 1914. That year, Russia entered World War I, fighting against Germany. It was a harsh war. Millions of Russian soldiers were killed or wounded. At home, people suffered severe food and fuel shortages. By March 1917, the Russian people began rioting. Troops were sent to put down the uprising. However, they joined the people instead. The czar was forced to give up his throne. A weak government took over.

In November 1917, Lenin and his supporters pushed the weak government aside. Lenin knew the Russians wanted peace more than anything else. In March 1918, Russia signed an agreement with Germany and withdrew from World War I. This was just what the Germans had hoped for.

As the new leader of Russia, Lenin wanted a communist government. **Communism** (KAHM yoo nizum) is a theory that says the government should own the farms and factories for the benefit of all the citizens. Everyone should share the work equally and receive an equal share of the rewards.

In theory, communism appealed greatly to many of the Russian people. Remember the deep split between Russia's rich and poor? For hundreds of years, Russia's poor had suffered terrible hardships while the rich lived in luxury. In a communist nation, everyone is supposed to be equal. Lenin told the workers and serfs that communism would bring fairness and equality to all Russians.

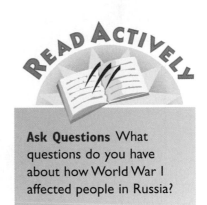

Ask Questions What questions do you have about how World War I affected people in Russia?

Building a Communist State

The treaty with the Germans ended the war, but peace did not come. After the Communists came to power, there was a terrible **civil war,** a war between groups inside a country. On one side were the Communists. On the other were many groups opposed to them.

The Russian civil war lasted three years and cost millions of lives. Finally, the Communists won. In 1922, Lenin created the Union of Soviet Socialist Republics (U.S.S.R.), also called the Soviet Union. The Soviet Union was made up of Russia and smaller areas, or republics, under Russian control.

Lenin began taking steps to turn the Soviet Union into a communist country. He jailed and even killed people who opposed him. Such people were enemies of the revolution, he said. Lenin died in 1924. He was followed by Josef Stalin, whose rule would be even more harsh.

▼ This World War II Soviet poster shows a worker holding up a red flag bearing the portraits of Lenin and Stalin. The slogan encourages the Soviet people to produce more for the war effort.

СОРЕВНУЙТЕСЬ
НА ЛУЧШУЮ ПОМОЩЬ ФРОНТУ!

Stalin's Dictatorship

Josef Stalin was a **dictator** (DIK tayt ur), a leader who has absolute power. Stalin did not care about the suffering his decisions caused. For example, he wanted to build industry in the Soviet Union. He knew that factory workers would need plenty of food. Therefore, Stalin forced serfs to give their farm products to the government. When the serfs opposed the plan, Stalin sent millions of them to prison camps in Siberia. Most died there. And when people questioned him about other actions, Stalin simply got rid of them. He sent them to the camps, or had them executed. All of the Soviet Union lived in terror of Stalin.

When the Germans invaded the Soviet Union during World War II, they had to contend with the combined forces of bad weather and the Soviet army. First, rain caused German tanks to get stuck in the mud. Then, bitterly cold temperatures gave soldiers frostbite and caused machinery to break down. Finally, they had to fight determined Soviet soldiers who were ready to defend their country regardless of the cost. This picture shows Soviet soldiers in their victorious battle for the city of Stalingrad, which is now known as Volgograd. **Critical Thinking** How do you think the weather helped the Soviet soldiers to win victory over the Germans?

World War II In 1939, Stalin signed an agreement with the Germans. It stated that the two countries would not fight each other. But the Germans invaded anyway. In 1941, three million German soldiers, with tanks and airplanes, drove deep into the Soviet Union.

For a time, a German victory appeared likely. Soviet cities were destroyed, and millions of soldiers died or were captured. But the Soviet people, helped by the harsh Russian winter, fought bravely. In 1943, the Soviets began pushing the Germans back toward their own borders. By 1945, Soviet troops had captured Berlin, the capital of Germany.

The Cold War

After World War II, the United States and the Soviet Union were the world's two strongest countries. They were so much stronger than other countries that people called them "superpowers." Relations between the superpowers were very tense, though the two sides never fought each other. This time of tension without actual war, which lasted roughly from 1945 until 1991, is called the **Cold War.**

Causes of the Cold War Two things caused the tension. First was the problem of Eastern Europe. During World War II, the Soviet army moved westward all the way to Berlin. As the army advanced, it freed Eastern European countries the Germans had conquered. But after the war, Soviet troops did not leave. The Soviets forced these countries

LINKS TO LANGUAGE ARTS

Worried About War Many people during the Cold War feared that the United States and the U.S.S.R. would attack each other and destroy the world. Grace Paley's "Anxiety" is a story about people living with this fear. In the story, an old woman tells a young father to treat his daughter well because her future "is like a film which suddenly cuts to white."

CITIZEN HEROES

to become communist. Most contact with the West was cut off. British leader Winston Churchill said that it was as if an "iron curtain" had fallen across Eastern Europe, dividing East and West.

Second, the Soviets tried to expand their power beyond Eastern Europe. They encouraged rebels in other nations to turn to communism. The United States was determined to stop this. The superpowers often backed opposing sides in conflicts in Asia and Africa. The superpowers also built powerful weapons to use against one another. By the 1960s, they had enough nuclear (NOO klee ur) bombs to destroy the entire world.

Collapse of an Empire During the Cold War, the Soviet Union's economy did not grow fast enough. The government invested most of its money in heavy industries, such as steel. It paid little attention to **consumer goods,** such as cars or blue jeans, that the common person might enjoy.

By the early 1980s, almost all of the Soviet people had lost faith in the communist system. They did not want the government to control almost every part of their lives. In the mid-1980s, one Soviet leader responded. Mikhail Gorbachev (mee khah EEL GOR buh chawf), who took power in 1985, made many changes in the Soviet system. He allowed more personal freedom. He also reduced government control of the economy.

▼ Under communism, food shortages and long lines became a daily fact of life for unhappy Soviet shoppers.

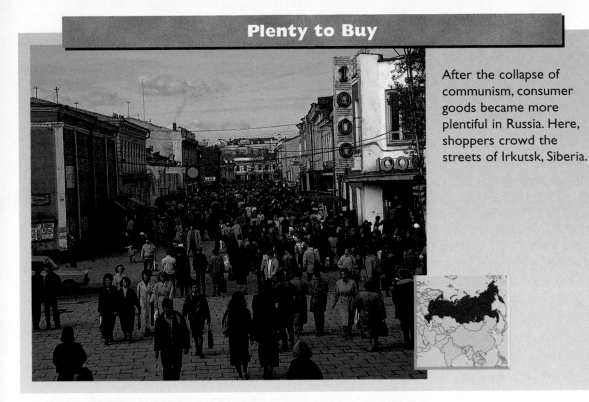

Plenty to Buy

After the collapse of communism, consumer goods became more plentiful in Russia. Here, shoppers crowd the streets of Irkutsk, Siberia.

Often, when people have a taste of freedom, it makes them want more. By the late 1980s, this happened across Eastern Europe and the Soviet Union. Eastern European countries abandoned communism. And the Soviet republics demanded their independence. They wanted to decide their own futures. Finally, at the end of 1991, the Soviet Union broke apart. Russia and most of the former Soviet republics became independent nations.

Today, Russia faces a huge challenge. For hundreds of years, the Russian people have suffered hardships, under the czars and under communism. Now Russians control their own fate. It is up to them to build a new way of life.

SECTION 5 REVIEW

1. **Define** (a) revolutionary, (b) communism, (c) civil war, (d) dictator, (e) Cold War, (f) consumer goods.

2. **Identify** (a) Vladimir Lenin, (b) Josef Stalin, (c) Mikhail Gorbachev.

3. How did Lenin become leader of the Soviet Union?

4. Why was Josef Stalin feared?

5. Why were the people of the Soviet Union unhappy with the communist government?

Critical Thinking

6. **Recognizing Cause and Effect** Why did the Germans send Lenin back to Russia?

Activity

7. **Writing to Learn** Some people in Russia want to go back to the old communist way of life. Write a paragraph arguing against returning to communism.

Review and Activities

Reviewing Main Ideas

1. What accomplishments of the ancient Greeks and Romans affect our world today?

2. How did Christianity and feudalism affect the lives of people in the Middle Ages?

3. How did renewed trade affect Europe's interest in the world?

4. List two important changes made during the Age of Revolution.

5. How did the Industrial Revolution change life for people in Europe?

6. How did nationalism help to cause World War I and World War II?

7. Explain how Russia gained territory and became an empire.

8. Why did the Russian people come to oppose the czars?

9. What changes did Lenin and Stalin make in the Soviet Union?

10. Why did the Soviet Union collapse?

Reviewing Key Terms

Use each key term below in a sentence that shows the meaning of the term.

1. democracy
2. empire
3. feudalism
4. Renaissance
5. humanism
6. monarch
7. colony
8. Scientific Revolution
9. Industrial Revolution
10. imperialism
11. nationalism
12. alliance
13. communism
14. civil war
15. dictator
16. Cold War

Critical Thinking

1. **Recognizing Cause and Effect** Describe causes that led to the fall of the Roman Empire.

2. **Making Conclusions** How were the main ideas of the Renaissance different from common ideas of the Middle Ages?

3. **Identifying Central Issues** How was Russia under the czars different from the Soviet Union under communism?

Graphic Organizer

Copy the chart on a sheet of paper. Fill in the empty boxes with important events that happened in Western Europe and in Russia for each century listed.

	Western Europe	Russia
1300s		
1500s		
1700s		
1900s		

Map Activity

Europe and Russia

For each place listed below, write the letter from the map that shows its location. Use the maps in the Activity Atlas to help you.

1. Athens
2. Rome
3. Italy
4. Great Britain
5. St. Petersburg

Place Location

Writing Activity

Writing an Interview

Choose a historical figure from this chapter. Write a "personal interview" with that person. First, think of questions that you would like to ask. Do research to learn how that person might have answered the questions. Then write the "interview" as if you were asking that person the questions and he or she were answering them.

Take It to the NET

Activity View artifacts of Russian czars and learn some fun facts about Russian history. For help in completing this activity, visit www.phschool.com.

Chapter 2 Self-Test To review what you have learned, take the Chapter 2 Self-Test and get instant feedback on your answers. Go to www.phschool.com to take the test.

Skills Review

Turn to the Skills Activity.

Review the steps for interpreting diagrams and illustrations. Then, find a diagram or illustration somewhere else in this book. Following the steps, write a brief paragraph detailing your interpretation.

How Am I Doing?

Answer these questions to help you check your progress.

1. Can I list the major accomplishments of the Greeks and the Romans?

2. Do I understand how people's views of the world changed during the Renaissance?

3. Do I understand how the Industrial Revolution changed European life?

4. Can I identify Russia's important rulers and their accomplishments?

5. Do I understand what communism is and why it did not work in the Soviet Union?

6. What information from this chapter can I include in my journal?

FROM
Pearl in the Egg

BY DOROTHY VAN WOERKOM

Reach Into Your Background

In Europe in the Middle Ages, an average day for a person your age looked quite different than an average day today. For one thing, a twelve-year-old at that time was seen as much closer to being an adult.

People in those days did not live as long as they do today. A 20-year-old person was considered middle-aged!

Pearl in the Egg was the name of a real girl who lived in the 1200s. Historians know little about her except her name. Dorothy Van Woerkom has written a book of historical fiction about Pearl. Her descriptions of Pearl's life are based on what historians know about life in the 1200s. At that time, people in Europe were just beginning to use family names. Usually they gave themselves names that described their work or their families in some way.

In this part of Pearl's story, you will see something of a typical day in her life.

Questions to Explore

1. What does this story tell you about the life of a serf?
2. What can you learn from this story about work on a feudal manor?

rushlight *n.:* a lamp made with grease and part of a rush, or swamp plant

dripping *n.:* fat and juices drawn from cooking meat

serf *n.:* peasant farmers who worked the land as slaves of wealthy landowners

Pearl set the bowl of cabbage soup down on the floor near the rushlight. She knelt beside the box of straw that was her father's bed. She wiped his forehead, listening to his heavy breathing.

"Please, Fa," she coaxed. She broke off a piece from a loaf of black bread and dipped it into the soup. She placed it on his lips, letting the soup trickle into his mouth. She ate the chunk of bread, and dipped another.

"I will be in the fields until the nooning," she said, "so you must try to eat a little now. See, I have put a bit of dripping in the soup."

She forced the warm, mild liquid down his throat until the bowl was half empty. She drank the rest herself, chewing hungrily on the lump of fat that the sick man had not been able to swallow.

Again she wiped his face, and then she blew out the light. She crossed the smooth dirt floor, and pulled a sack from a peg on the wall near the door as she left the hut. Outside, the sky was gray with the dawn. Ground fog swirled around her feet. The air smelled of ripening grain and moist earth.

From other huts of mud and timber, serfs hurried out into the early morning mist. Some, like Pearl, would spend the day in their own small holdings in the fields. It was the time for harvesting their crops, which would feed their families through the winter. Others, like Pearl's older brother, Gavin, had already left for work in the manor fields to bring in Sir Geoffrey's crops.

Sir Geoffrey was lord of the manor, which included his great stone house and all the land surrounding it. He owned this tiny village. He even owned most of the people in it. A few, like the baker, the miller, and the soapmaker, were freemen and free women. They worked for themselves and paid the lord taxes. For tax, Sir Geoffrey collected a portion of everything they produced. No one in the village had money.

But the serfs were not free. They could never leave the manor, or marry without the lord's permission. They could not fish in the streams or hunt in the forest. They owned only their mud huts and small gardens, called holdings, and an ox or cow, or a few geese or sheep. The serfs also paid taxes. Each year they gave Sir Geoffrey a portion of their crops. He took a share of their eggs; if a flock of sheep or geese increased, he took a share; and if a cow had a calf, he took that also. On certain days of the week each family had to send a man—and an ox if they had one—to help plow the lord's fields, harvest his crops, and do their work. Each woman had to weave one garment a year for the lord and his family.

The sun was up when Pearl reached the long furrows of her field, where the flat green bean pods weighed down their low bushes. She bent to see if the leaves were dry. Wet leaves would wither when she touched them.

The sun had dried them. Pearl began filling her sack, wondering how she could finish the harvest all by herself before the first frost. She had other plots to work as well.

Now that their father was ill, twelve-year-old Gavin was taking his place for three days each week in the manor fields. Sir Geoffrey would get *his* crops safely in! But if the frost came early, or if the only one left at home to work was an eleven-year-old like Pearl, that was of small matter to Sir Geoffrey.

Pearl stood up to rub her back. A serf's life was a hard life. Her father's was, and his father's before him. She sighed. Who could hope to change it?

Old Clotilde came swaying up the narrow path between her field and Pearl's. She waved her empty sack by way of greeting and squatted down among her plants.

"How be your Fa this morning?" she asked Pearl.

"He took some soup. But he wanders in his head. He thinks I am my mother, though she's been dead three summers now."

furrows *n.:* rows in the earth made by a plow
Clotilde (kluh TILD)

▼ This painting from the Middle Ages shows peasants working in a field.

► This wall painting from the 1300s shows the kind of hunt Pearl saw.

bowmen *n.:* men with bows and arrows; archers
defiant *adj.:* bold or resistant

Connect Why does Pearl shed tears of anger?

"Ah, and he'll join her soon, Big Rollin will." Clotilde's wrinkled face was nearly the same dirty gray as her cap. "They all do, soon as they take a mite of sickness. For the likes of us to stay alive, we must stay well! Get the priest for him! He won't plow these fields again."

Before Pearl could reply, the shrill blare of a hunting horn sounded across the meadow, followed by the baying of hounds on the trail of a wild boar. Startled to their feet, the serfs watched the terrified boar running in and out among the rows of crops.

"Run, lest you get trampled!" Clotilde screamed, dashing down the path toward the forest. The others followed her. Someone pulled Pearl along as she stumbled forward, blinded by angry tears, her fingers tightly gripping her sack.

The hounds came running in pursuit of the boar. Behind the hounds rode the hunting party of twenty horsemen, led by Sir Geoffrey. At the rear was another man Pearl recognized. Jack, one of Sir Geoffrey's bowmen, had come upon her one day as she scrounged for dead branches near the edge of the forest. He had baited her with cruel words, rudely ruffling her hair with the shaft end of an arrow.

"Jack's my name. What's yours?" he had demanded, taking pleasure in her discomfort. For answer she had spat at him, and he had pressed the arrow's metal tip against her wrist until she'd dropped her bundle. Laughing, he had scattered the branches with his foot and grabbed her hair.

"Spit at me again, girl, and that will be the end of you!" Though his mouth had turned up in a grin, his eyes had been bright with anger. His fingers had tightened on the nape of her neck, bending her head back. She stared up at him, frightened, but defiant.

"Perhaps you need a lesson in manners right now," he'd said, raising his other hand. He probably would have struck her, but for the rattle of a wagon and the tuneless whistle signaling someone's approach. He had let her go with a suddenness that had left her off balance, and had stalked away.

Shaken, Pearl had turned to see Sir Geoffrey's woodcutter driving out of the forest with a wagonload of wood for the manor house.

Now Pearl shuddered at the memory; but Jack was taking no notice of her. His eyes were on the boar and on his master. If the boar became maddened during the chase and turned on one of the hunters, Jack was ready with his arrows to put an end to the beast.

Over the meadow they galloped, and onto the fields. They churned up the soft earth, trampled down the precious bean plants, crushed the near-ripe ears of the barley and oats, tore up the tender pea vines. They chased the boar across the fields and back again, laughing at the sport.

When they had gone, Pearl ran back to her field. She crawled in the turned-up earth, searching for unbroken bean pods. The other serfs were doing the same.

"What is the matter with us?" she demanded of Clotilde, "Why do we stay silent, with spoiled crops all around us, just so Sir Geoffrey will have his sport?"

"Shish!" Clotilde warned, looking quickly around to see who might have heard. "Do you want a flogging for such bold words? Hold your tongue, as you see your elders do."

For the rest of the morning they worked in silence. At midday, Pearl picked up her half-filled sack. It should have been full by now. She glared fiercely across the meadow at the manor house, but she held her tongue.

Pearl returned home to find that her father had worsened. When she could not rouse him, she went for the priest.

flogging *n.:* beating or whipping

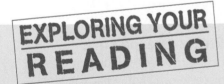

EXPLORING YOUR READING

Look Back
1. Why does Pearl work alone in her family's holdings?

Think It Over
2. Why did the serfs give Sir Geoffrey a portion of their crops every year?

3. What did the serfs use instead of money?

4. What did Clotilde mean when she said, "Do you want a flogging for such bold words?"

Go Beyond
5. The feudal system existed for more than 400 years. Why do you think it did not change for such a long time?

6. Based on what you know about Pearl, how do you think she might act the next time she sees the lord or one of his men?

Ideas for Writing: Story
7. Write an addition to Pearl's story that tells how she got the name Pearl in the Egg.

Cultures of Europe and Russia

PICTURE ACTIVITIES

In many cities and towns in Europe and Russia, people live and work among things that remind them of their cultural backgrounds. This is a picture of Cologne (kuh LOHN), Germany. To learn more about Cologne's culture, complete the following activities.

Study the picture
Find a modern building and a historic one. For what use do you think each building was constructed?

Draw conclusions
From looking at the picture, what conclusions can you draw about the people of Cologne? Do they have a modern way of life? Do they value their cultural background? How do you know?

The Cultures of Western Europe

SECTION 1

Reach Into Your Background

Think about your community and your way of life. Now think of another community that you have visited or heard about from relatives or friends. How are the ways of life in each community different? How are they the same? List some differences and similarities.

Questions to Explore

1. What makes the cities of Western Europe great cultural centers?

2. How do people of the many countries of Western Europe interact with one another?

Key Terms

urbanization
immigrant
multicultural
tariff

Key Places

Paris
London
Madrid
Berlin

The train speeds down the track with hardly a whisper. As the passengers sit in their comfortable seats, they can look out the window at the highway next to the railroad. They know that the cars are traveling at 60 miles (96 km) per hour, but the cars seem to be moving backward. That's because the train is traveling *three times faster* than the cars—about 180 miles (289 km) per hour.

Would you like to take a trip like that? You can if you go to France, which has the world's fastest trains. Great Britain, too, has speedy rail travel. Some British trains reach speeds of 140 miles (225 km) per hour. In Western Europe, high-speed trains have made travel between countries easy and fast. Europeans can be in another country in a matter of hours. You will soon see how such easy movement through Western Europe affects the culture of the region.

▼ France's high-speed trains travel about 47 times faster than a person can walk.

READ ACTIVELY

Visualize Visualize a European city street with modern and old buildings.

Cultural Centers

When people travel in Europe, they are usually heading for a city. People travel from small towns and villages to cities to find jobs. Some people go to cities to go to school. People also travel to cities to enjoy the cultural attractions. These include museums, concerts, restaurants, nightclubs, and stores.

Most Western European cities are a mix of the old and the new. Public buildings and houses from the Middle Ages are a common sight. They stand next to modern apartments and office buildings. Cars and buses drive along cobblestone streets once used by horse-drawn carriages. Monuments stand for leaders who lived hundreds of years ago.

Each city in Western Europe is different from the other. Paris, the capital of France, attracts scholars, writers, and artists from all over the world. England's capital, London, is known for its grand historic buildings and lovely parks. The Spanish capital city of Madrid (muh DRID) is known as a friendly place where people meet in cafes to relax after work. The German city of Berlin is always full of activity.

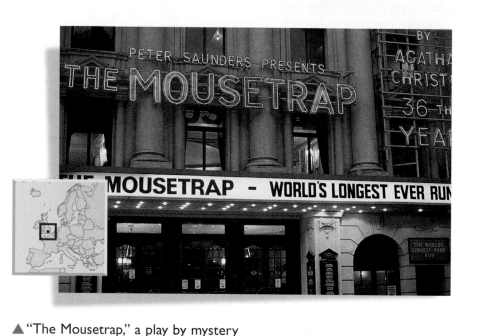

▲ "The Mousetrap," a play by mystery writer Agatha Christie, has been playing continuously in London since its opening in November 1952.

▼ This glass pyramid houses the entrance to the Louvre, a famous art museum in Paris.

Let's focus on life in Germany for a moment. Most visitors to Germany think that the Germans are efficient. In other words, Germans do their work without waste or extra effort. Visitors get this idea from what they see. In Germany, cities, streets, and buses are clean. Hotels are well run. German cars are well designed and long-lasting. Travel is swift on an excellent system of four-lane highways. Travel is equally fast on high-speed trains.

But life in Germany is not all hard work and fast-paced activity. Many workers enjoy up to six weeks of vacation each year. Outdoor recreation is popular. Mountains and highlands allow skiing, hiking, and camping. The country's many rivers, as well as the North and Baltic seas, are good for swimming and boating. Those who prefer city life enjoy the museums, concerts, and plays.

Growing Cities, Growing Wealth

People in most Western European countries enjoy a similar lifestyle. That's because these countries are prosperous, or wealthy. This prosperity is based on industry. Factories in Western Europe make consumer goods that are in great demand around the world. Western European workers also make steel, cars, machines, and many other vital products.

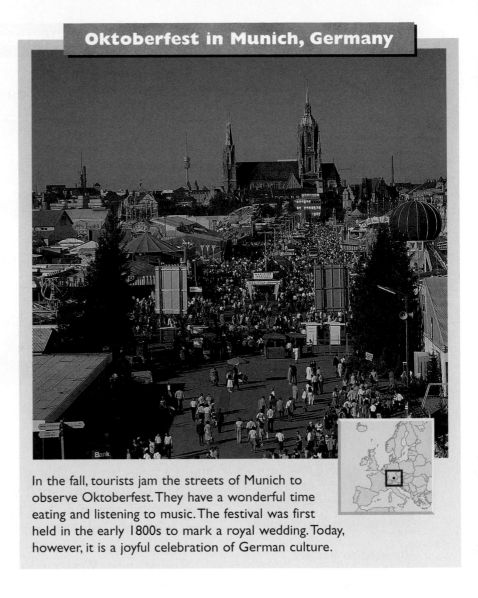

Oktoberfest in Munich, Germany

In the fall, tourists jam the streets of Munich to observe Oktoberfest. They have a wonderful time eating and listening to music. The festival was first held in the early 1800s to mark a royal wedding. Today, however, it is a joyful celebration of German culture.

Industry and the Growth of Cities Industry has been developing in Western Europe since the late 1700s. It has not always been so important to the economy, however. In the past, farming played a bigger role.

About 200 years ago, there were few machines to help do farmwork. To meet basic food needs, most of the people worked on farms. Gradually, things changed. New and better farm machines were invented. These machines could do tasks that once required many workers. Farmers also learned ways to improve soil quality and fight insects. With these advances, farms could produce more and better crops with fewer workers.

This revolution in farming came at the same time as the Industrial Revolution. Thus, as the need for farmworkers fell, the need for industrial workers grew. Many people began moving to cities, where

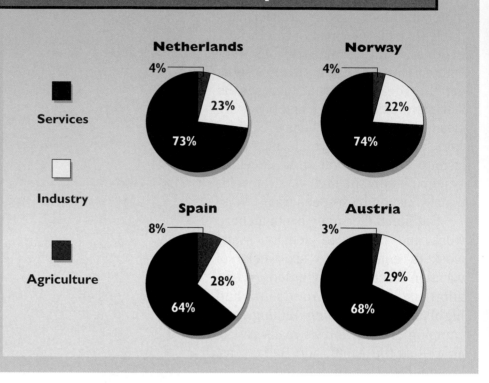

The Labor Force in Selected Western European Countries

Chart Study Today, most people in the Netherlands, Norway, Spain, and Austria make a living as service workers. A service is any task that one person does for another—like selling groceries, typing a letter, or teaching a class. Workers in industry make products, such as clothing, automobiles, and video games. Agricultural workers grow crops and raise livestock.

Critical Thinking Of the four countries shown here, which two have the most service workers? Which two have the most industrial workers? Would you expect to find service and industrial workers in cities or rural areas? Why?

Services

Industry

Agriculture

Netherlands 4% · 23% · 73%

Norway 4% · 22% · 74%

Spain 8% · 28% · 64%

Austria 3% · 29% · 68%

LINKS TO LANGUAGE ARTS

Devoted to Nature
Writers of the English Romantic Age (1798–1832) reacted strongly to the events of their time. They disliked the way the Industrial Revolution changed the ways people lived. In "My Heart Leaps Up When I Behold," William Wordsworth describes the beauty of a rainbow and wishes every day was bound "each to each by natural piety," which means living each day in devotion to nature.

the factories were. This growth of cities, known as **urbanization** (ur bun ih ZAY shun), sped up after World War II. The United States provided billions of dollars to help Western Europe recover from the war. With this help, the region's industries came back stronger than ever. And even more people left rural areas to work in cities.

Today most Western Europeans work in factories or in service industries such as banking and food service. And most Western European workers earn good wages and have a comfortable life.

A Home for Immigrants Life in Western Europe was not always so good. In the 1800s and early 1900s, millions of Western Europeans left Europe. Most went to the United States, Canada, and the countries of South America. They left in search of a better life.

Since World War II, the direction of human movement has changed. No longer are large numbers of people leaving Western Europe. As industry developed in the postwar years, more workers were needed. As a result, people began moving to Western Europe. Today, **immigrants** (IM uh grunts), or people who move to one country from another, make up about 6 percent of the workers in Western Europe. Most are from Eastern Europe, North Africa, South Asia, and the Middle East.

Yang-Mee Tang is an example. She moved to London to start a career in business. Her homeland was Mauritius (maw RISH ee us), an island in the Indian Ocean, off the eastern coast of Africa. Yang-Mee is learning to get around London on the "tube," or subway. She is learning a much different lifestyle from her lifestyle in Mauritius. "There is so much to do here!"

says Yang-Mee. "In my hometown in Mauritius, everything shuts down at around 10:00 P.M. But every night in central London, the streets are still crowded with people at 1:00 A.M."

Immigrants do not simply leave their cultures when they leave their homelands. They bring their languages, religious beliefs, values, and customs. But most immigrants make changes in their ways of life. They may change the way they dress. They may try new foods and discover new ways of cooking. Most of them learn the language of their new country.

In many ways, immigration has changed the cultures of Western Europe. In countries like Britain and France, people from many different backgrounds live and work together. They learn about one another's way of life. In the process, the cultures blend and change. In this way, many Western European countries have become multicultural. A **multicultural** (mul tih KUHL chur ul) country's way of life is influenced by many different cultures.

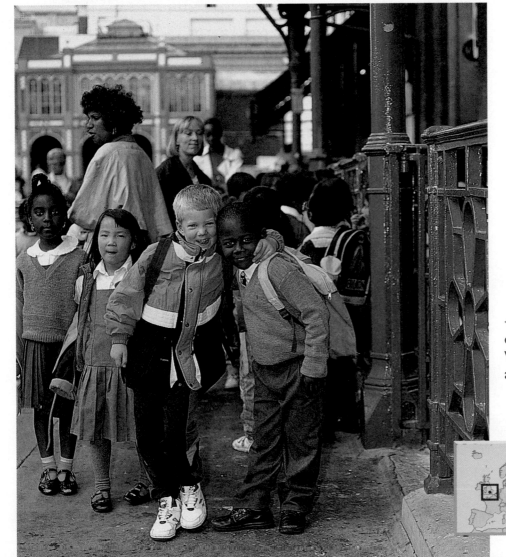

◀These British children are on a school field trip to the West End, London's shopping and entertainment district.

Predict How do you think open borders help Western Europe grow and succeed?

Open Borders

Turn to the political map of Europe in the Activity Atlas in the front of your book. Notice that most European countries are small and close together. Picture a high-speed train traveling across Europe. It's little wonder that travelers can get from one country to another in a matter of hours. Ideas, goods, and raw materials can travel quickly as well. The open exchange of ideas and goods has helped make Western Europe prosperous.

It was not always so easy for people, goods, and ideas to move throughout Western Europe. Changes began around 1950, when France and Germany agreed to work together to help rebuild after World War II. Other nations soon joined them. Now there is an organization called

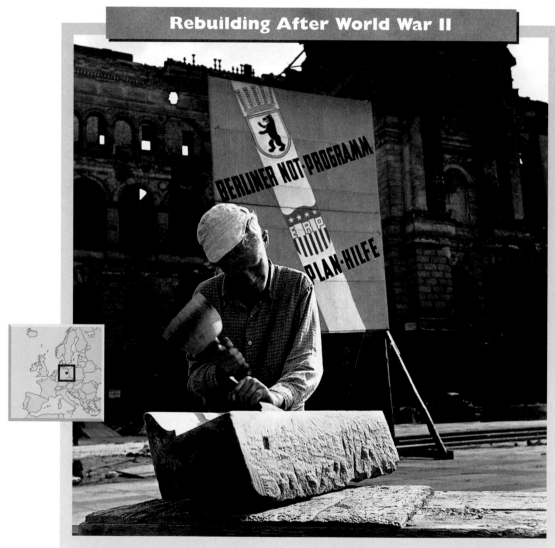

Rebuilding After World War II

After World War II, Germany lay in ruins. The Allied countries worked together to rebuild West Germany and make it a democracy. This man is helping to repair and repaint the Titaina Palace, West Berlin's largest concert hall. The Allies also helped to rebuild homes and factories. **Critical Thinking** Why do you think it was important to the Allies to rebuild Germany as a democracy?

Europe's New Money—the Euro

To make it easier for member nations to trade among themselves, the European Union adopted a single currency called the European Currency Unit, or ECU. Later, the ECU was renamed the Euro. In 1999, consumers began using the Euro, but only through checks, credit cards, or bank transfers. Actual bank notes and coins replaced the national currencies of participating EU members in 2002. **Critical Thinking** How might the Euro make travel and trade among the European countries easier?

the European Union (EU). In 1999, the EU had 15 member nations and plans for adding at least three more. The EU works to expand trade in Europe. One way to do this is to end **tariffs**, or fees that a government charges for goods entering the country. The EU hopes to create a "united states" of Europe, where people, money, goods, and services move freely among member countries.

SECTION 1 REVIEW

1. **Define** (a) urbanization, (b) immigrant, (c) multicultural, (d) tariff.

2. **Identify** (a) Paris, (b) London, (c) Madrid, (d) Berlin.

3. How did the growth of industry affect cities in Western Europe?

4. Why is there ease of movement among the countries in Western Europe?

Critical Thinking

5. **Drawing Comparisons** This section describes how the lives of many immigrants to Western Europe change when they settle in their new country. What effect do you think the immigrants have on the way of life in their new home?

Activity

6. **Writing to Learn** Write down two facts about Western Europe that you were surprised to learn. How has this new information changed the way you think about Western Europe?

Summarizing Information

How many words are in this sentence? You should count seven words. How many words do you think are in this paragraph? When you finish reading it, count them.

You can easily count the words in a sentence or a paragraph. But how many ideas do you think are on this page? What about in this entire book?

Think of all the books, magazines, and newspapers you read at school and at home. They all give you a mind-boggling amount of information. No one person could remember them all. You are not expected to. But you can summarize the basic ideas to help yourself remember them.

Get Ready

Summarizing information is a good skill to have. It will help you pick out the main points of what you read. It will also help you study for tests. Most important, it will help you make sense of all the ideas you read or hear about.

You may not know it, but you have already done a lot of summarizing. How can that be? People summarize without even knowing it. For example, suppose someone asked you, "How was math class?" You would not answer with every detail. You would tell the main things that happened, along with a just a few important details. That is just what a summary is: a description of the main points along with a few important details.

Try It Out

To see how easy summarizing is, try this exercise. Write a summary of yesterday. Your goal will be to describe the main points of your day from when you woke up to when you went to sleep. Follow these steps to write your summary.

A. Work from start to finish. When you summarize, you will do best to start at the beginning and work through to the end. When summarizing your day, start with when you woke up.

B. List the main points. Remember that a summary describes the main points, not every little detail. List only the main things that you did yesterday.

C. Add some details to the list. Although you do not want to list too many details, it helps to list a few that will later jog your memory. For example, you might write "ate breakfast" as a main point. You can add the details of what you ate if the meal was special in some way. As you make your list, add details after some of the main points.

D. Turn your list into a summary. Summaries are often in paragraph form. Once you have made your list, you can add transitions to make it into a paragraph. Transitions are words that connect one idea

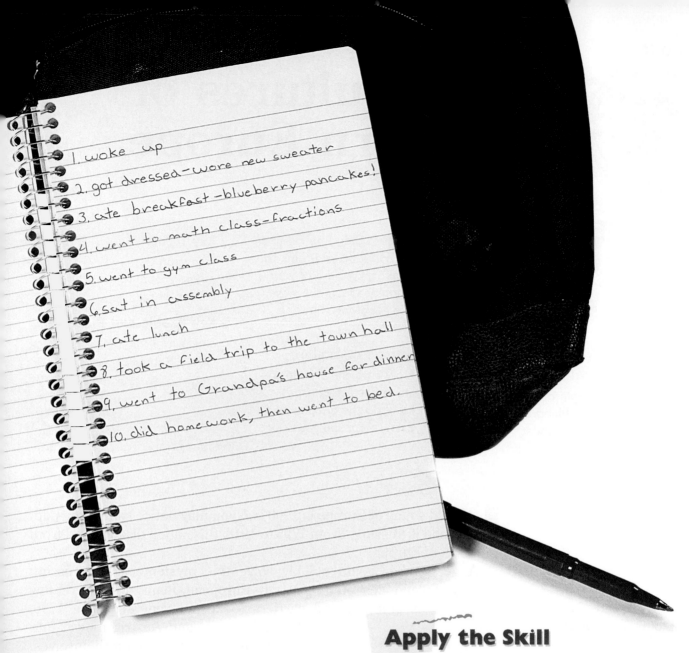

1. woke up
2. got dressed—wore new sweater
3. ate breakfast—blueberry pancakes!
4. went to math class—fractions
5. went to gym class
6. sat in assembly
7. ate lunch
8. took a field trip to the town hall
9. went to Grandpa's house for dinner
10. did homework, then went to bed.

Apply the Skill

to the next by showing how the ideas are related to each other. For example, if your list reads "1) woke up, 2) got dressed, 3) ate breakfast," you might write, "First, I woke up. Then, after I got dressed, I ate breakfast."

Congratulations! You have just summarized an entire morning in a single paragraph.

Summarizing a day is good for diary writing, but not much help in your schoolwork. However, the steps you just took will help you in school when you apply them to what you read or hear.

Practice by writing a summary of this chapter. Follow the four steps you took when summarizing your day. The headings in the chapter will help you pick the main points to list. Topic sentences in paragraphs will also help you find main points and interesting details. Remember to turn your list into a written summary. When you have finished, reread your summary. How can your summary help you remember what was in the chapter and help you prepare for a test?

The Cultures of Eastern Europe

BEFORE YOU READ

Reach Into Your Background

Are the people of your community a blend of several cultures? Or do most people come from the same cultural group? How do you think the cultural background of your community affects the way people get along with one another?

Questions to Explore

1. How have the Slavs shaped life in Eastern Europe?
2. How do the peoples of Eastern Europe get along?

Key Terms
migration
ethnic group
dialect

Key People and Places
Slovakia
Czech Republic

Look at a map of Europe in 1900 and you may notice something odd. Poland is missing. From 1795 to 1918, this nation disappeared from the maps of Europe.

A geographer could quickly solve this mystery of the missing country. Poland lies on the North European Plain. There are few mountains or other natural barriers to keep invaders out. In 1795, Russia, Prussia, and Austria moved into Poland and divided it among themselves. Poland did not become independent again until the end of World War I.

Movement throughout much of Eastern Europe is easy. For thousands of years, groups have entered or crossed this region. This movement from place to place, called **migration** (my GRAY shun), is still happening today.

There are many reasons for migration in Eastern Europe. Long ago, people moved to find places with a good supply of natural resources. Sometimes people moved to escape enemies. In more recent times, people have fled places where their religious or political beliefs put them in danger. And they have often moved to find a better life.

▼ Poland is not shown on this map of Europe, which was drawn in 1870.

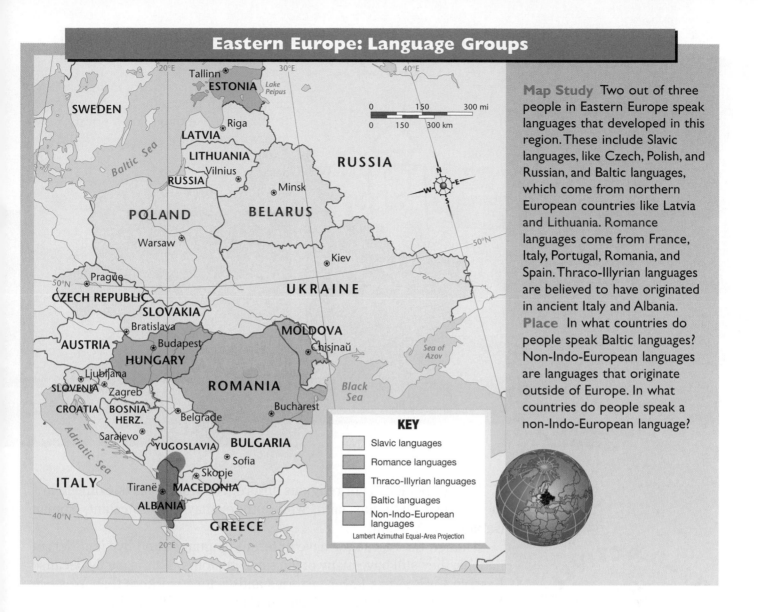

Eastern Europe: Language Groups

Map Study Two out of three people in Eastern Europe speak languages that developed in this region. These include Slavic languages, like Czech, Polish, and Russian, and Baltic languages, which come from northern European countries like Latvia and Lithuania. Romance languages come from France, Italy, Portugal, Romania, and Spain. Thraco-Illyrian languages are believed to have originated in ancient Italy and Albania. **Place** In what countries do people speak Baltic languages? Non-Indo-European languages are languages that originate outside of Europe. In what countries do people speak a non-Indo-European language?

KEY

- Slavic languages
- Romance languages
- Thraco-Illyrian languages
- Baltic languages
- Non-Indo-European languages

Lambert Azimuthal Equal-Area Projection

Ethnic Groups in Eastern Europe

Among the groups that long ago migrated to Eastern Europe were the Slavs (slahvz). These people first lived in the mountains of modern Slovakia (sloh VAH kee uh) and Ukraine. By the 700s, they had spread south to Greece, east to the Alps, and north to the coast of the Baltic Sea.

Slavic Cultures Today, the Slavs are one of the major ethnic groups in Eastern Europe. People of the same **ethnic group** share things, such as a culture, a language, and a religion, that set them apart from their neighbors. Two thousand years ago, there was a single Slavic language. But as the Slavs separated, different Slavic languages developed. Today, some 10 Slavic languages are spoken in Eastern Europe. These include Czech, Polish, and Russian.

Also, even two Slavs who speak the same language may not speak the same dialect. A **dialect** (DY uh lekt) is a different version of a language that can be found only in a certain region.

Religion in Eastern Europe

Eastern Europeans practice many religions. Some Eastern Europeans are Muslims (left); others, like these Polish priests (below), are Roman Catholics. Still others belong to the Eastern Orthodox Church.

READ ACTIVELY

Predict What happens when different groups cannot solve their differences?

There are also major religious differences among Slavs. Some follow the Eastern Orthodox faith, while others may be Protestant, Roman Catholic, or Muslim.

Though the Slavs now have different languages and live in different nations, they still have many of the same customs. This is partly because Eastern Europe has fewer factories and factory workers than Western Europe. Large numbers of Eastern Europeans still live in rural areas and work as farmers. Customs change more slowly in rural areas than in cities.

Other Ethnic Groups Such countries as Poland, Croatia (kroh AY shuh), Slovenia (sloh VEE nee uh), and the Czech Republic are almost entirely Slavic. But many other ethnic groups live in Eastern Europe. About 90 percent of the people of Hungary belong to an ethnic group called the Magyars (MAG yarz). In the country of Romania, most people belong to yet another ethnic group, the Romanians. Similarly, the Bulgars of Bulgaria and the Albanians of Albania are separate ethnic groups. And people belonging to the German ethnic group live in several of the countries of Eastern Europe.

Ethnic Conflict

In some Eastern European countries, people of different ethnic groups live together in harmony. But in other places, there have been ethnic conflicts.

Czechs and Slovaks: A Peaceful Division   For most of the 1900s, Czechoslovakia (check uh sloh VAH kee uh) was a single country. The two main ethnic groups were the Czechs and the Slovaks. The Czechs lived mostly in a western region called Bohemia. Czechs and Slovaks lived in the central region of Moravia. The Slovaks lived mostly in the eastern region of Slovakia. Hungarians, Ukranians, Germans, and Polish people also lived in these areas.

Czechoslovakia was a parliamentary democracy from 1918 to 1935. After World War II, the Soviet Union controlled Czechoslovakia. Almost overnight, the Communist party took over the country. Many people were not happy with the Communist government. For example, writers and scientists could not gain work unless they were members of the Communist party. From the 1960s to the 1980s, students and writers formed groups promoting a return to democracy. Vaclav Havel, a playwright, was a major voice of protest. He spoke out against the government for more than 20 years and was repeatedly put in jail. The government urged him to move out of the country, but he always refused. In 1988, he explained his reasons for staying in Czechoslovakia.

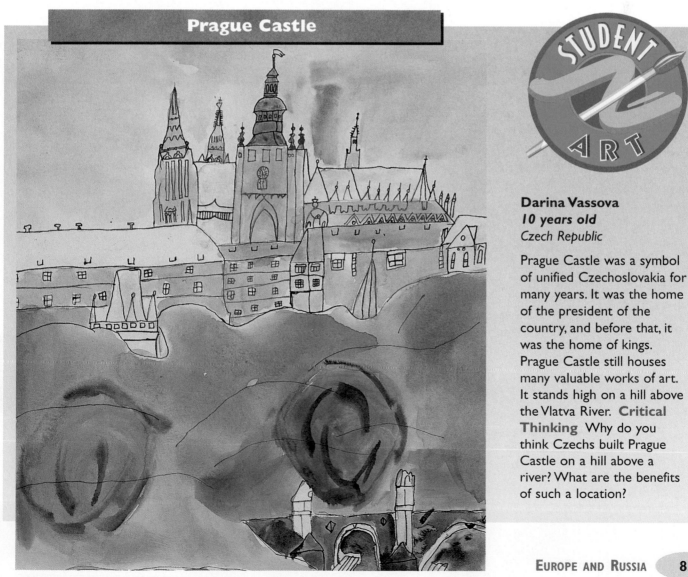

Prague Castle

Darina Vassova
10 years old
Czech Republic

Prague Castle was a symbol of unified Czechoslovakia for many years. It was the home of the president of the country, and before that, it was the home of kings. Prague Castle still houses many valuable works of art. It stands high on a hill above the Vlatva River. **Critical Thinking** Why do you think Czechs built Prague Castle on a hill above a river? What are the benefits of such a location?

> **"I** am Czech. This was not my choice, it was fate. . . . This is my language, this is my home. I live here like everyone else. I don't feel myself to be patriotic, because I don't feel that to be Czech is to be something more than French, English, or European, or anybody else. . . . I try to do something for my country because I live here.**"**

Mass protests forced the communist government to consider changes. In 1989, the Communist party gave up its power and worked in cooperation with the democratic groups. This generally nonviolent change in power from a communist government to a democratic system is called the Velvet Revolution. Havel later was elected president of Czechoslovakia.

The Czechs and the Slovaks had strong ideas about the future of their groups. Both sides disagreed about how to carry out the goals of the newly democratic country. In 1993, they agreed to separate, and the countries of the Czech Republic and Slovakia were born. Perhaps because most Czechs and Slovaks already lived in separate parts of the country, the split was peaceful.

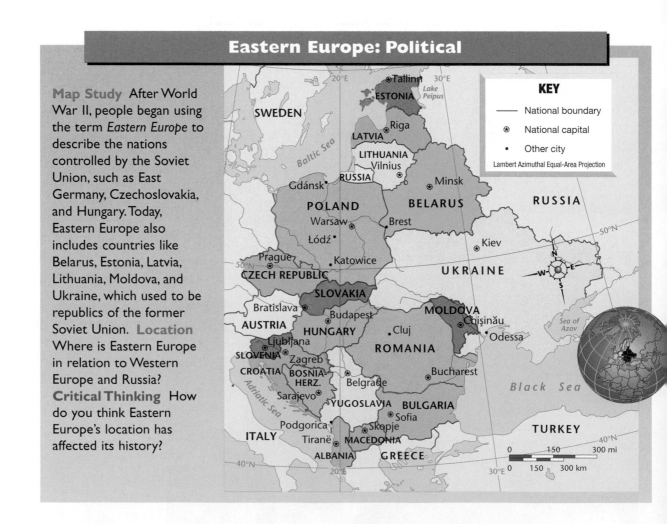

Eastern Europe: Political

Map Study After World War II, people began using the term *Eastern Europe* to describe the nations controlled by the Soviet Union, such as East Germany, Czechoslovakia, and Hungary. Today, Eastern Europe also includes countries like Belarus, Estonia, Latvia, Lithuania, Moldova, and Ukraine, which used to be republics of the former Soviet Union. **Location** Where is Eastern Europe in relation to Western Europe and Russia? **Critical Thinking** How do you think Eastern Europe's location has affected its history?

KEY

— National boundary

⊛ National capital

• Other city

Lambert Azimuthal Equal-Area Projection

◄ In the war-torn country of Bosnia-Herzegovina, United Nations troops struggle to keep a fragile peace among the warring parties.

When Ethnic Groups Clash   But not all ethnic conflicts in Eastern Europe have ended peacefully. In Yugoslavia (yoo goh SLAH vee uh), most Yugoslavs were part of the same ethnic group—the Slavs. However, various groups within the country had distinct religions and cultures. These differences led to the breakup of Yugoslavia in the early 1990s. The new countries of Bosnia-Herzegovina (BAHZ nee uh hert suh goh VEE nuh), Croatia, Slovenia, Serbia and Montenegro, and Macedonia were formed. The breakup of Yugoslavia led to many problems in the new countries of the region. War broke out, and thousands of people, mainly Bosnians, were killed. In 1995, NATO forces helped bring peace to the region. NATO (North Atlantic Treaty Organization) is an alliance between the United States, Canada, and other western nations. NATO was formed in 1949 with the goal of protecting the interests of the member nations and promoting international cooperation.

By 1999, conflict had again broken out, this time between the Serbs and ethnic Albanians who live in Kosovo, a province of Serbia. As a result, NATO forces were again sent to the region. Though a cease-fire was reached, tensions remain, and the future of the region is uncertain.

SECTION 2 REVIEW

1. **Define**   (a) migration, (b) ethnic group, (c) dialect.

2. **Identify**   (a) Slovakia, (b) Czech Republic.

3. Why are the Slavs important in Eastern Europe?

4. Give an example of Eastern Europeans (a) getting along with one another and (b) being in conflict with one another.

Critical Thinking

5. **Recognizing Cause and Effect**   This section explains that Slavs in rural areas follow customs that have lasted for centuries. Why do you think customs change more slowly in rural areas than in urban areas?

Activity

6. **Writing to Learn**   Write a paragraph about how you think ethnic conflicts affect the ways in which people think of other ethnic groups. How can people's attitudes make it harder to solve these conflicts?

The Cultures of Russia

BEFORE YOU READ

Reach Into Your Background

Do you and your family celebrate certain holidays each year? Why are these holidays important? Do other people in your community observe these holidays, or do they observe different ones?

Questions to Explore

1. How have ethnic groups in and around Russia affected Russian history?

2. How are the people of Russia reconnecting with their traditions?

Key Terms

heritage
repress
propaganda

Key People and Places

Leo Tolstoy
Peter Tchaikovsky
St. Petersburg

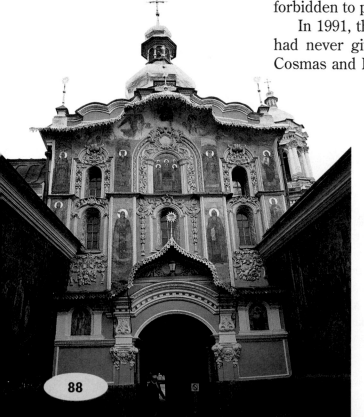

▼ Under communism, worship in Soviet churches was forbidden. Now, the doors of churches all over the former Soviet Union are open again for worshippers.

For many years, Russians passing the Church of Saints Cosmas and Damian in Moscow never heard a choir. They never saw a bride and groom leave the church. They never heard religious services. The only sound they heard was the hum of machines printing government documents. The communist government of the Soviet Union owned the church and used it as a printing shop. In the Soviet Union, people were forbidden to practice religion.

In 1991, the Soviet Union collapsed. Two years later, Russians who had never given up their faith took back their church. Now Saints Cosmas and Damian is filled with people singing songs of worship. In recent years, hundreds of other churches in Moscow have reopened their doors. The same return to religion can be seen in places of worship across all of Russia.

Russia's Ethnic Mix

The Russian Orthodox religion, a branch of Christianity, has been a powerful bond among Russians for hundreds of years. It is part of the Russian **heritage** (HEHR ut ij), or the customs and practices that are passed from one generation to the next. Another part of the Russian heritage is ethnic. More than 80 percent of the Russian people belong to the ethnic group of Russian Slavs. These people generally speak the Russian language and live in western parts of the country.

Other Ethnic Groups Besides the Slavs, more than 75 different ethnic groups live in Russia. Most of the minority groups live far from the heavily populated western areas. The Finns and Turks live in regions of the Ural and Caucasus (KAW kuh sus) mountains. Armenians and Mongolians live along Russia's southern edges. The Yakuts (yah KOOTS) live in small areas of Siberia. These groups speak languages other than Russian. They also follow different religions. Muslims make up Russia's second-largest religious group, after Russian Orthodox believers. Many followers of Buddhism (BOOD izum) live near Russia's border with China.

United or Divided? When the Soviet Union came apart, some non-Russian ethnic groups broke away from Russia and formed their own countries. Since that time, other ethnic groups have tried to break ties with Russia.

The new Russian government has tried to keep the country unified by giving ethnic groups the right to rule themselves. At times, however, groups have called for complete independence from Russia. In response, the Russian government has sent the army to **repress,** or put down, the independence movements.

ACROSS THE WORLD

The East-West Split In 1054, it was official. The Christian Church was split into the Eastern Orthodox Church (which included the Russian Orthodox Church) and the Roman Catholic Church. The leaders of each church excommunicated each other; each man said that the other man could not belong to his church. It was not until 1965 that the two sides officially removed the excommunications.

Families in Siberia

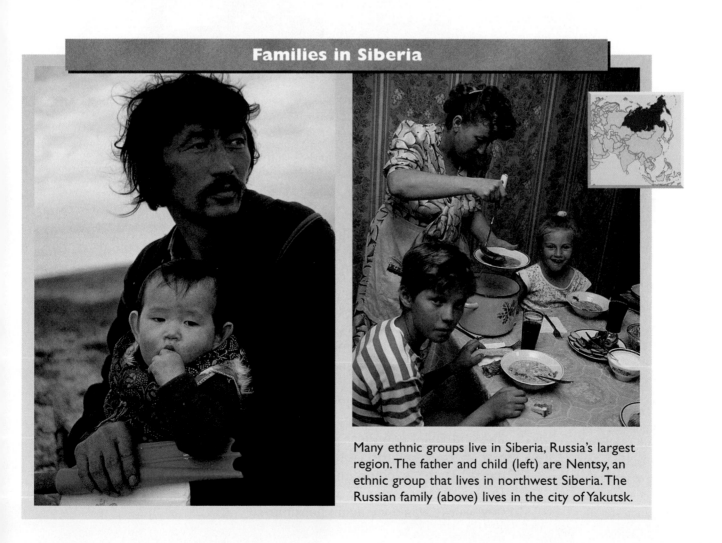

Many ethnic groups live in Siberia, Russia's largest region. The father and child (left) are Nentsy, an ethnic group that lives in northwest Siberia. The Russian family (above) lives in the city of Yakutsk.

A Monument to Heroic Workers

Socialist realism was the only acceptable style of art in the Soviet Union. Socialist realist paintings and sculptures showed idealized—or perfect—views of heroic workers and farmers, often struggling against great odds. The only purpose of socialist realist art was to further the aims of the Soviet government. **Critical Thinking** This sculpture in Moscow is a monument to Soviet workers. The two workers are holding aloft a hammer and sickle, the symbols of the Soviet Union. What aspects of socialist realist art does this sculpture illustrate?

Russian Ballet Sergei Diaghilev created the Ballets Russes—a Russian ballet company—in 1909. He had a flair for using unusual dance and music in his shows. In one ballet, the music was so strange that the audience complained—and the dancers were unable to hear the music from the nearby orchestra pit.

Russian Culture and Education

Russia has produced many great artists, thinkers, and writers. Russia's artistic heritage includes outstanding architecture, fine religious paintings, great plays, and intricate art objects like the Fabergé (fah ber ZHAY) egg on the opposite page. Novelist Leo Tolstoy (TOHL stoy) wrote powerful stories of life in Russia in the 1800s. Peter Tchaikovsky (chy KAWF skee) composed moving classical music. Russian painters, such as Vasily Kandinsky (kan DIN skee), were leaders in the modern art movement in the early 1900s. In a way, creating works of art is a tradition among Russians.

Under communism, the creation of great new works of art nearly came to a halt. The Soviet government believed that the purpose of art was to glorify communism. The government banned any art it did not like and jailed countless artists. The only art that the government did like was **propaganda**—the spread of ideas designed to support some cause, such as communism. With the collapse of communism, the Russian people eagerly returned to their artistic traditions. Creating new works was once again possible.

Elegant St. Petersburg   An important center of Russian culture is the city of St. Petersburg. Visitors to the city can clearly see the Russian mixture of European and Slavic cultures. This city has many Western influences. Peter the Great founded it in 1703. His goal was to create a Russian city as beautiful as any Western European city.

Elegant is the best word for St. Petersburg. The Neva (NEE vuh) River winds gracefully through the city. Along the river's banks are palaces, and public buildings hundreds of years old. St. Petersburg's

A Fabergé Egg

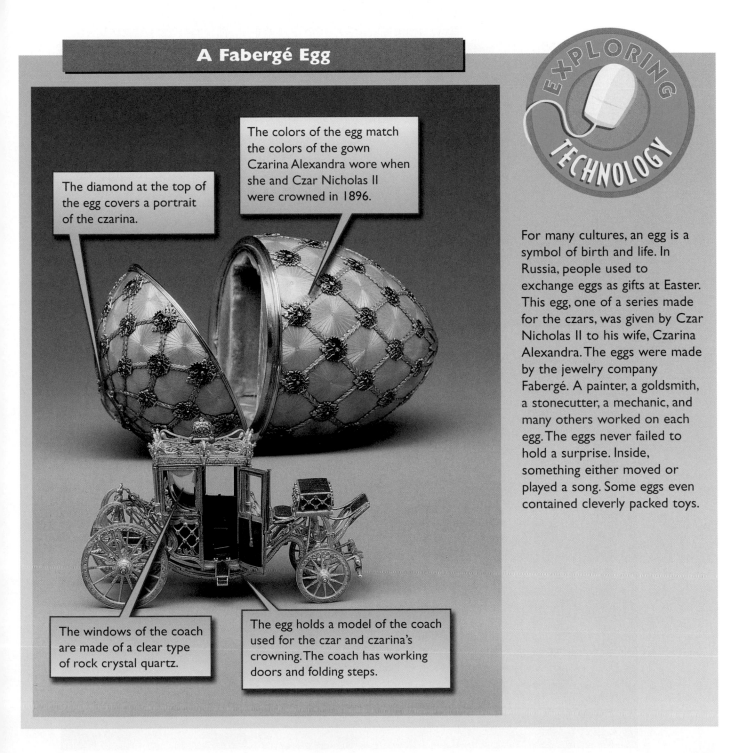

The diamond at the top of the egg covers a portrait of the czarina.

The colors of the egg match the colors of the gown Czarina Alexandra wore when she and Czar Nicholas II were crowned in 1896.

The windows of the coach are made of a clear type of rock crystal quartz.

The egg holds a model of the coach used for the czar and czarina's crowning. The coach has working doors and folding steps.

EXPLORING TECHNOLOGY

For many cultures, an egg is a symbol of birth and life. In Russia, people used to exchange eggs as gifts at Easter. This egg, one of a series made for the czars, was given by Czar Nicholas II to his wife, Czarina Alexandra. The eggs were made by the jewelry company Fabergé. A painter, a goldsmith, a stonecutter, a mechanic, and many others worked on each egg. The eggs never failed to hold a surprise. Inside, something either moved or played a song. Some eggs even contained cleverly packed toys.

grandest sight, the Winter Palace, is on the Neva. This more than 1,000-room palace, shown in the pictures below, was the winter home of Russia's czars. Part of the palace is the Hermitage (HUR mih tij) Museum. This museum houses one of the world's finest art collections.

Education in Russia   One of the few strengths of the old Soviet Union was its offer of free public education. Under this system, the number of Russians who could read and write rose from about 40 percent to nearly 100 percent.

Russian Treasures

Visitors to St. Petersburg's Hermitage Museum can view priceless art objects in the Emblem Hall (below) and climb the Grand Staircase where czars once walked (left). **Critical Thinking** Why do you think it is important to Russians to preserve the homes of czars even though Russia is no longer ruled by a czar?

The new Russia has continued free public schooling for children between ages 6 and 17. Schools are updating their old courses of study, which told only the communist point of view. New courses, such as business management, are preparing students for the new, noncommunist Russia. Some private schools run by the Orthodox Church offer similar courses, as well as religious instruction.

These changes show that Russia is trying to recover the riches of its past even as it prepares for a new future. Religion and art, two important parts of Russia's cultural heritage, can now be freely expressed. And Russia's young people, unlike their parents, can grow up deciding their future for themselves.

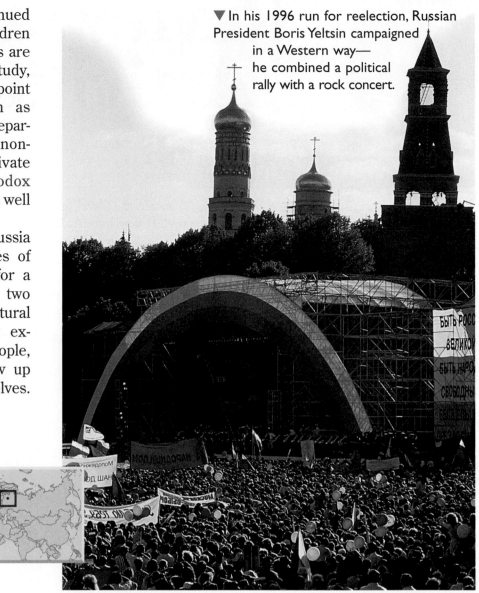

▼ In his 1996 run for reelection, Russian President Boris Yeltsin campaigned in a Western way— he combined a political rally with a rock concert.

SECTION 3 REVIEW

1. **Define** (a) heritage, (b) repress, (c) propaganda.

2. **Identify** (a) Leo Tolstoy, (b) Peter Tchaikovsky, (c) St. Petersburg.

3. (a) What is Russia's major ethnic group? (b) How has the government treated Russia's smaller ethnic groups?

4. What are some examples of ways in which Russians are reconnecting with their past?

Critical Thinking

5. **Recognizing Cause and Effect** How have the political changes in Russia led to changes in education?

6. **Expressing Problems Clearly** How has Russia's ethnic mix created challenges for the new Russian government?

Activity

7. **Writing to Learn** What predictions might you make about Russia's culture in the next 10 years? Give reasons for your predictions.

CHAPTER 3 Review and Activities

Reviewing Main Ideas

1. What features make many cities in Western Europe great centers for culture?

2. How do open borders and free trade affect the way Western Europeans live?

3. (a) Who are the Slavs? (b) Why are the Slavs an important part of the population of Eastern Europe?

4. How was the breakup of Czechoslovakia different than the breakup of Yugoslavia?

5. How have non-Russian ethnic groups reacted to recent events in Russia?

6. What traditions are Russians reviving following the collapse of the Soviet Union?

Reviewing Key Terms

Match the definitions in Column I with the key terms in Column II.

Column I

1. to put down
2. the movement of people from place to place
3. people who share a language, culture, and religion
4. a variation of a language
5. customs passed on from one generation to the next
6. influenced by many different cultures
7. spread of ideas designed to support a cause
8. a fee that the government charges for goods entering the country

Column II

a. multicultural
b. migration
c. heritage
d. ethnic group
e. dialect
f. propaganda
g. repress
h. tariff

Critical Thinking

1. **Drawing Conclusions** Why do Western Europeans generally have a higher standard of living than Eastern Europeans?

2. **Identifying Central Issues** How has life changed for the Russian people since the collapse of the Soviet Union?

Graphic Organizer

Copy the chart onto a separate sheet of paper. Then fill in the empty boxes to complete the chart.

	How the Lives of Its People Are Changing	What Is Special About Its Cultures	Relations Among Different Ethnic Groups or Countries
Western Europe			
Eastern Europe			
Russia			

Map Activity

Europe and Russia

For each place listed below, write the letter from the map that shows its location. Use the maps in the Activity Atlas to help you.

1. France
2. Ukraine
3. Russia
4. Germany
5. Slovakia
6. St. Petersburg

Place Location

Writing Activity

Writing a Travel Guide

If you had friends who were visiting Europe and Russia for the first time, what information would you want to share with them? Starting with the title "A Guide to Europe and Russia," write a brief travel guide your friends can use to plan an educational and enjoyable trip. Mention interesting places and activities, and provide background information on the cultures of the people they will meet.

Take It to the NET

Activity Explore the Web sites of Russian cities and use the information to create a brochure on Russian culture. For help in completing this activity, visit www.phschool.com.

Chapter 3 Self-Test To review what you have learned, take the Chapter 3 Self-Test and get instant feedback on your answers. Go to www.phschool.com to take the test.

Skills Review

Turn to the Skills Activity.

Review the steps for summarizing information. Then, write a one-paragraph summary of your last weekend.

How Am I Doing?

Answer these questions to help you check your progress.

1. Do I understand how and why the people of Western Europe are coming together?
2. Can I identify different ethnic groups in Eastern Europe?
3. Can I describe the heritage of the Russian people?
4. What information from this chapter can I include in my journal?

CHAPTER 4

Exploring Western Europe

MAP ACTIVITIES

This map shows Western Europe, the region you will be reading about in this chapter. To help you get to know Western Europe, complete the following activities.

Understanding geography

Western Europe is sometimes called a "peninsula of peninsulas." Use information from the map to explain why.

Study the map

Follow the outlines of the countries. Look for familiar shapes. For example, Italy looks like a boot. Spain and Portugal look like a square attached to the rest of Europe. Describe the shapes of other countries.

Great Britain

A DEMOCRATIC TRADITION

BEFORE YOU READ

Reach Into Your Background

What does the word *tradition* mean to you? Identify two or three American traditions.

Compare them to the British traditions you read about in this section.

Questions to Explore

1. How did democracy develop in Britain?
2. How does Britain's status as an island nation affect the way of life of its people?

Key Terms

Parliament
representative
constitutional monarchy

Key People and Places

Queen Elizabeth II
King John
Buckingham Palace

The line of tourists seems to go on forever. Every few feet along the line, a different language is spoken. You can hear English, French, Arabic, and Japanese. Despite the difference in languages, all the tourists are talking about the same thing: the British crown jewels.

The jewels are kept under guard in a large building called the Tower of London. The beautiful collection includes crowns worn by Great Britain's kings and queens. After a long wait, the tourists reach a motorized walkway, which slowly carries them past the bulletproof case. Their eyes widen with wonder at the sight of huge diamonds, bright rubies, and cool sapphires (SAF eyerz).

British history comes alive in and around the Tower. On Tower Green, nobles went to their deaths on the executioner's block. In the Bloody Tower, the young King Edward V and his brother were said to have been murdered. The Wakefield Tower holds rings and royal symbols of

▼ St. Edward's crown, one of several crowns kept at the Tower of London, is a copy of a crown worn by Edward the Confessor. He ruled England from 1042 to 1066.

kings and queens. All these places are watched [by] Beefeaters. They wear colorful red costumes lik[e] guards in the 1500s.

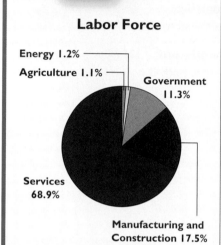

COUNTRY · PROFILE

United Kingdom: Resources and the Ec[onomy]

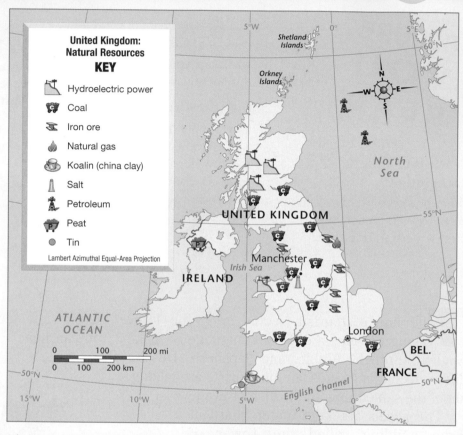

United Kingdom: Natural Resources
KEY
- Hydroelectric power
- Coal
- Iron ore
- Natural gas
- Koalin (china clay)
- Salt
- Petroleum
- Peat
- Tin

Lambert Azimuthal Equal-Area Projection

Shetland Islands
Orkney Islands
North Sea
UNITED KINGDOM
Manchester
Irish Sea
IRELAND
ATLANTIC OCEAN
London
BEL.
FRANCE
English Channel

0   100   200 mi
0   100   200 km

Labor Force

Energy 1.2%
Agriculture 1.1%
Government 11.3%
Services 68.9%
Manufacturing and Construction 17.5%

Source: CIA World Factbook 2000

Major Export Destinations

Ireland 5%
Netherlands 7%
France 9%
Germany 11%
United States 13%
Other 55%

Major Sources of Imports

Japan 5%
Netherlands 6%
France 9%
Germany 12%
United States 14%
Other 54%

Source: Dorling Kindersley World Desk Reference

Take It to the NET Data Update For the most recent data on the United Kingdom, visit **www.phschool.com**.

Economics The map and charts show the natural resources, workforce, and trading partners of the United Kingdom. **Map and Chart Study** (a) Describe the location of energy sources—coal, oil, and natural gas—found in the United Kingdom. (b) Which type of economic activity employs the most people in the United Kingdom? (c) From which country does the United Kingdom receive the most imports?

A Democratic Heritage

Visitors standing inside the Tower of London may forget that Great Britain is a modern nation. In the Tower, Britain's long tradition of kings and queens seems as strong as ever. Great Britain is still a monarchy, headed by Queen Elizabeth II. She is a symbol of Britain's past and its customs. But Great Britain also has a strong democratic government. This country served as one of the first models of a modern democracy.

The roots of British democracy go back many hundreds of years. During the Middle Ages, British kings could not take major actions without the approval of a group of rich nobles. Over time, the power of this group grew. In 1215, the group forced one English monarch, King John, to sign a document called the Magna Carta, or "Great Charter." The Magna Carta strengthened the power of the nobles and limited the power of the king.

In time, the group of nobles became known as the **Parliament.** This word comes from the French word *parler* (PAHR lay), which means "to talk." The Parliament later gained more power. It helped to decide the kinds of taxes paid by citizens. It elected people from each area to serve as **representatives.** A representative represents, or stands for, a group of people. In time, the people themselves elected these representatives. Such changes helped to make Britain a true democracy.

Ask Questions What questions would you like answered about Great Britain's system of government?

British Parliament, Present and Past

The modern Parliament consists of the House of Commons, whose members actually govern the nation, and the House of Lords (above). This 300-year-old illustration of Parliament in session (right) shows how the governing body looked in 1295 when King Edward I reigned.

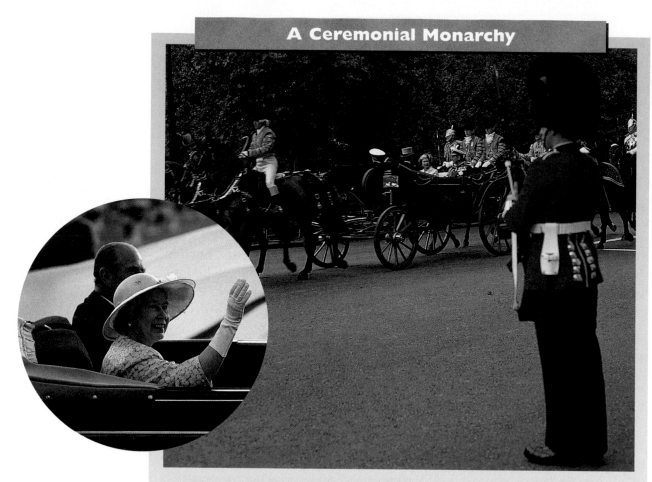

Britain's Queen Elizabeth II (above left) was crowned in 1953. The red-coated officers (above right) who guard her stand at stiff attention. The Queen may approve or reject laws passed by Parliament, but no British monarch has rejected a law since the 1700s. The Queen and members of her family also sponsor charity events, participate in important national ceremonies and parades, and represent Britain on trips to other countries.

Democracy and Monarchy

Today, the monarchy serves as an important symbol of Britain's past. It also helps to unify, or bring together, the British people. The British honor the monarchy in many ways. When the queen is in London, a royal flag is flown over her home at Buckingham (BUK ing um) Palace. Whether she is there or not, a short ceremony called the changing of the guard takes place every day. Trumpets blare and guardsmen march back and forth at the palace gate.

However, Britain's monarchs today do not have the power to make laws or collect taxes. Great Britain is now a **constitutional monarchy.** A constitution is a set of laws that describes how a government works. In a constitutional monarchy, the power of kings and queens is limited. The laws state what they can and cannot do. This is very different from the absolute monarchy in France during the time of Louis XIV. British laws are made by Parliament, not by the king or queen.

Britain Looks Outward

Parliament today governs all of the United Kingdom, which includes Great Britain (England, Scotland, and Wales) and Northern Ireland. The southern part of the island of Ireland became an independent country in the 1920s. Though *United Kingdom* is the country's official name, people often use *Britain* or *Great Britain* instead. This is because most of the people live on the island of Great Britain.

Building an Empire As an island nation, Great Britain is more difficult to invade than other European countries. During World War II, it was one of the few European countries that was not captured by the Germans. But as an island, Britain has limited natural resources. It must trade with other nations for resources. For this reason, trade has always been important to Britain.

In the 1500s, Britain began building a large empire. Its empire grew to include colonies on six continents. The colonies provided Britain's factories with raw materials. They also provided places to sell the goods made in Britain's factories. The colonies, then, helped Britain become a world economic power.

ACROSS THE WORLD

The Brightest Jewel Rare spices, silks, and other riches attracted the British East India Company to India in the 1600s. In time, the company gained great power in India. But the company misused its power, so the British government took over. By the mid-1800s, Britain controlled three fifths of India. Many people called India the "brightest jewel" in the British "crown" of colonies.

British Empire, 1900

ARCTIC OCEAN

ALASKA (U.S.)

CANADA

GREAT BRITAIN

RUSSIAN EMPIRE

UNITED STATES

CHINA

ATLANTIC OCEAN

EGYPT

INDIA

BURMA

PACIFIC OCEAN

FRENCH WEST AFRICA

ANGLO-EGYPTIAN SUDAN

Arabian Sea

PACIFIC OCEAN

BRAZIL

BRITISH EAST AFRICA

INDIAN OCEAN

N W E S

UNION OF SOUTH AFRICA

AUSTRALIA

NEW ZEALAND

KEY
British Empire, 1900
Robinson Projection

0   2,000   4,000 mi
0   2,000   4,000 km

Map Study By 1900, the British Empire had reached its high point. At that time, it included approximately one fourth of the world's land and people. As the 1900s dawned, one writer noted that the area under British control had grown by "over two acres of new territory every time the clock has ticked since 1800." **Location** List, along with their continents, at least three British colonies.

At one point, Britain had so many colonies around the world that people said, "The sun never sets on the British Empire." Fighting the two World Wars weakened Britain, however. After the World Wars, Great Britain's empire fell apart. Most of its colonies gained their independence. Britain maintained close economic ties with its former colonies. However, it now had to compete with other countries to buy and sell in these markets.

A Community Member Britain's industrial base remains strong. It has good supplies of fossil fuels—especially oil from deposits beneath the North Sea. It continues to export many manufactured goods, such as clothing and electronic products. However, Britain is not as strong a world power as it was before the World Wars.

A Natural Gas Refinery

Great Britain uses natural gas in factories that produce automobiles, ships, steel, textiles, and many other products. Several deposits of natural gas lie under the North Sea, east of Great Britain. Great Britain produces most of the natural gas that it needs from these fields. **Critical Thinking** Unlike gasoline, which is a liquid, natural gas is a gas, like air and steam. What do you think the challenges of shipping a gas might be?

Flags of the European Union

In 2001, the European Union had 15 members. Some of their flags are shown here. Many more European countries are working their way through the EU application process. **Critical Thinking** How might membership in the EU benefit the British economy?

Britain can no longer rely on its colonies to boost its economy. To be successful in the modern world, Britain has had to change its approach to trade. In 1973, Britain joined what is now called the European Union (EU), a group of nations that promotes trade among its members.

Britain today is a leading member of the EU. Its expertise in areas such as shipping and finance have strengthened the EU in global trade. In turn, easier access to European markets has helped replace the trade Britain lost when its empire collapsed. With new links to the resources and markets of other European countries, the British look forward to a bright economic future.

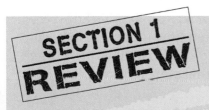

SECTION 1 REVIEW

1. **Define** (a) Parliament, (b) representative, (c) constitutional monarchy.

2. **Identify** (a) Queen Elizabeth II, (b) King John, (c) Buckingham Palace.

3. How did Britain become a constitutional monarchy?

4. How has the location of Great Britain affected how the country has developed?

Critical Thinking

5. **Drawing Conclusions** Why do you think Britain holds on to its monarchy even though the monarch now has very little power?

Activity

6. **Writing to Learn** Write one or two paragraphs describing the places you would go and the things you would do if you visited London.

France

PRESERVING A CULTURE

Reach Into Your Background

Do you have a special way of doing something? Is it dancing, playing a sport, dressing, or something else? As you read this section, you will see that the French, too, have special ways of doing things.

Questions to Explore

1. In what parts of their culture do the French people take special pride?
2. How is the culture of other nations affecting French culture?

Key Terms
emigrate

Key Places
Aix-en-Provence
Paris

▼ Carrying baguettes—long, crusty loaves of bread—two young girls stroll through France's countryside.

Catherine and Victoire are sisters. Both are in their 20s—just one year apart in age. The two look so much alike that some people think they are twins. They grew up in the south of France, in a city called Aix-en-Provence (eks ahn praw VAHNS). It is a quiet, pretty town, a trading center for olives, almonds, and wine.

Catherine and Victoire may look alike, but they are very different. Catherine still lives in Aix. She is married and has two children. Her husband works as a pastry chef, making cakes and other desserts. He learned how to make them from a master chef. He follows French recipes that were created 150 years ago.

Victoire is single and lives in Paris, the capital of France. She works for a publisher. Her job is to get American books translated into French. She has worked on science fiction books, westerns, and even vampire novels! Of course, she speaks English very well. In her apartment, she listens to American rock bands or watches American television programs. Her favorite restaurant serves only American food.

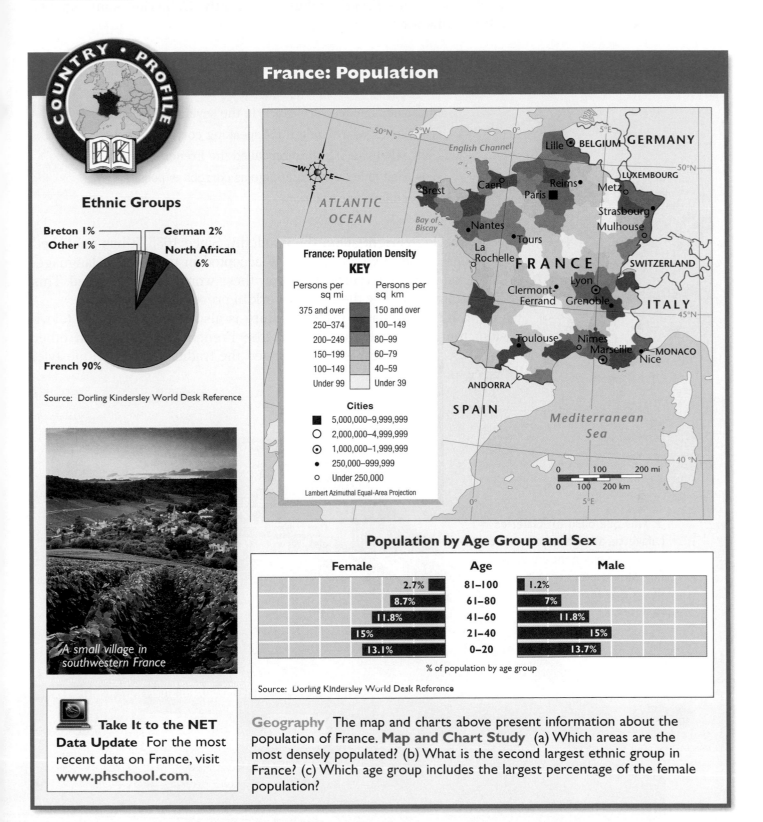

COUNTRY · PROFILE

DK

France: Population

Ethnic Groups

Breton 1%
Other 1%
German 2%
North African 6%
French 90%

Source: Dorling Kindersley World Desk Reference

A small village in southwestern France

France: Population Density
KEY

Persons per sq mi	Persons per sq km
375 and over	150 and over
250–374	100–149
200–249	80–99
150–199	60–79
100–149	40–59
Under 99	Under 39

Cities

■	5,000,000–9,999,999
○	2,000,000–4,999,999
◉	1,000,000–1,999,999
•	250,000–999,999
○	Under 250,000

Lambert Azimuthal Equal-Area Projection

Population by Age Group and Sex

Female	Age	Male
2.7%	81–100	1.2%
8.7%	61–80	7%
11.8%	41–60	11.8%
15%	21–40	15%
13.1%	0–20	13.7%

% of population by age group

Source: Dorling Kindersley World Desk Reference

Take It to the NET
Data Update For the most recent data on France, visit **www.phschool.com**.

Geography The map and charts above present information about the population of France. **Map and Chart Study** (a) Which areas are the most densely populated? (b) What is the second largest ethnic group in France? (c) Which age group includes the largest percentage of the female population?

Pride in French Culture

Catherine and Victoire show us two sides of the French character. Each side values French culture differently. Catherine sums up her attitude this way:

> **W**e French are as modern as anyone else. But there is something very special about our culture. Take our language. It's very exact. In the seventeenth century [we] invented a standard for speaking correct French. Since then, an organization called the French Academy has tried to keep our language as correct as possible. We French love our traditions.

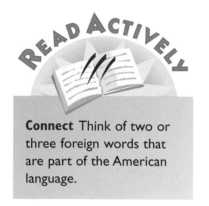

Connect Think of two or three foreign words that are part of the American language.

Catherine is right about the Academy. Since 1635, it has published dictionaries that give all the words accepted in the French language. The Academy makes rules about how these words should be used. This is an example of how the French work to preserve their culture.

On the other hand, French culture is also changing. Films, television, tourists, and trade have put the French in contact with other cultures. These cultures have changed the traditional French lifestyle. As Victoire explains:

▶This billboard on Galeries Lafayette, a huge department store in Paris, announces to English speakers that it is the "Capital of Fashion."

"There are plenty of articles in the French papers about the need to keep the French language pure. How are we going to do that, is what I want to know! At my publishing company most of us use a few foreign words to describe some of our activities. In the new France there are plenty of modern things that we didn't have any words for. We had to borrow them from the Americans!"

Building Chartres Cathedral

"The bigger the better" may have been the motto of architects and builders in the Middle Ages. Without the help of modern machinery or electric power, they built towering cathedrals like this one at Chartres, France. At the time, many people could not read or write, so cathe- drals were built with scenes from the Bible carved in stone or shown in stained-glass windows. It took over 100 years to build most cathedrals, but the people of Chartres built this one in only 30 years. What part of the cathedral do you think was the hardest to build? Why?

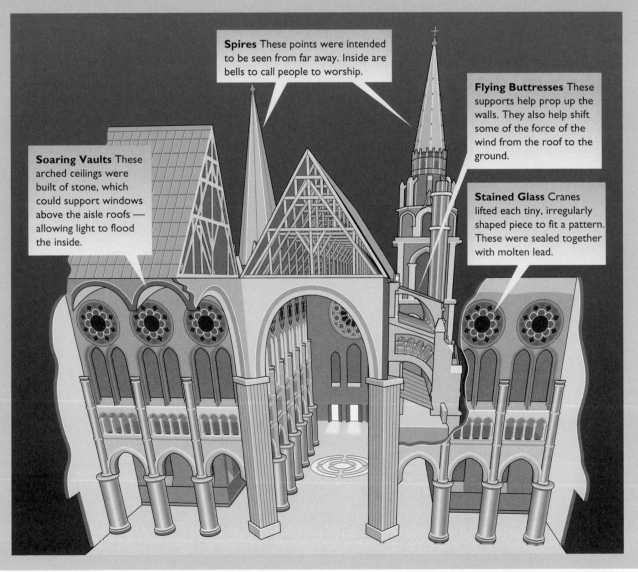

Spires These points were intended to be seen from far away. Inside are bells to call people to worship.

Flying Buttresses These supports help prop up the walls. They also help shift some of the force of the wind from the roof to the ground.

Soaring Vaults These arched ceilings were built of stone, which could support windows above the aisle roofs — allowing light to flood the inside.

Stained Glass Cranes lifted each tiny, irregularly shaped piece to fit a pattern. These were sealed together with molten lead.

Going Home to Paint Paul Cézanne was one of the greatest painters of his time. He lived in both Paris and Aix-en-Provence—where he was born—for most of his life. In 1883, he went to the countryside near his home town. He painted mountains, seashores—even his gardener. When he was outdoors, Cézanne tried to learn from nature. He believed that nature showed him what he needed to paint.

Victoire is referring to words like *sandwich, weekend, toast,* and *parking.* These words are a sign of France's close ties with other nations. These close ties mean that other cultures affect life in France. They also mean that French culture affects life in other nations.

Highlights of French Culture In 1805, a French pastry chef named Marie-Antoine Carême (muh REE ahn TWAHN kuh REM) began making desserts for rich and powerful people in France. His cakes and puddings delighted all. Some cakes looked like buildings or monuments. Some puddings looked like birds or flowers.

In 1833, Carême wrote a book on the art of French cooking. His book was similar to the dictionary of the French Academy. It set strict standards of excellence. Ever since Carême's book was published, French cooking has been one of the most respected kinds of cooking in the world.

The French have also set standards in the fashion industry. In 1947, a French fashion designer named Christian Dior (dee OR) caught the attention of the industry. His clothing designs were fresh and new. During World War II, women had worn shoulder pads and short, straight skirts. In contrast, Dior's "New Look" featured narrow shoulders and long, full dresses. His fashions became popular all over the world. Dior made Paris the center of the fashion industry.

Fashion's "New Look"

Women in your grandmother's generation might have worn evening dresses such as these, designed in the 1950s by French fashion designer Christian Dior (center).
Critical Thinking High-fashion clothing by European designers remains popular today. Why do you think this is so?

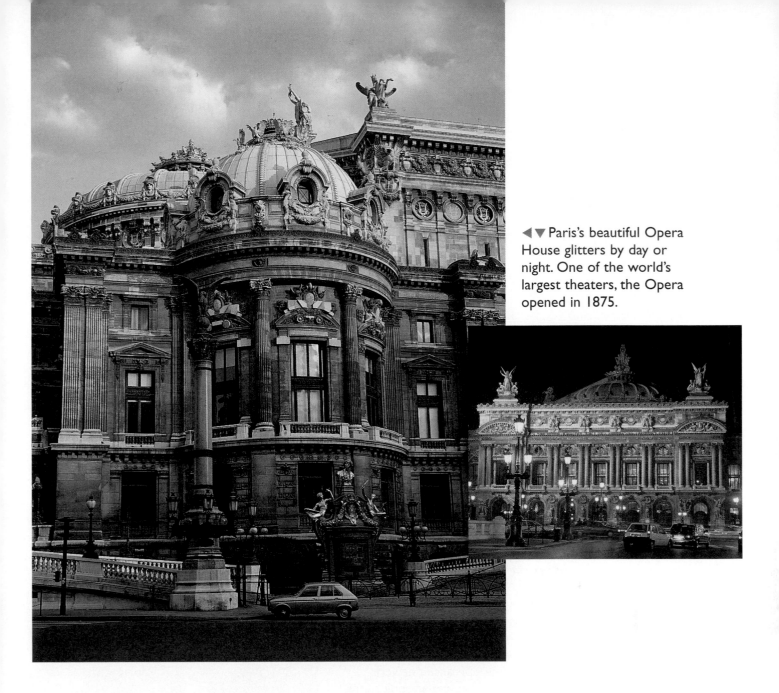

◀▼ Paris's beautiful Opera House glitters by day or night. One of the world's largest theaters, the Opera opened in 1875.

French cooking and fashions are only two examples of the influence of French culture on the rest of the world. France has also produced world-famous poets, philosophers, painters, and politicians. And some of the best wine in the world comes from France. The roots of this success go back centuries. They are based on the French system of education, methods of farming, and outlook on life.

Holding on to Tradition   In Aix, many French traditions continue. Catherine feels that the city of her birth is an important part of who she is. Her father, grandmother, and great-grandmother live in Aix. Her family has lived there since the 1400s! Catherine says that good French pastry chefs, like her husband, are born with the talent "in their blood." Once she even checked the city's records to see if her husband's ancestors were pastry chefs.

Changes in French Life

Like many French citizens, Catherine believes French culture is unique and valuable. Yet she, too, agrees that life in France is changing. And the French people and government are beginning to deal with the changes.

Predict When immigrants move to a new place, how do they change the culture?

The New Immigrants Immigrants have been moving to Western Europe since World War II. Many people in French colonies started **emigrating,** or moving away, from their homelands to France. They came from Algeria (al JIR ee uh), Senegal (sen ih GAWL), Vietnam (vee ut NAHM), and other former French colonies.

When France joined the European Union, immigrants from other countries in Europe moved to France in search of work. The native French people had questions about the immigrants. Would the newcomers take jobs away from people already in France? Would the newcomers understand French culture? Would the cultures of the newcomers change French traditions?

The debate about the new immigrants continues. But their influence can be seen, especially in the big cities. In Paris, Arab, African, and Asian cultures are very strong. In other large cities in France, it is common to hear people speaking languages other than French. Every year, there are more and more restaurants and grocery stores that sell foreign food.

Paris Street Scenes

In an immigrant neighborhood in Paris, people buy and sell foods that are both new and familiar (below). Immigrants from West and North Africa, some of France's newest residents, can browse at book shops that feature Arabic and French-language books about Islam and Africa (right).

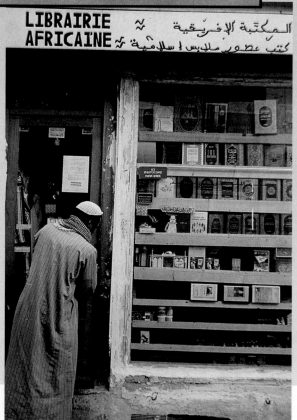

Some French people, like Catherine, continue to follow traditional French ways. And some French politicians support her point of view. The French government passed a law that makes it illegal to use certain foreign words in advertisements, business, and education. This law aims to protect the French language from foreign influences. Another law was passed to deal with citizenship. This law states that children born in France of parents born in other countries are not all French citizens.

Like her sister, Victoire is proud of French culture. But Victoire disagrees with the new language law. She believes France should accept foreign influences. Victoire also disagrees with the citizenship law. A few years ago, she and some friends protested against it in public.

American Influence In 1992, a strong foreign influence showed up just outside of Paris: the EuroDisney (YOO roh diz nee) theme park. This was the first Disney park to be built in Europe. Many French people cannot believe how big it is. The park is one fifth of the size of Paris.

At EuroDisney, visitors from all over Europe get to sample American culture. EuroDisney has a section called Main Street, U.S.A., with an American-style city hall. It also has a hotel that looks like a Wild West town, a camp with log cabins, and a California-style restaurant.

When the theme park opened, French reactions were mixed. Some French people loved it and brought their families to enjoy the rides, exhibits, and food. Other people were not so happy. They disliked the bright colors, cartoon characters, and fake scenery in the park.

After a slow start, EuroDisney has become a success. However, most visitors come from Great Britain, Germany, and other European countries—not France. Many French people prefer to go to another, smaller theme park called Parc Astérix (uhs STA riks). It is based on a French comic strip character.

▲ The theme park based on France's favorite cartoon character, Astérix, has added a new attraction every year since it opened.

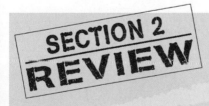

SECTION 2 REVIEW

1. **Define** emigrate.

2. **Identify** (a) Aix-en-Provence, (b) Paris.

3. How has Catherine shown pride in French culture?

4. How has Victoire shown that she is open to new ideas from outside of France?

Critical Thinking

5. **Recognizing Bias** Describe the views of those who agree and those who disagree with France's language law.

Activity

6. **Writing to Learn** Think about making a visit to Catherine or Victoire. What would you like to talk about? What would you like to see in Aix or Paris?

Using the Writing Process

James ran the entire three blocks home from the library. He threw open the front door and dropped his books and coat in the hall. Then he ran upstairs. His uncle Steven found him an hour later at his desk, scribbling madly.

"What are you doing, James?"

James barely looked up from his paper. "I'm writing about the Berlin Wall. I can't believe it stood in place for all those years and then the people just knocked it down!"

Uncle Steven picked up the paper. He read a few sentences and frowned.

"James, I can see in your writing that you're very excited about it, but it's kind of a jumble. What are you trying to say?"

James shrugged. "I just want to write down everything I know."

"It's tempting, I know, but you can't just throw everything into one pot like a soup. You have to plan your work. Remember, writing is a process."

Get Ready

Using the writing process means following a certain kind of method when writing. It means that people do not just sit down and write a paper all at once. Writing is not a single act. Instead, writing is a process, or a series of steps.

Most things you do in life are processes. For example, when you brush your teeth, you might follow these steps: 1) pick up your toothbrush and toothpaste, 2) put toothpaste on the brush, 3) brush your teeth, and 4) rinse. When you think about it, you can see how you go through processes every day of your life.

Writing is the same way. It involves a series of steps called the writing process. By simply following the steps, you can complete any writing assignment.

Try It Out

The writing process is shown in the diagram at right. Refer to the diagram as you read the description of each step. Use it to complete the activity that follows.

A. Prewriting This first step is what you do before you start to write. (*Pre-* means "before.") Prewriting involves two steps: deciding what you will write about, and finding the information you will need.

B. Drafting Drafting means organizing your information in a logical and interesting way. Make an outline and write a rough draft of your work. If you discover that you need more information, return to the prewriting step.

C. Revising Revising is, in many ways, the most important step. Professional writers often revise their work three, four, or even more times until they are happy with it. When you revise, you change your writing to make it clearer and more enjoyable to read. If necessary, you can reorganize your ideas by returning to the drafting stage.

D. Proofreading Reread your writing and correct any errors in grammar, usage, spelling, and punctuation. Fix even the smallest problems to make your writing as good as it can be. This step is especially important because a lot of little mistakes can hurt a piece of writing as much as a few big mistakes can.

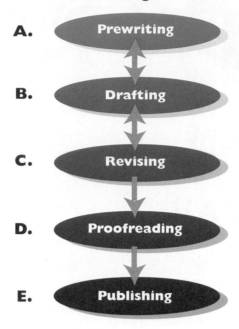

The Writing Process

A. Prewriting
B. Drafting
C. Revising
D. Proofreading
E. Publishing

E. Publishing Publishing is the final step. Publishing means sharing your writing with an audience. You might do this by turning it in to the teacher, posting it on the bulletin board, or reading it aloud to your classmates.

To help you apply the skill next time you have a writing assignment, do the following now. On a clean sheet of paper, copy the flowchart that shows the writing process. Write a brief description of each step underneath the step in the flowchart.

Apply the Skill

Use the writing process every time you have a writing assignment, from one-paragraph reports to long themes. You should even use it to answer essay questions on tests.

Now that you understand the writing process, put it to work. Your assignment is to use the writing process to write a paragraph that describes life in present-day rural France.

Sweden
A WELFARE STATE

BEFORE YOU READ

Reach Into Your Background

Do you know someone who has received some kind of help from the government? Do you think people need more government help, or should they do more for themselves? In Sweden, the government provides many services—such as hospital care and a college education—at little or no cost.

Questions to Explore

1. How does the Swedish government care for the needs of its people?

2. What economic challenges face the Swedish government, and how is it meeting these challenges?

Key Terms
benefit
welfare state
national debt

O lof Hylten-Cavallius (OHL uhf HIL tuhn kuh VAHL yuhs) is a Swedish banker. He thinks his third heart attack was the luckiest thing that ever happened to him. That is because it was not until the third heart attack that doctors agreed to give Olof an operation. Now his heart is close to normal.

The doctors who performed Olof's operation were experts in their field. The hospital had all the latest equipment, and the care afterwards was excellent. The operation would have cost Olof about $20,000 in the United States. But in Sweden, it cost him next to nothing. How did Olof manage to get such an expensive operation at such a low cost?

▼ Highly skilled surgeons use the most up-to-date equipment to perform heart surgery.

Life in a Welfare State

Olof's operation is just one example of the free—or nearly free—services in Sweden. Elisabet Ray, a school teacher, provides another example. She is happy that her daughter is going to college. This education costs nothing. Does this sound amazing to you? As you may know, college in the United States can cost more than $20,000 a year.

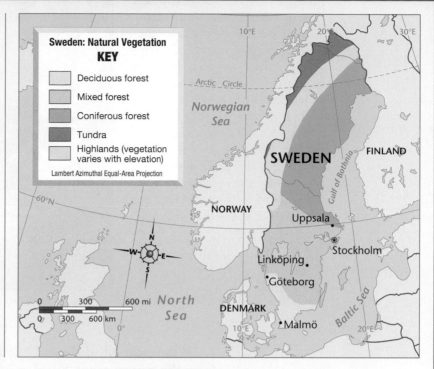

Sweden: Natural Vegetation
KEY

- Deciduous forest
- Mixed forest
- Coniferous forest
- Tundra
- Highlands (vegetation varies with elevation)

Lambert Azimuthal Equal-Area Projection

The Five Most Populated Cities

Cities	Population
Stockholm	
Göteborg	
Malmö	
Uppsala	
Linköping	

= 100,000 people

Source: New York Times Almanac

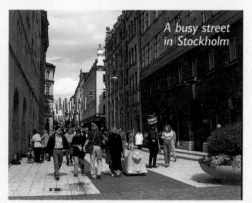

A busy street in Stockholm

Take It to the NET Data Update For the most recent data on Sweden, visit **www.phschool.com**.

Weather Chart

°F/°C — Average daily temperature — Rainfall — in/cm

Source: Dorling Kindersley World Desk Reference

Geography The map and charts above present information about land use and climate in Sweden. **Map and Chart Study** (a) In which months does Sweden experience the lowest average temperature? (b) In which vegetation regions are the five most populated cities located?

Elisabet's family received other forms of help, too. When Elisabet's son Patrick was born, she took nine months off work so that she could take care of him. Her husband also took the time off from his job. During their time away from work, they received monthly checks for 90 percent of their salaries.

When Elisabet went back to work, she needed to take her son to a childcare center. Elisabet's family received help for this care, too. Until her son reaches the age of 16, Elisabet will receive more than $100 a week to pay for child care. Most countries do not have such benefits. A **benefit** is a free service or a payment.

READ ACTIVELY

Predict How do you think the Swedish government pays for services for its citizens?

Consumer goods are expensive in Sweden. For the most part, this is because of the taxes the Swedish government collects. First, consumer goods are more expensive to make because companies pay heavy taxes on the raw materials they need. Second, a sales tax is charged when the goods are sold in stores. **Critical Thinking** How might your life be different if you had to pay more for goods like shoes than you currently pay?

Where do all of these benefits come from? In Sweden, they come from the government. Sweden is a **welfare state.** This means that many services are paid for by the government. The government provides benefits so that the people can live well. To pay for these services, the government collects high taxes.

Most people in Sweden live this way. They pay high taxes on the money they earn. Food, clothing, and other consumer goods are costly because these items have a sales tax of about 20 percent. In exchange for this, all Swedes have security. Whether they are rich or poor, they know their children will get a good education. Medical costs are low. Rents are affordable.

Sweden's Difficult Past

Life in Sweden was not always so secure. By the late 1800s, industry had grown in the United States and most of Europe. But Sweden was far behind. There were few factories or railroad lines, or even good roads. Farming methods had not changed much since the Middle Ages. Many people were very poor. By the end of the century, 1.5 million Swedes had left the country in search of a better life. Most of them settled in the United States.

Building a Welfare State

After World War II, a political party called the Social Democrats became powerful in Sweden. The Social Democrats promised a better life for Swedes. From 1946 to 1976, the party changed Sweden into a welfare state.

As part of the government benefits program, all workers receive five weeks of paid vacation. Most workers generally take their vacation at the same time during the summer. For five weeks in the summer, the nights in this far-northern country are very short. It is daylight for most of the day. Many factories and businesses shut down during this period.

Swedish people take more days off for being sick—and get paid for them—than the workers of any other Western country. Some of this money comes from the government. And when Swedish workers retire, they receive a monthly payment from the government that nearly equals the pay they received when they were working.

In Sweden, welfare benefits are for everyone. Many Swedes do not mind paying high taxes because they enjoy the benefits. Mona Sahlin (MOH nuh SAH lin), a Swedish politician, summed up the Swedish way of thinking:

> **"I**f you are a Social Democrat, you think it is terrific to pay taxes. For me, taxes are the finest expression of what politics are all about.**"**

A welfare system means something very different in the United States than it does in Sweden. Our welfare system only helps people in great need—people who cannot afford medical care or food. And the rules about who can receive welfare benefits in the United States are becoming stricter. Sweden, too, is changing its rules about welfare benefits.

LINKS TO SCIENCE

The Forecast: Sunny All Day and Night Near the Earth's polar regions, the sun can be seen 24 hours a day in six-month periods. At the North Pole, the sun is out from about March 20 to September 23. At the South Pole, the sun remains above the horizon from September 23 to March 20. In the northern part of Sweden, the sun stays out day and night for a few days around June 21. The Swedes celebrate this as Midsummer's Eve, with maypoles, dancing, and music.

▼ In midsummer, when the sun shines 24 hours a day, many people in Sweden stay up and celebrate with traditional dances.

Peter Wallenberg is a Swedish banker. His family owns more than 40 percent of Sweden's corporations. Most businesses in Sweden, like most businesses in the United States, are owned by individuals. **Critical Thinking** How do businesses help people in the community?

Problems and Solutions

Everyone in Sweden receives benefits, but some people are wealthier than others. The Wallenberg family, for instance, owns more than 40 percent of the corporations in Sweden. Families like the Wallenbergs live in great luxury. But in Sweden, some people are struggling with the costs of living. Lately, a number of Swedes have been just getting by.

Connect What would you do if you had to wait a long time for medical help when you really needed it?

Sweden's Troubles For the last 20 years, Sweden's economic growth has stalled. Because of the high taxes on groceries, clothing, and other goods, people buy fewer items than they would like to. Thus there is less spending to boost the economy. Also, Sweden's long vacations mean that workers spend less time on the job. This makes Swedish companies less productive.

There are also problems with the health care system. Medical care is not always available when it is needed. People often wait a long time to receive help.

The government is facing budgetary problems. To supply more benefits, the government has had to borrow money. Some Swedes think the amount their government owes, or the **national debt,** has gotten out of control. The government has increased taxes and cut some spending to try to control national debt.

Finding Solutions   Government and private businesses must both try to solve these problems. The government needs to reduce benefits and spend less money. And businesses need to earn more. The more money businesses earn, the more money, in the form of taxes, will go to the government.

One way for businesses to grow is to take advantage of Sweden's natural resources. Sweden has high-grade iron ore and makes enough steel for itself and for export. Each year, half of Sweden's electricity is made by hydroelectric turbines that use Sweden's fast rivers and many waterfalls. Sweden's vast forests support the timber industry, which supplies Sweden's needs and those of other countries.

Swedish companies have had trouble competing with firms in other countries. Most Swedish products are of high quality. But the Swedes have not been able to make them as quickly and cheaply as other countries. Some companies have found a solution to this problem. A Swedish automaker, for example, has made a partnership with an American company. Using the methods of American auto factories, the Swedes can now make a car in less than 40 hours. It used to take them four days.

The Graying of Sweden
Sweden has 1.5 million retired people out of a population of about 8.9 million. This means that about one out of six people is retired. This is the highest proportion in the world. The Swedish government is having trouble taking care of so many retired people. Some studies say that unless the government reforms its welfare benefits, there will not be any money left by 2015. Raising taxes to cover benefits for everyone has been proposed— but it is not a popular idea.

◄▼ Natural resources, such as large forests (left), helped Sweden to build thriving industrial cities such as Stockholm (below). Wood products make up a large amount of Sweden's exports.

Sweden's Dala Horses

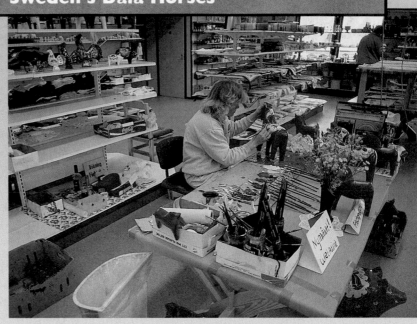

In this picture, a craftworker puts the finishing touches to a dala horse. These small figures are carved out of wood, painted red or blue, and decorated with floral designs. For Swedes, the dala horse is a symbol of hope and good luck. And for Swedes who no longer live in Sweden, it represents their homeland. In fact, the dala horse has become an important export item. Some 20 percent of dala horses made in Sweden are exported to the United States alone.

Improving the economy means changing the ways things are done in Sweden. Mats Thourslund (mahts THORZ luhnd), a professor at a Swedish university, said:

> **"S**weden will not be that different from other countries in the future. We have been used to having our kids in day-care centers and old people cared for by the system, leaving the rest of us free to do whatever we want. But the party is over.**"**

When Thorslund says, "the party is over," he means the country will be providing fewer services in order to spend less money. Making this happen is Sweden's biggest challenge today.

SECTION 3 REVIEW

1. **Define** (a) benefit, (b) welfare state, (c) national debt.

2. Describe some of the benefits that Swedish citizens receive.

3. What natural resources can help the Swedish economy?

Critical Thinking

4. **Recognizing Cause and Effect** What has caused Sweden to want to change its welfare system?

Activity

5. **Writing to Learn** Think about the welfare systems in the United States and Sweden. Write a paragraph about what you think the United States and Sweden might learn from each other.

Italy

TWO WAYS OF LIFE

BEFORE YOU READ

Reach Into Your Background

Do you think the region in which you live should help other regions develop new industries? Why or why not?

Questions to Explore

1. How have the differences in the environments of northern and southern Italy affected the lives of Italians?
2. How are Italians attempting to speed the development of southern Italy?

Key Term
manufacturing

Key Places
the Vatican
Rome
Milan
Locorotondo

Can you solve this riddle? A magazine photographer spent about a year exploring a certain country, yet the country is so tiny that he was able to walk around it in 40 minutes. Its population is only about 1,000. But one billion people look to its leader for guidance. What is the country?

The tiny nation is called the Vatican (VAT ih kun). It is the world headquarters of the Roman Catholic Church. Its leader is the pope. Every day, Roman Catholics all over the world look to him for leadership.

Country Within a Country

The Vatican is a country within a country. Located within Rome, the capital of Italy, the Vatican is an independent city-state. A city-state is both a city and an independent nation. The Vatican has its own money and stamps. It is a member of the United Nations. It also has its own radio station, newspaper, fire department, and supermarket.

▼ This aerial view of Vatican City shows the grand dome of St. Peter's Church, which dominates the skyline.

Italy: Land Use and the Economy

Labor Force

Agriculture 7%

Industry 32%

Services 61%

Source: CIA World Factbook 2000

Italy: Land Use
KEY

- Manufacturing
- Wheat, rice & dairy
- Livestock
- Fruit, mixed farming
- Grapes
- Forest
- Little use

Albers Equal-Area Projection

SWITZERLAND
AUSTRIA
SLOVENIA
Milan
Venice
CROATIA
45°N
BOSNIA-HERZEGOVINA
Florence
SAN MARINO
Ligurian Sea
Corsica (Fr.)
VATICAN CITY
Rome
Adriatic Sea
ITALY
Naples
Tyrrhenian Sea
40°N
Sardinia
Ionian Sea
Mediterranean Sea
Sicily

N W E S

0   100   200 mi
0 100 200 km

10°E   15°E   5°E   10°E   15°E

Mt. Etna in southern Italy

Take It to the NET
Data Update For the most recent data on Italy, visit **www.phschool.com**.

Major Exports

Metal Manufacturing

Textiles

Chemicals

Other

0   10   20   30   40   50   60

Percent of exports

Source: United Nations Statistics Division

Economy The map and charts show information about land use and the economy in Italy. **Map and Chart Study** (a) What do you notice about the location of the farming regions in Italy? (b) Study the graphs and write a short paragraph describing industry and the economy in Italy.

READ ACTIVELY

Visualize What would it be like to visit the Sistine Chapel? What would it feel like to be surrounded by art?

Every day, Catholics and non-Catholics stream into this little country. They come here to see St. Peter's Church. The Vatican's palace and art museum is also a popular attraction.

The Sistine (SIS teen) Chapel, located inside the Vatican, contains many world-famous paintings, sculptures, and other works of art. Tourists crowd into this chapel, but there is nearly perfect silence inside. No one is allowed to speak above a whisper. Everyone leans back to see the scenes painted on the ceiling. Some scenes were painted by the famous artist Michelangelo. It is the most famous and perhaps the most beautiful ceiling in the world.

Church and Family

Roman Catholicism unites about one billion people around the world. And it especially unites Italians. Not every Italian is Catholic, but Italy's history is closely tied to the history of Catholicism. Until recently, Catholicism was the official religion of the country.

The Roman Catholic Church provides a common focus for Italians throughout the country. For most Italians, the pope is symbolic of a father. The Church is a giant family to which they belong. Many Italians expect the Church to help them with their daily decisions—just as good parents help their children.

This way of living has existed for hundreds of years. Today, in the small towns of the countryside, life is organized around the larger family of the Church and the smaller family in the home. In the cities, these ties may not be as strong.

Divisions Between North and South

A common belief in Catholicism has helped Italians unify their nation. Until the 1800s, Italy was made up of many separate city-states, territories, and small kingdoms. In 1870, the Italian people unified these areas into one nation. Still, the Italy of today seems divided into two different countries—the north and the south. The ways of life in the two areas set them apart.

The Risorgimento: "Rising Again" The Risorgimento was a movement in the 1800s to inspire the Italian people to unite as one nation. Poets and philosophers tried to create a sense of nationalism. Today, Italian schoolchildren learn about and celebrate the movement. Cities have streets and squares that bear the names of many of the Risorgimento's heroes.

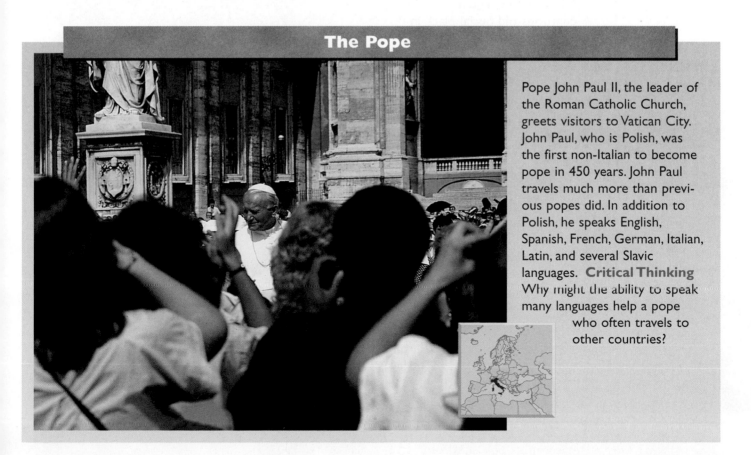

The Pope

Pope John Paul II, the leader of the Roman Catholic Church, greets visitors to Vatican City. John Paul, who is Polish, was the first non-Italian to become pope in 450 years. John Paul travels much more than previous popes did. In addition to Polish, he speaks English, Spanish, French, German, Italian, Latin, and several Slavic languages. **Critical Thinking** Why might the ability to speak many languages help a pope who often travels to other countries?

A Cross Between Art and Fashion Futurism was an artistic movement that centered in Italy in the early 1900s. Futurists celebrated the future and criticized traditions. They glorified technology by painting images of a speeding car or the motion of a powerful train. An artist named Fortunato Depero, a Futurist painter, also designed men's vests. These vests had "Futurist" designs on them—such as mechanical figures.

Life in the North Milan (mih LAN) is typical of northern Italy. Abundant minerals, fast rivers, and a developed economy have brought wealth to the area. Many international businesses are located here.

Milan is one part of a triangle of cities—with the cities of Turin and Genoa—that are home to most of Italy's **manufacturing** industries. Manufacturing is the process of turning raw materials into finished products.

Milan has a flashier side, too. Every season, people interested in fashions crowd into Milan to see collections from clothing designers. Italian fashion has become so important that Milan is second only to Paris as a fashion capital. Milan's factories also produce cars, planes, leather goods, and plastics.

Like many European cities, Milan is a mix of the old and the new. In a 300-year-old palace, you can see what may be the oldest public library in Europe. Millions of dollars have been spent to keep it in good condition. Less than a mile away, you can drive past modern steel-and-glass office buildings. These buildings cost millions of dollars to construct.

▼▶ Italy has both new and old attractions, such as this high-tech shoe factory in Milan (below) and a centuries-old burial place in Rome (right).

▲ This band is playing music for the tarantella, one of southern Italy's most popular folk dances. Tarantella music is lively, so the dancers must skip, run, and hop as they dance. Italian legend states that dancing the tarantella can cure someone who has been bitten by a tarantula spider.

A Town in Southern Italy   Southern Italy is very different from Milan. Southern Italy is mostly agricultural. Fertile areas near the coast get enough rainfall to grow abundant crops. Olives, tomatoes, fruits, and other crops are grown here. Inland, people barely make a living because of the thin soil and dry climate. These people follow a traditional way of life.

Locorotondo (loh koh roh TAWN doh) is a small town located in the southernmost part of Italy. It is on the "heel" of the Italian "boot." Farming is the way most people here make a living. Wheat, olives, and fruits are grown here. Fishing is also an important industry.

The people here talk about northern Italy as if it were another country. They know little of the high fashions of Milan or the noisy city of Rome. Southern Italian traditions and the family still rule everyday life.

Many religious events are celebrated in the streets of town. The procession of the Feast of Corpus Christi takes place every year, several weeks after Easter. It celebrates the presence of Jesus Christ. In this festival event, women hang their wedding clothes over their balconies and place flowers on them. Additional such displays are set up on the streets around town. People walk together around the town, from church to church and display to display.

The traditional way of life may change as the economy of southern Italy changes. After World War II, Puglia (POOL yah)—the region that Locorotondo lies within—became one of the main areas for land reform. Large farms were divided into smaller farms and sold. Today the Italian government is using tax money to modernize parts of the southern region. New schools and hospitals are being built. The government is also rebuilding factories in the south's large cities, such as Naples (NAY pulz) and Syracuse (SIHR uh kyoos).

Politics and the Two Italys

Northern and southern Italy are so different that some Italians think the two regions should be separate countries. In 1996, a political party known as the Northern League won 10 percent of the vote in a national election. The Northern League wants to turn northern Italy into a separate country. If this happens, people in northern Italy will no longer have to support the poorer southern part of Italy with their taxes.

It is not likely that the Northern League will get its way. No matter how much Italians disagree, they will never lose their strong Italian identity. Religion and family will probably keep the people of Italy unified for many years to come.

A Call for Independence

During a speech in Venice in 1996, Umberto Bossi, the leader of the Northern League, demanded independence for Padania, the League's name for northern Italy.

SECTION 4 REVIEW

1. **Define** manufacturing.

2. **Identify** (a) the Vatican, (b) Rome, (c) Milan, (d) Locorotondo.

3. List three differences between life in Milan and life in a southern Italian village.

4. How has the government tried to help the development of southern Italy?

Critical Thinking

5. **Drawing Conclusions** Do you think northern Italy should try to help develop southern Italy? Why or why not?

Activity

6. **Writing to Learn** Work with a partner. One of you will write a letter to a relative about life in northern Italy. The other will write a response from the point of view of a southern Italian.

Germany

A NATION REUNITED

Reach Into Your Background

What is it like to see a friend whom you have not seen in a long time? Do you sometimes find that you do not know the person as well as you once did? As you read this section, you will see how two parts of Germany separated and then came together again.

Questions to Explore

1. Why was Germany divided and how did it become reunited?
2. How are Germans dealing with the issues of a reunited nation?

Key Terms
Holocaust
reunification

Key People and Places
Adolf Hitler
Berlin

One day in 1961, Conrad Schumann, a 19-year-old policeman, stood guard at a barbed-wire fence. His job was to shoot anyone who tried to get across the fence. East Berlin (bur LIN), where Schumann was standing, was part of East Germany. East Germany had a communist government. The fence was built to prevent East Berliners from escaping to West Berlin. From West Berlin, people could reach democratic West Germany.

To Schumann, the fence was a terrible thing. He could see the buildings of West Berlin on the other side. They seemed very beautiful. On television, he had seen a program from West Berlin. It showed people dancing to American music, shopping for colorful clothing, and speaking their views freely. In East Germany, the government did not approve of American music and free speech. The stores had few interesting things to buy.

Schumann thought about all these things. Then he made a decision and jumped over the barbed wire. A moment later, he was on the other side—in the freedom of the West.

Just a few days after Schumann jumped to freedom, the barbed-wire fence was replaced by a concrete wall. The Berlin Wall separated families and friends. On one side of it, communism ruled. On the other side, the people did.

▼ At first, the Berlin Wall was only barbed wire. As you can see, Conrad Schumann jumped over it easily. Later, he said, "I had no desire to shoot my fellow citizens, and I knew that they were about to put up a much stronger wall."

Germany: Population

Germany: Population Density
KEY

Persons per sq mi	Persons per sq km
838 and over	300 and over
418–837	150–299
278–417	100–149
138–277	50–99
63–137	25–49
Under 62	Under 24

Cities
- ○ 2,000,000–4,999,999
- ◉ 1,000,000–1,999,999
- ● 250,000–999,999
- ○ Under 250,000

Albers Equal-Area Projection

Population by Age Group and Sex

Female		Age	Male	
	2.8%	81–100	1%	
	10.1%	61–80	7.5%	
	13.2%	41–60		13.5%
	14.7%	21–40		15.7%
	10.5%	0–20		11.1%

% of population by age group

Source: Dorling Kindersley World Desk Reference

Urban and Rural Population

87%   13%

Source: Dorling Kindersley World Desk Reference

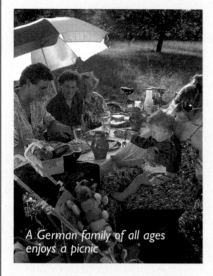

A German family of all ages enjoys a picnic

Geography The map and charts on the right describe the people of Germany and where they live. **Map and Chart Study** (a) Which regions of Germany are least populated? (b) In Germany's oldest age group, are more people male or female?

Take It to the NET Data Update for the most recent data on Germany, visit **www.phschool.com.**

Germany's Tragic Past

To understand the importance of the Berlin Wall, you need to understand part of Germany's past. After losing World War I in 1918, the German government had to pay billions of dollars as punishment for attacking other countries. To make things even worse, the German economy collapsed. Prices soared. Germans everywhere felt desperate.

Hitler and World War II Adolf Hitler (AY dahlf HIT lur), a young German soldier, had wept bitterly in 1918 when he learned that Germany had lost the war. He promised himself that his country would never suffer such a defeat again. Hitler became deeply involved in politics. In speech after speech, he promised to make Germany great again. By 1933, this once unknown soldier was dictator of Germany.

Hitler blamed Germany's economic problems on German Jews. He spread hateful theories about Jews, Gypsies, and other ethnic groups in Germany. He claimed they were inferior to, or not as good as, other Germans. He claimed that Germans were a superior ethnic group—and should lead Europe.

Many people did not believe Hitler's threats. But Hitler was deadly serious. He ordered attacks on neighboring countries and forced them under German rule. His actions led to the start of World War II in 1939. Great Britain, the Soviet Union, and the United States joined other nations to stop Hitler and the Germans. By the end of the war, Europe was in ruins. People around the world learned that the Germans had forced countless Jews, Gypsies, Slavs, and others into brutal prison camps. Millions of people were murdered in these camps. Most of them were Jews. This horrible mass murder of six million Jews is called the **Holocaust** (HAHL uh kawst).

The Cold War   At the end of the war, the Americans, the British, the French, and the Soviets divided Germany. The American, British, and French sections were joined into a democratic country called West Germany. The Soviet Union created a communist system in East Germany.

Albert Einstein Born in 1879 to Jewish-German parents, Albert Einstein was a quiet child who grew into one of the greatest scientists of all time. His famous equation, $E=mc^2$, describes the relationship between mass and energy and led the world into the atomic age. Einstein settled in the United States in 1933 and gave up his German citizenship. He became a citizen of the United States in 1940.

Divided Berlin

Map Study When the United States, Great Britain, France, and the Soviet Union divided Germany into two parts, they also divided Germany's capital, Berlin. The city of Berlin was located well inside East Germany. At one point, the Soviet Union tried to take over West Berlin by blocking all the roads, railways, or waterways leading to the city, so that the two million people living in West Berlin could not get food or supplies. The United States, Great Britain, and France organized a huge airlift to supply West Berlin until the Soviet Union ended its blockade. **Movement** What challenges do you think would face people living in a city that is isolated within enemy territory?

Berlin was in the Soviet part of Germany. But the western half of it, called West Berlin, became part of democratic West Germany. This turned the Western half into an island of democracy in the middle of communism. The Berlin Wall separated the two halves of the city. But it divided more than Berlin. It was a symbol of a divided world. Little wonder that some people called it the "Wall of Shame."

During the Cold War, the United States and Western Europe became partners. These countries had democratic governments and were against communism. Eastern European countries had communist governments and were partners with the Soviet Union. Soviet troops stayed in Eastern Europe to make sure that these countries remained communist.

Think about the effects of the Cold War on European countries. Recall that these countries are small and close together. Family, friends, and relatives were separated by Cold War borders. Even some who had managed to escape to the West suffered. For example, Conrad Schumann, who jumped over to the western side, could no longer see his sister, brother, and mother. They remained in East Berlin. The idea that he could not even visit his mother filled him with sadness.

East Germans led far different lives than West Germans. The communist government required people to obey without asking questions. It even encouraged people to spy on family members and

Easing International Tensions

Soviet and Western leaders often met to try to ease tensions. Soviet leader Nikita Khrushchev is shown meeting with French President Charles de Gaulle (above right) and U.S. President John F. Kennedy (above).

During the summer of 1989, many East Germans took vacations in other Eastern European countries. They had no intention of returning, however. Rather, they planned to flee to West Germany. Here, a group of East Germans celebrate as they prepare to go through the Czech-West German border. **Critical Thinking** In the summer of 1989, the Soviet Union and Eastern European countries such as Czechoslovakia were still under communist rule. Why do you think that no efforts were made to prevent East Germans from fleeing to the West?

neighbors. Children were taught to respect only those things that helped communism. Things from the West—including movies, music, books, and magazines—were seen as harmful to communism.

The Communists Weaken   In time, communist rule started to change. One reason was that the East German economy was falling further behind the West German economy. The average West German had a much better life than the average East German. To keep East Germans happy, the government softened its rules. Some East Germans could then visit West Germany. Conrad Schumann's mother, who was then in her late seventies, was allowed to see him. But he still was not allowed to go to East Berlin to see her. If he crossed the border, he would be arrested and put in prison.

In the late 1980s, changes in the Soviet Union helped to cause the collapse of East Germany. Soviet leader Mikhail Gorbachev made it clear that he would not use force to protect communism in Eastern Europe. Fear of the Soviets had helped keep the East German government in power. Now this fear was gone. Gorbachev told the East German leaders to make more reforms, but they refused. Without any support from the people, East Germany's government collapsed.

The Berlin Wall collapsed as well. On November 9, 1989, crowds of Germans began scrambling over the wall. Some people raced to see friends and relatives. Others just wanted to enjoy a different life. People

Visualize Visualize the collapse of the Berlin Wall. Describe some of the sights and sounds of this momentous event.

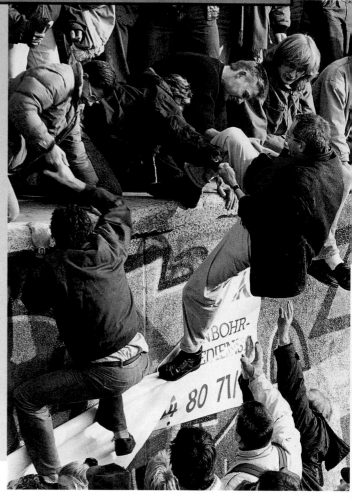

Crowds began to destroy the Berlin Wall on November 9, 1989. They held a huge party on and around the wall, while people from both sides helped each other up and over. Three million people from East Germany visited West Germany the first weekend after the wall came down, and 2,500 decided to stay there permanently. **Critical Thinking** Judging from the behavior of the crowds, how do you think Germans felt about the Berlin Wall?

Ask Questions What questions might you ask East Germans about their views on reunification?

helped each other over the top of the wall to the other side. Crowds tore at the wall and took it apart block by block. Less than a year later, the governments of East and West Germany united. Germany had become a single country again.

Germany Reunited

Most Germans were thrilled about the fall of the Berlin Wall. The cultures of East and West Germany had remained similar in many ways. People in both Germanys spoke the same language and ate the same foods. They knew the same German composers, writers, and painters. Still, the process of becoming unified again, called **reunification** (ree yoo nuh fih KAY shun), would not be easy.

Germans spent millions of dollars to rebuild the economy of what was East Germany. For the first time since World War II, East Germans are enjoying modern televisions, cars, and washing machines. They have new shopping malls and better roads.

Easterners may have more televisions and cars, but they have fewer jobs. In communist East Germany, people were guaranteed a job and

▲ Since the fall of communism, many new stores and coffee shops have opened in Alexanderplatz, East Berlin's main shopping area.

food to eat. There are no such guarantees under the Western democratic system. This is one of the prices of freedom, and most former East Germans are willing to pay it.

When Germany was reunited in 1990, so was Berlin. The next year, the German legislature restored this city to its traditional role as the nation's capital. By 1999, most government offices had moved back to Berlin from the West German capital of Bonn.

The cost of moving the capital has been enormous. It has led to budget cuts and the elimination of many public service jobs. Still, Germans believe that the move will benefit the "new Germany." Berlin's central location, they say, will aid reunification by linking Germans in the east with Germans in the west.

SECTION 5 REVIEW

1. **Define** (a) Holocaust, (b) reunification.

2. **Identify** (a) Adolf Hitler, (b) Berlin.

3. Describe (a) the events that led to the division of Germany and (b) the events that led to its reunification.

4. How has the reunification of Germany affected life in the former East Germany?

Critical Thinking

5. **Making Comparisons** Compare personal freedom in East and West Germany during the Cold War.

Activity

6. **Writing to Learn** Write a journal entry from the point of view of an East Berliner. Describe the night the Berlin Wall was torn down. How did you feel? Whom and what did you want to see?

Review and Activities

Reviewing Main Ideas

1. How does the monarchy unify Great Britain?
2. If Great Britain were on the European continent, would life for the British be different? Explain your answer.
3. Why have the French made laws forbidding the use of foreign words?
4. What aspects of foreign culture are becoming a part of France?
5. How do Sweden's mineral reserves benefit its economy?
6. Why have most Swedes not worried about medical care or money for retirement in the past?
7. Why might a person from Milan have a hard time adapting to life in southern Italy?
8. How has northern Italy tried to develop southern Italy?
9. (a) How was Germany divided? (b) Why was it reunified?
10. What kept Germans unified in their thinking even when their country was divided?

Reviewing Key Terms

Decide whether each statement is true or false. If it is true, write *true*. If it is false, change the underlined term to make the statement true.

1. <u>Parliament</u> is the group of people that governs Britain.
2. A <u>representative</u> is someone who represents, or stands for, a group of people.
3. In a <u>welfare state,</u> the power of kings and queens is controlled by laws about what they can and cannot do.
4. To <u>immigrate</u> is to move away from a country.
5. Swedes enjoy the <u>national debt</u> they receive from the government.
6. Milan is a <u>manufacturing</u> center.
7. Many European Jews were killed during the <u>Holocaust</u>.
8. Germans celebrated the <u>reunification</u> of their nation.

Critical Thinking

1. **Making Comparisons** (a) How is Sweden like the former East Germany? (b) How is it different?
2. **Drawing Conclusions** How do you think Germany will change in the future? How might Germans react to these changes?

Graphic Organizer

Copy the chart onto a separate sheet of paper. Then fill in facts you have learned about each country.

Country	Government	Economy	Culture
United Kingdom			
France			
Sweden			
Italy			
Germany			

Map Activity

Western Europe

For each place listed below, write the letter from the map that shows its location.

1. Aix-en-Provence

2. London

3. Sweden

4. Italy

5. Berlin

Writing Activity

Writing a Travel Journal
Imagine that you have traveled to each country in this chapter. Write a journal entry describing some of the traditions you encountered.

Take It to the NET

Activity Use a clickable map to take a virtual tour around the museums and monuments of Paris. For help in completing this activity, visit **www.phschool.com**.

Chapter 4 Self-Test To review what you have learned, take the Chapter 4 Self-Test and get instant feedback on your answers. Go to **www.phschool.com** to take the test.

Skills Review

Turn to the Skills Activity.
Review the steps for using the writing process. Then, follow the steps to write a one-page paper about one aspect of life in Western Europe.

How Am I Doing?

Answer these questions to help you check your progress.

1. Do I understand why tradition is important in Great Britain?

2. Do I understand why France has tried to preserve its traditional culture?

3. Do I understand what kind of welfare state Sweden is?

4. Do I understand how and why people are working to unify two separate regions in both Italy and Germany?

5. What information from this chapter can I include in my journal?

Tracking the Midnight Sun

In Hammerfest, Norway, people who look up in the middle of a December afternoon see a dark sky full of stars. In the summer, though, people who go to bed at midnight can see the sun shining through their windows.

All around the world, the length of daylight changes throughout the year. The amount of change in daylight is greatest in areas near the North or South Pole. Because Hammerfest is in the Arctic, near the North Pole, there is a huge difference in the number of light hours during summer days and winter days.

Purpose

The length of daylight changes as the Earth makes its yearly orbit around the sun. Because of the tilt of the Earth's axis, the Northern Hemisphere faces the sun during summer. It faces away from the sun during winter. In this activity, you will make a model that shows why arctic Scandinavia and Russia have midnight suns in summer and dark days in winter.

Materials

- unshaded lamp
- tangerine or orange
- masking tape
- marker
- pencil
- metric tape measure

Procedure

STEP ONE

Make a model of the Earth. Holding your tangerine or orange around its middle, push your pencil through the fruit's core. The fruit represents the Earth. The pencil represents the Earth's axis, or the imaginary line around which the Earth turns. The point where the pencil emerges represents the North Pole. With your marker, draw a line all the way around the fruit, halfway between the two ends of the pencil. This circle represents the Equator. Next, measure the distance in centimeters between the "Equator" and the "North Pole." Then use your marker to draw a circle around the fruit approximately seven ninths of the distance from the "Equator" to the "North Pole." This circle represents the 70° latitude. Areas north of the 70° latitude are considered arctic areas. Make a dot just above this line to represent Hammerfest, Norway.

STEP TWO

Make a model of the Earth's path around the sun. Place the unshaded lamp on the floor. With the masking tape, mark a circle on the floor with the lamp at its center. This line shows the Earth's orbit. Next, mark the tape at four points equally spaced around the orbit. Label the points "arctic spring," "arctic summer," "arctic autumn," and "arctic winter." Turn on the lamp.

STEP THREE

Show what happens when it is summer in the Arctic. Hold the fruit at the level of the lamp's lightbulb and place it above the spot on the floor labeled "arctic summer." Refer to the diagram to tilt the "Earth's" axis correctly. The Earth turns on its axis about once every 24 hours, or once each day. Where the Earth faces the sun, it is daytime. Where the Earth faces away from the sun, it is night. Slowly turn the "Earth" on its axis. Notice where the lamp's light hits the fruit. Notice what parts of the fruit are in shadow. Study the amount of light and shadow in the Arctic.

STEP FOUR

Show what happens when it is winter in the Arctic. Hold the fruit at the level of the lightbulb and place it above the spot on the floor marked "arctic winter." Line up the axis as before. Slowly turn the fruit on its axis. Study the amount of light and shadow that hits the Arctic.

Observations

1. In the Arctic, is the length of daylight more affected by the Earth's rotation or the tilt of the Earth's axis? Explain your answer.

2. During summer, how much of the day is light in Hammerfest? How much is light during winter? Why?

ANALYSIS AND CONCLUSION

1. If the Earth were not tilted on its axis, how do you think life in the Arctic would be different? Explain your answer.

2. Suppose that the Earth orbited around the sun but never rotated on its axis. How much daylight would Hammerfest receive during the summer? Autumn? Winter? Spring? Explain your answer.

CHAPTER 5

Exploring Eastern Europe and Russia

SECTION 1
Poland
TRADITION AND CHANGE

SECTION 2
Yugoslavia
A REGION TRIES TO REBUILD

SECTION 3
Ukraine
PEOPLE WORKING TOGETHER

SECTION 4
Russia
A LARGE AND DIVERSE COUNTRY

Eastern Europe and Russia:
Political
KEY

—— National boundary

⊛ National capital

Two-Point Equidistant Projection

MAP ACTIVITIES

The countries of Eastern Europe and Russia have undergone many changes. Some have come about peacefully and others have come about with much struggle. To help you get to know Eastern Europe and Russia, complete the following activities.

Study the map
Which countries border the Baltic Sea? Which countries do not share a border with any bodies of water?

Make historical connections
Many countries in Eastern Europe once had communist governments. How do you think the location of these countries helped communism dominate the area?

Poland

TRADITION AND CHANGE

BEFORE YOU READ

Reach Into Your Background

Think of your own hometown 20 years from now. Do you think it will be very different?

What things about it would you like to see changed? What would you like to stay the same?

Questions to Explore

1. What traditions remain strong in the Polish countryside?
2. How is life changing in Polish towns and cities?

Key Terms

free enterprise
shrine

Key People

Pope John Paul II

In 1989, Poland's communist government came to an end, and many things changed. Meet two brothers-in-law who are like the two faces of Poland. One man has changed with the times. The other sticks to old ways.

The first is Janusz Rajtar (YAHN uhsh RY tuhr). He owns a grocery store in a small city. The new non-communist government lets him keep most of his profits. He has saved money and gotten a loan. Now he is thinking of expanding his business. You can tell how well he is doing when you see his family. He and his wife dress in the latest fashions. His three young sons have new clothes, too.

Janusz Rajtar's brother-in-law, whose name is Janusz Podolak, has not been quite so lucky. He still wears the loose-fitting overalls that people wore during communist days. When the communist government fell, he grew poorer. He is a peasant farmer in a region where most farmers still use horses to plow the land. During the time of communist rule, the government kept his farm going by paying some of his costs. Now all of that is over.

▼ Now that Poland is no longer communist, its businesses are thriving.

Poland: Land Use and the Economy

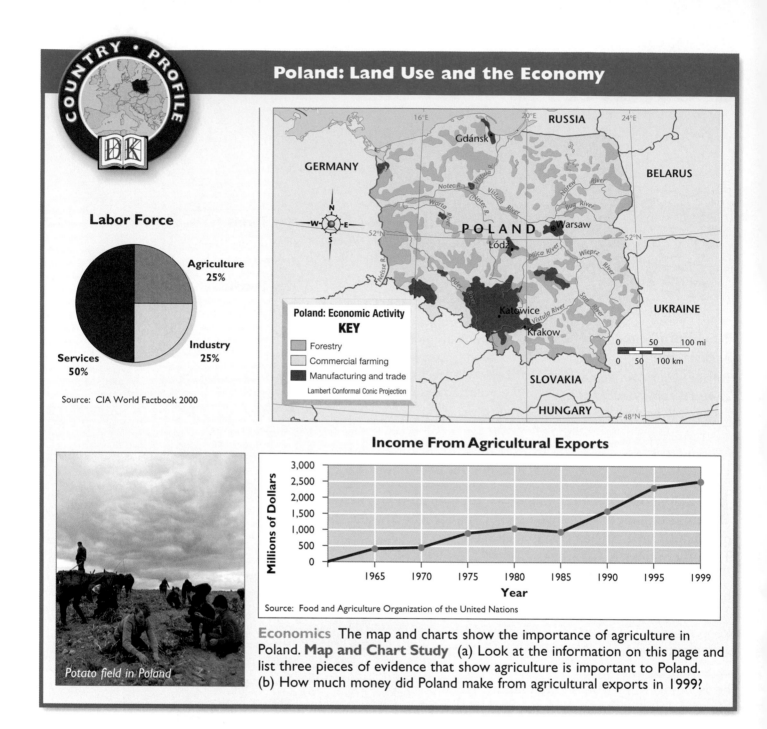

Labor Force

- Agriculture 25%
- Industry 25%
- Services 50%

Source: CIA World Factbook 2000

Poland: Economic Activity
KEY
- Forestry
- Commercial farming
- Manufacturing and trade

Lambert Conformal Conic Projection

Potato field in Poland

Income From Agricultural Exports

Millions of Dollars (vertical axis: 0, 500, 1,000, 1,500, 2,000, 2,500, 3,000)

Year (horizontal axis: 1965, 1970, 1975, 1980, 1985, 1990, 1995, 1999)

Source: Food and Agriculture Organization of the United Nations

Economics The map and charts show the importance of agriculture in Poland. **Map and Chart Study** (a) Look at the information on this page and list three pieces of evidence that show agriculture is important to Poland. (b) How much money did Poland make from agricultural exports in 1999?

Take It to the NET
Data Update For the most recent data on Poland, visit www.phschool.com.

Tradition in Poland

Since Poland's communist government fell, the country has moved away from a communist economy in which the government owned and ran all the businesses. Instead, Poland has adopted the **free enterprise** system, or capitalism. In it, people can run their own businesses. But not all of life in Poland has changed. As you travel in the countryside, you see signs of a way of life that existed long before communist rule.

The Polish Countryside For a look at tradition in Poland, you might visit the northeast corner of the country. Here, the Polish border has shifted many times. Again and again, other countries have seized this area. Sometimes, it belonged to Russia. At other times, it was controlled by Lithuania (lith oo AY nee uh) or Germany. There were even times when other countries took over all of Poland. But no matter what happened, the traditions of Polish life stayed the same. This is true even today.

After World War II, Poland became a communist nation. At public festivals, Poles had to pledge loyalty to communism. When crops did not grow, Poles relied on money from the communist government. When Poles were sick, they went to doctors who were paid by the government. When they were too old to farm, they knew they would receive a government pension.

Now all that has changed. It is up to the farmer to save money for old age. If the crops fail, the farmer must try to borrow money to start again. Learning this new way of life has been hard for some Poles.

Polish Catholicism The years of communist rule did not change the love most Poles have for the Roman Catholic Church. For hundreds of years, Catholicism has been at the center of Polish tradition. The communist government tried to discourage Catholicism, but it did not succeed. Today, most Poles still are Catholic.

Polish Catholicism is unique. Poles have their own way of observing Catholic holidays and their own way of prayer. An example of Polish religious life can be seen in northeastern Poland, in the forest of

Ask Questions What questions might you ask about life in Poland under communism?

Poland's Solidarity Movement

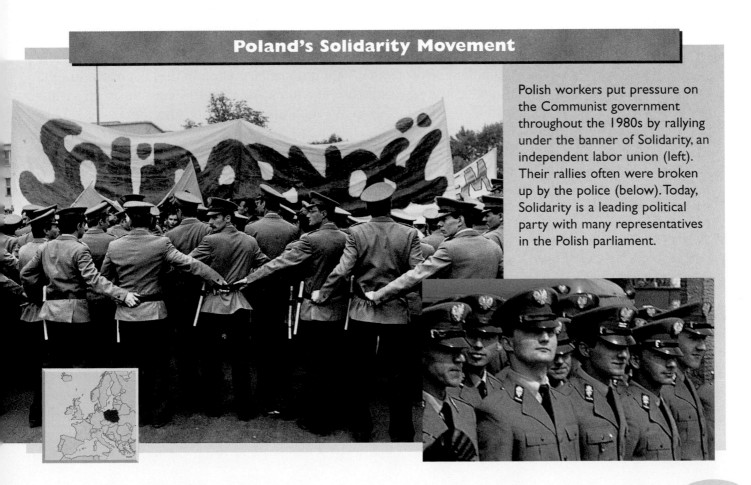

Polish workers put pressure on the Communist government throughout the 1980s by rallying under the banner of Solidarity, an independent labor union (left). Their rallies often were broken up by the police (below). Today, Solidarity is a leading political party with many representatives in the Polish parliament.

Brightly Colored Eggs

Christians across the world give decorated eggs as gifts at Easter. The brightly colored eggs pictured here are similar to those Polish people might exchange. Don't try to peel off the shells, however. These eggs are made of wood. **Critical Thinking** What other celebrations or religious holidays involve the exchange of special gifts?

LINKS ACROSS TIME

The Wisent For centuries the European bison, or wisent, roamed forests from Western Europe to Siberia. These animals are related to the North American buffalo. The wisent eat grasses, ferns, leaves, and tree bark. By 1600, loss of habitat wiped out almost all of the wisent. Now, thanks to special programs, about 1,500 wisent live in Poland. They make their home in the forest of Biaolowiza.

Biaolowiza (bee AHL uhv yezh uh). Not far from the forest is the holy mountain of Grabarka. A church sits at the top of the mountain. In mid-August, visitors climb this mountain to visit the church. Each visitor plants a cross in the earth. Among the trees on the mountainside are hundreds of crosses. Some are as tall as trees, others as tiny as flowers. You can see such **shrines,** or holy places, all over Poland.

Polish Catholics felt tremendous pride in 1978, when a Pole was selected as pope of the Catholic Church. Pope John Paul II quickly became the most widely traveled Catholic leader in history. He also made the world more aware of Poland, which was struggling under communism. On his visit to Poland in 1979, about one million Poles went wild with joy in greeting him. Mothers held babies over their heads for the pope's blessing. The crowd sang hymns and threw flowers toward the stage on which he sat. For most of these people, the pope stood for traditional Poland. He was a symbol of a part of Poland that they hoped would never die.

The Polish Language   Like Roman Catholicism, the language of the Poles has also stood the test of time. Some foreign rulers banned the use of Polish in schools and in the government. The communists did not ban Polish but did force Polish schoolchildren to learn Russian, the main language of the Soviet Union.

Today, the Polish language is alive and well. It ties the people of the nation together. And it gives them the strong feeling that being Polish is something different and special. As a Slavic language, it also links the nation to other Slavic nations in Eastern Europe.

Changes in Towns and Cities

If you are looking for the newer Poland, you will find it in the larger towns and cities. Ever since the fall of communism, Poland has undergone rapid change. The biggest of these changes have come in Poland's economy.

Making Business Grow With the end of communist rule, Poles were free to find new ways to make money. Small businesses soon blossomed all over Poland's capital, Warsaw. At first, traders set up booths on the streets. They sold everything they could find, from American blue jeans to old Soviet army uniforms.

Slowly but surely, some traders earned enough money to take over stores that the government had once owned. Poland's economy began growing faster than any other in Eastern Europe. Today, the standard of living of its people is growing stronger every day.

Predict What do you think new businesspeople in Poland must do to succeed?

Standard of Living in Eastern European Countries

Country	Number of Televisions per 1,000 People	Number of Telephones per 1,000 People
Albania	89	40
Czech Republic	446	371
Hungary	438	405
Lithuania	364	321
Poland	414	228
Romania	201	167
Yugoslavia	27	214
United States	847	653

Source: The World Almanac 2001

Chart Study One way to study a country's economic health is to take a look at its basic services, such as communications. Televisions and telephones are two important tools of communication in today's world. This chart lists several Eastern European countries and shows how many people have TVs and telephones in each. It also shows the same for the United States. **Critical Thinking** Study the information in the chart. Which country probably has the weakest economy? Why?

People like store owner Janusz Rajtar are doing well in the new Poland. To find the best products for his store, Rajtar rises at 4:00 A.M. to buy fruits and vegetables at the local farmers' market. By 7:00 A.M., he is behind his desk at a second job, working in an office. Then, at 3:00 P.M., he is back at the grocery store.

Looking Toward the Future Janusz Rajtar is benefiting from his hard work. But people like Janusz's brother-in-law are working harder and are not benefiting. Farmers, with no government support, find it hard to compete in the European market. Many young people in rural areas feel that they have little chance to make a decent living. Some have moved to the city in the hope of finding jobs.

Migration to the cities, however, can cause overcrowding. Today, 65 percent of all Poles live in towns or cities, a huge increase from just 50 years ago. In response, the government is building apartment buildings and expanding suburban areas.

The new life is good in some ways and hard in others. Many Poles have things they never had before. In 1989, only half of the homes in Poland had color televisions. Now, almost every home has one. On the streets of Warsaw, some people make telephone calls on cellular phones and wear the new clothing fashions. For these people, the new way of life is good.

▼ Forests once covered Poland's flat landscape, but for centuries most of the country has been cleared for farming. This picture shows Poland's fertile farmland and the traditional wooden houses near the city of Krakow, in the foothills of the Carpathian Mountains. Many of Poland's farmers still sow their fields by hand.

Old Market Square, Warsaw, Poland

Years ago, merchants sold their wares in Warsaw's Old Market Square. People did their shopping on special market days. Today, Old Market Square is not only a shopping area, but also a place to meet friends and watch free entertainment. Street performers regularly attract large and enthusiastic audiences.

But in Warsaw, you can also see people with nothing to do. This, too, is a change. There are more people without jobs than there were under communism. The Poles will have to find ways to deal with such challenges. The Polish people are ready to do whatever is needed because for the first time in many years, their future is in their own hands.

SECTION 1 REVIEW

1. **Define** (a) free enterprise, (b) shrine.

2. **Identify** Pope John Paul II.

3. What features of country life show the traditional side of Poland?

4. What are some of the changes taking place in Poland?

Critical Thinking

5. **Making Predictions** What do you predict will happen to the Polish economy in the future? Give reasons for your predictions.

Activity

6. **Writing to Learn** Use library resources to find a book or encyclopedia article about Polish history. Read about the fall of communism in Poland. Then, write a brief summary of what you have read.

SECTION 2

Yugoslavia
A REGION TRIES TO REBUILD

BEFORE YOU READ

Reach Into Your Background

Think about how you identify yourself as a person. How would you feel if someone who didn't know you disliked you just because of who your parents were? In Yugoslavia, people have been in this situation for many years.

Questions to Explore

1. What are some of the differences among the people who live in Yugoslavia?

2. What happened to Yugoslavia after communist leader Tito died?

3. What changes have taken place in Yugoslavia since the signing of the peace treaty in the 1990s?

Key Terms
United Nations
economic sanctions

Key People and Places
Sarajevo
Belgrade
Marshal Tito

▼ The Olympic Center was destroyed during the civil war that took place in Yugoslavia in the 1990s.

In January 1984, the people of Sarajevo (sah rah YAY voh), a beautiful old city in Yugoslavia, were filled with a spirit of anticipation. They had proudly won the right to host the Winter Olympics of 1984. To prepare for these games, they had built new hotels and restaurants. They had erected ski lifts and carved ski racing trails into the mountains. New bobsled runs and an elegant skating complex were waiting for the athletes. A shiny new Olympic Village had been built to welcome athletes and visitors to the Games.

Ten years later, most of these facilities lay in ruins. So did much of Sarajevo. Bombings destroyed many of its fine old buildings. How could this have happened? The answer is war—civil war that broke up Yugoslavia and shattered the grand city.

Land of Many Cultures

Yugoslavia is located in a region of southeastern Europe called the Balkans. Most of its people are Slavs. However, the Slavs are made up of many ethnic groups. Before the breakup of Yugoslavia, the largest Slavic groups in the country were the Serbs and Croats (kroh ATS). Slovenes,

Yugoslavia: Population and History

COUNTRY · PROFILE

Religious Groups

- Protestant 1%
- Roman Catholic 4%
- Other 11%
- Muslim 19%
- Eastern Orthodox 65%

Source: Dorling Kindersley World Desk Reference

Yugoslavia: Ethnic Groups
KEY
- Serbs
- Albanians
- Montenegrins
- Other ethnic groups

Lambert Equal-Area Projection

Reshaping Yugoslavia

1945
Yugoslavia is made up of Bosnia-Herzegovina, Croatia, Macedonia, Montenegro, Serbia, Slovenia, Kosovo, and Vojvodina.

1991 June
Slovenia and Croatia declare independence from Yugoslavia.

1991 September
Macedonia declares independence from Yugoslavia.

1992 March
Bosnia-Herzegovina declares independence from Yugoslavia.

1992 April
Serbia and Montenegro name themselves the "Federal Republic of Yugoslavia," known as Yugoslavia.

1940	1950	1960	1970	1980	1990	2000

1989
Serbia takes control of Kosovo and Vojvodina.

1997–1999
Ethnic Albanians in Kosovo, a province of Serbia, fight for Kosovo's independence from Serbia. Fighting ends with Kosovo remaining part of Yugoslavia.

Take It to the NET
Data Update For the most recent data on Yugoslavia, visit **www.phschool.com**.

Culture The map and charts above present information about the people and history of Yugoslavia. **Map and Chart Study** (a) What are the two major religious groups of the people in Yugoslavia? (b) How is the Yugoslavia of today different from the Yugoslavia of 1945?

Montenegrins (mahn tuh NEH grinz), and Macedonians (mas uh DOH nee unz) were smaller Slav groups.

While many of these groups share a Slavic heritage, there are also differences among them. One is language. Three different languages are used by the groups—Serbo-Croatian, Slovenian, and Macedonian. Both Serbs and Croats speak Serbo-Croatian, but they use different alphabets to write the language.

Religion is another major difference among the groups. Most Serbs, Montenegrins, and Macedonians belong to the Christian Orthodox Church. Croats and Slovenes are mainly Roman Catholic. Other Serbs are Muslim.

READ ACTIVELY

Connect What kinds of ideas can cause barriers between people?

Writer in War During World War II, Germany invaded Yugoslavia. To protest against this, people in Sarajevo started a newspaper called *Oslobodjenje* in 1943. It is still published today, despite the civil war. *Oslobodjenje's* office has been bombed. The newspaper has suffered from shortages of electricity, paper, and ink. It has few reporters left. And still it continues, keeping hope alive.

▼ Yugoslav soldiers approach a German fort in what is now Slovenia during World War II.

Historic Regional Tensions How did these differences arise? They began centuries ago when the Roman Empire broke up into eastern and western regions. The Cyrillic alphabet and the Christian Orthodox Church became dominant in the eastern empire, and the Latin alphabet and Roman Catholic Church were dominant in the western empire. Serbs, Montenegrins, and Macedonians developed cultures influenced by the east. The Croats and Slovenes who had settled to the northwest developed cultures influenced by the west.

Then, in the 1300s, a group known as the Ottoman Turks conquered much of the Balkan region. They brought their religion, Islam, with them. Some Serbs converted to Islam. After that, differences between Christians and Muslims added to the ethnic tensions in the region.

Yugoslavia—A Nation Torn Apart

For hundreds of years, the Ottoman Turks ruled the peoples of the Balkans. When the Ottoman empire broke up in the early 1900s, some Balkan peoples formed independent states. The nation of Yugoslavia was formed in 1918. This new nation joined together various ethnic and religious groups. But making one united nation out of these separate groups was not easy. The Serbs, who were Yugoslavia's largest ethnic group, set up a central government in the city of Belgrade. This government failed to win the support of other ethnic groups, and resentment of it grew. Yugoslavia faced a new challenge in 1941. During World War II, Germany and Italy invaded and occupied Yugoslavia.

Communism—Its Rise and Fall In 1945 the war ended. The leader of the Yugoslav fight against Germany, Joseph Broz Tito, became head of the government. Marshal Tito, as he was usually called, built the government on communist political and economic principles. Yugoslavia was a federal state, divided into smaller units called republics. Each ethnic group lived in a republic where it was in the majority. For example, Croatia was home to most of the Croats. All republics, however, contained peoples of other ethnic groups.

Yugoslavia became a firm ally of the Soviet Union. Later Tito wanted to develop his own policies and relations with other countries, especially those of the West. This put him in conflict with the Soviet dictator, Joseph Stalin. In 1948, Stalin expelled Yugoslavia from the Soviet Union's communist group of nations in Eastern Europe. Tito then became less hostile to the United States and nations of Western Europe. He continued to rule Yugoslavia according to communist principles, but he also had good relations with anti-communist nations.

Breakup Leads to War Tito's strong government reduced ethnic tensions. During Tito's time, people began to identify themselves as citizens of Yugoslavia. But after his death in 1980, politicians struggled for power. Their struggle encouraged ethnic nationalism and

Map Study In the 1990s, several regions declared themselves independent of Yugoslavia. Yugoslavia is now half the size it was during Tito's rule. **Location** What countries now occupy areas that were once part of Yugoslavia? In what country is Sarajevo now located?

Connect How would you feel if you and some of your friends or members of your family were on opposite sides in a war?

independent movements. The first republics to break away from Yugoslavia were Slovenia and Croatia. They declared themselves independent nations in 1991. Macedonia and Bosnia-Herzegovina followed later that year. By 1992 only two republics—Serbia and Montenegro—remained part of Yugoslavia.

The breakup of Yugoslavia led to terrible violence and bloodshed. Croats and Serbs battled over disputed borders. Croats forced Serbs living in Croatia to return to Serbia. Serbia made Croats living in Serbia return to Croatia. Bosnia-Herzegovina was torn apart by civil war.

Bosnia-Herzegovina

In Bosnia-Herzegovina, tensions among different ethnic groups led to a long and bitter war. Sometimes Christian Serbs and Croats fought on the same side to win land controlled by Bosnian Muslims. At other times Serbs, backed by Yugoslavian president Slobodan Milosevic, fought Croats for land. People on all sides were mistreated by their enemies. Many people were killed. Others had their homes blown up and were forced to move away from where they had lived peacefully for years, just because they were Serbs or Croats.

During the war, Sarajevo, the capital of Bosnia-Herzegovina, was almost completely destroyed. Homes and schools were bombed. People were shot as they tried to go about their daily business. Serb armies cut Sarajevo off from the rest of the world, causing people to run out of food and other supplies.

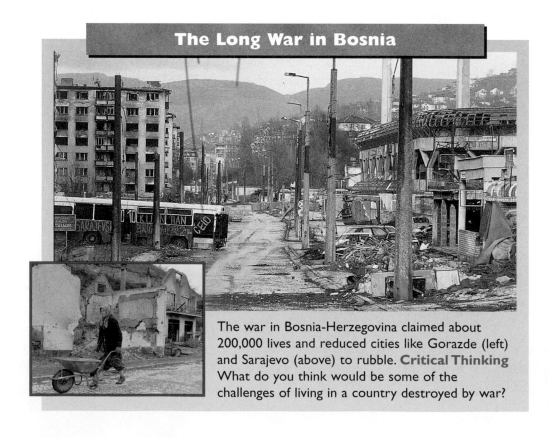

The Long War in Bosnia

The war in Bosnia-Herzegovina claimed about 200,000 lives and reduced cities like Gorazde (left) and Sarajevo (above) to rubble. **Critical Thinking** What do you think would be some of the challenges of living in a country destroyed by war?

In 1992 the United Nations sent troops to the city to bring in supplies. The **United Nations** is an international group that was founded in 1945, after World War II. Its member countries work together to bring about peace and cooperation. A few years later, the Serbs, Croats, and Bosnian Muslims signed a peace treaty. After years of war, the people of a much smaller Yugoslavia hoped that the peace would last.

The Region's Future

Though a peace treaty was signed, trouble in the region did not end. Tensions between different ethnic groups still existed. Russian and NATO forces, sent in by Western countries, helped keep peace but often introduced new conflicts.

Many Serbs were unhappy with President Slobodan Milosevic, known for his cruel treatment of people who were not Serbs. The United States and Europe held Milosevic responsible for the violence. They placed **economic sanctions** on Yugoslavia to show their disapproval. Economic sanctions are actions to limit trade with nations that have violated international laws.

In 2000, Yugoslavia held new presidential elections. Vojislav Kostunica was elected, replacing Milosevic. To show their approval of the new president, the United States and European nations promised to lift the sanctions against Yugoslavia.

What lies ahead for Yugoslavia? The destruction that occurred in the 1990s presents its population of over 10 million with deep economic problems. The country hopes to move toward a more stable and peaceful time, but it will have to overcome its recent history of ethnic conflict.

▼ Slobodan Milosevic was arrested in Yugoslavia in 2001 and turned over to a United Nations tribunal to face charges of crimes against humanity.

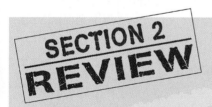

SECTION 2 REVIEW

1. **Define** (a) United Nations, (b) economic sanctions.

2. **Identify** (a) Sarajevo, (b) Belgrade, (c) Marshal Tito.

3. Describe the similarities and differences among Yugoslavia's ethnic groups.

4. What challenges face Yugoslavia and the former nations of Yugoslavia in the future?

Critical Thinking

5. **Recognizing Cause and Effect** Why might the presence of NATO peace-keeping forces in Yugoslavia lead to new conflicts?

Activity

6. **Writing to Learn** Suppose that you work for the United Nations. Write a letter to the leader of one of Yugoslavia's ethnic groups explaining why the group should strive for peace.

Recognizing Cause and Effect

Have you ever played with dominoes? It's fun to stand them up in a line and then topple them over. By pushing just the first domino, you set up a chain reaction that eventually knocks all of the dominoes down. In 1988, students in the Netherlands set up 1.5 million dominoes! By pushing just one, they were able to topple nearly all the rest.

Cause
Someone taps a domino.

Effect
Domino falls against a second domino.

Effect
Second domino falls.

Get Ready

Toppling dominoes is fun, but it also teaches a lesson in cause and effect. A *cause* is something that makes something else happen. The *effect* is what happens. Someone taps the first domino. It falls over. The falling domino hits a second domino and it falls, too. The tapping of the first domino is the cause, and the effect is the fall of the second domino.

Cause and effect can explain the relationship between events. History is full of causes and effects. For example, a big cause of the French Revolution was the fact that a small number of people owned most of the country's wealth. An effect of the revolution was that France's king, who was very wealthy, was thrown out of power.

A single event can have more than one cause or more than one effect. In France, for example, the revolution had many effects besides the fall of the monarchy.

Also keep in mind that not all events are linked by cause and effect. For example, if a girl claps her hands, and it then begins to rain, her claps did not cause it to rain. Learning to correctly recognize causes and effects will help you understand history.

Try It Out

Causes and effects can be shown in cause-effect diagrams, like the one pictured to the left. You can see how events can have more than one cause or more than one effect.

To understand how cause-effect relationships work, make a cause-effect diagram about the most recent presidential election. You can learn about this event by looking it up in an almanac or other source. To make your cause-effect diagram, complete the following steps:

A. Identify the event. Your diagram will explain the most recent presidential election. Write the event in the middle of a clean sheet of paper and circle it.

B. Identify the causes. What caused the election to take place? You should be able to identify at least two causes. Write them to the left of the event, and draw a circle around each one. Then, draw an arrow from each cause to the event to show that they made the event happen.

C. Identify the effects. Identify at least two effects of a presidential election. For example, was the President reelected? Write the effects to the right of the event, and circle each one. Then, draw an arrow from the event to each effect to show that they resulted from the event.

Now look your diagram over to see how it works. Notice that it reads from left to right, just as books do. By following the arrows, you can trace the causes and effects of events.

▼ A line of falling dominoes is an example of the relationship between cause and effect.

Apply the Skill

Read the paragraph below. Look for cause-and-effect relationships between the events. Words and phrases such as "because," "so," and "as a result" will give you clues that a cause-and-effect relationship exists.

Poland After Communism

In 1989, communism in Poland ended, and Poland adopted the free enterprise system. In this kind of system, people can open and run their own businesses free from government control. The fall of communism meant that the government no longer controlled the creation of jobs. As a result, many government jobs disappeared. The loss of jobs forced people to look for jobs elsewhere. Because of free enterprise, small companies now have the freedom to grow naturally. Growing companies have created new and better jobs for some people, but other people remain jobless.

When you have finished reading the paragraph, go back and read the underlined events. Find at least one cause and one effect of each underlined event, and write them down. As you are looking, remember that the effect of one event can also be the cause of another.

Ukraine

PEOPLE WORKING TOGETHER

BEFORE YOU READ

Reach Into Your Background

Have you gained more independence as you have grown older? What kinds of problems has your new independence brought you?

How have you solved them? The newly independent people of Ukraine have solved many of their problems by working together.

Questions to Explore

1. How have the natural resources of Ukraine shaped the history of that nation?

2. How did the accident at Chernobyl affect the environment of Ukraine?

Key Terms
chernozem
collective

Key Places
Kiev
Chernobyl
Kharkov

How many people, linked hand-to-hand, would it take to cover 300 miles (483 km)? The people of Ukraine can tell you, because they did it in 1990. It took about 500,000 Ukrainians to make a human chain this long. It stretched from Kiev, Ukraine's capital, to the city of Lvov (lvawf). The chain was a symbol of their protest against Soviet control of Ukraine. It also proved that Ukrainians know how to work together to solve their problems. Today, people in Ukraine are enjoying independence and still working together.

▼ In 1990, the people of Ukraine rallied to protest Soviet control of their country.

Ukraine's Path to Freedom

For hundreds of years, Ukraine had struggled to be independent. You can see why if you look at Ukraine's location. This huge land lies between the nations of Europe and Russia. In fact, the name *Ukraine* means "borderland." Look at the political map of Eastern Europe and Russia at the beginning of this chapter. Notice that to the west of Ukraine are Poland, Slovakia, and Hungary. To the east of Ukraine is Russia. The map makes it easy to see that Ukraine is open to invasion by its neighbors.

Ukraine: Agriculture and the Economy

Major Export Destinations

Germany 4%
Syria 5%
Turkey 5%
Belarus 5%
Russia 22%
Other 59%

Source: Dorling Kindersley World Desk Reference

Take It to the NET
Data Update For the most recent data on Ukraine, visit **www.phschool.com**.

Ukrainian port on the Black Sea

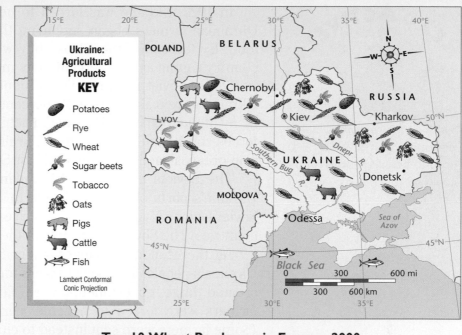

Ukraine: Agricultural Products
KEY
Potatoes
Rye
Wheat
Sugar beets
Tobacco
Oats
Pigs
Cattle
Fish
Lambert Conformal Conic Projection

POLAND • BELARUS • RUSSIA
Chernobyl • Lvov • Kiev • Kharkov
UKRAINE • Donetsk
MOLDOVA • ROMANIA • Odessa • Sea of Azov
Black Sea
0   300   600 mi
0   300   600 km

Top 10 Wheat Producers in Europe, 2000

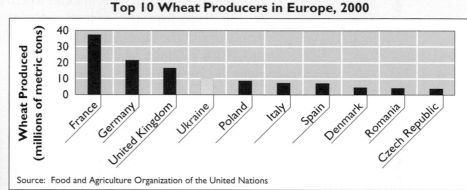

Wheat Produced (millions of metric tons): 40, 30, 20, 10, 0

France, Germany, United Kingdom, Ukraine, Poland, Italy, Spain, Denmark, Romania, Czech Republic

Source: Food and Agriculture Organization of the United Nations

Economics The map and charts highlight the importance of agriculture to Ukraine's economy. **Map and Chart Study** (a) How does Ukraine rank among European wheat producers? (b) Near what cities is wheat grown in Ukraine? (c) What country receives the most exports from Ukraine?

Location has been only part of the problem. The other has been Ukraine's vast natural resources, which attract invaders. As a result, at one time or another, Poland, Czechoslovakia, and Romania have taken slices of Ukraine. During World War II, the German army invaded Ukraine to gain its natural resources. But the most difficult neighbor of all has been Russia. It ruled Ukraine for much of the time between the late 1700s and the fall of the Soviet Union in 1991.

Supplying the Soviets A hundred years ago, Ukraine, which then was part of the Russian empire, was one of Europe's leading grain producing regions. Ukraine produced so much grain that people

READ ACTIVELY

Predict What kinds of natural resources would encourage one country to try to take over another?

Connect How would you feel if all the resources of the United States were used to benefit another country?

called it the "breadbasket of Europe." Why is Ukraine so productive? Over half of the country is covered by a rich, black soil called **chernozem** (CHER nuh zem).

In 1922, Ukraine was forced to become part of the Soviet Union. Ukrainian farmers began supplying the rest of the Soviet Union with food. By the end of the 1980s, they were producing 25 percent of the country's grain and 30 percent of its meat.

Under Soviet rule, Ukrainian industries grew. In time, factories in Ukraine were making about 25 percent of the country's goods. Further, many of the weapons, ships, and machines for the Soviet Union's armed forces came from Ukraine. And Ukrainian mines supplied much of the iron ore, coal, and other minerals for Soviet industries.

The Soviets used other Ukrainian resources as well. Ships used Ukraine's ports on the Black Sea to bring goods into and out of the Soviet Union. Several of Ukraine's rivers reach like highways into other countries. The Soviets made use of these rivers to ship goods.

All the economic changes under Soviet rule changed the lives of Ukraine's people. The Soviet rulers took farms away from farmers and created huge government-owned farms called **collectives.** Most farmers were forced to become workers on these collective farms. (Some farmers were sent instead to cities to work in the new factories.) All the crops from the collectives went to the government. The people who worked the land got very little of the food they grew. As a result, in the 1930s millions of Ukrainians died of hunger. Over the years, however, life improved on the farms.

Golden Fields of Wheat

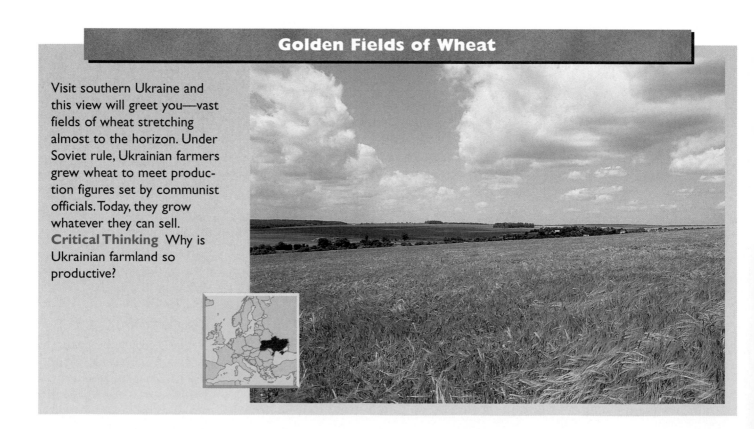

Visit southern Ukraine and this view will greet you—vast fields of wheat stretching almost to the horizon. Under Soviet rule, Ukrainian farmers grew wheat to meet production figures set by communist officials. Today, they grow whatever they can sell. **Critical Thinking** Why is Ukrainian farmland so productive?

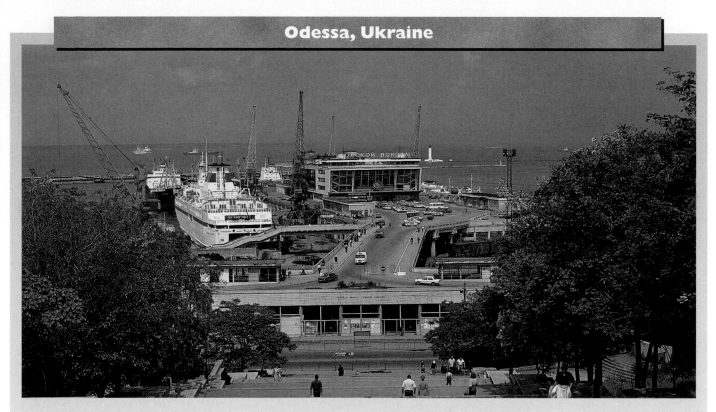

Odessa, Ukraine

The city of Odessa is one of Ukraine's greatest assets. Located on the Black Sea, it is a center of shipping and manufacturing.

Building an Independent Economy   Ukrainians won their independence from the Soviets in 1991. Since then, they have worked together to build up their economy and change to a new way of life. Like people in other former Soviet republics, Ukrainians are having to learn how to start new businesses, make goods, and keep prices under control. However, they have had some important successes. For example, very few Ukrainians are without work. Recently, less than 4 percent of the people who could work were unemployed. In contrast, 5 to 15 percent of workers are unemployed in the rest of Europe.

Issues After Independence

Now that Ukrainians are independent, they must decide many important issues for themselves. For example, should their national language be Russian or Ukrainian?

Choosing a Language   Under Soviet rule, the official language was Russian. Books and newspapers were published only in Russian. Lessons in school were taught only in Russian, using Russian textbooks. As a result, many Ukrainians speak only Russian, especially in the cities and in the eastern part of the nation. Russian is also the language of ethnic Russians, who make up about one fifth of the people. Ukrainian is widely spoken only in rural areas and in the western part of the nation.

After the Nuclear Accident at Chernobyl

In the days after the Chernobyl nuclear power accident, there was always at least one helicopter in the air near the reactor. From the helicopters, people used hand-held radiation counters (right) to check the levels of radiation in the air. Despite the unsafe conditions, the Soviet Union began operating the Chernobyl reactor again six months later. People returned to Chernobyl to work, but not to live. Years after the accident, the Chernobyl area (below) remained deserted. **Critical Thinking** What challenges do you think might face people who returned to work at Chernobyl after the accident?

READ ACTIVELY

Ask Questions What do you want to know about the explosion at the nuclear power plant in Chernobyl?

Still, many people want the country to return to its own language. Speaking Ukrainian could tie the country together. It could also free Ukraine from its Soviet past. Elementary schools have begun using Ukrainian in the early grades. In later grades and high school, Russian is still used. In the coming years, however, that will change. Most Ukrainians are pleased about the change. One teacher said, "Language is the anchor of our independence."

Accident at Chernobyl One of the biggest issues facing independent Ukraine grew out of a terrible event during the Soviet period. When it was under Soviet rule, Ukraine sent resources to the Soviet Union. In return, it received Soviet natural gas and oil. But Ukraine's industries needed even more energy. So the Ukrainians built five nuclear power plants. These supply about one third of the country's electricity.

Nuclear power is created with a special radioactive metal called uranium. When atoms, or very tiny pieces, of uranium are split, heat is released. The heat turns water into steam. The steam turns large machines called generators, which produce electricity.

This process must be kept under tight control. If too much heat is produced too quickly, it could destroy the entire building. Then poisonous gas would escape into the air.

In 1986, there was an explosion at the Chernobyl (CHER noh bul) nuclear plant, 65 miles (105 km) from the city of Kiev. Poisonous gases filled the air. Some people died at once. Others had serious health problems that killed them slowly or left them suffering. More than 100,000 people had to be moved out of the area because it was no longer safe to live there.

Even after 10 years, much of Ukraine's soil and water was still poisoned. Some towns and farmland remain abandoned to this day. With the help of other nations, the Ukrainians are cleaning up the poison around Chernobyl. It may take up to a hundred years to repair the damage. But the Ukrainians are determined to bring back the land they love.

Antinuclear Protests

Ukraine has a strong antinuclear movement. Some Ukrainians who are opposed to nuclear power wear masks and hoist banners in protest.

Life in Ukraine

Independence has already changed life in Ukraine. For example, the Kreshchatik (kree SHAH tik), the main street in Kiev, often is jammed with people. Along this street are many parks, stores, and restaurants. People sell ice cream and hot dogs covered with a thin red sauce that Ukrainians love. Newsstands are filled with magazines and newspapers, many of which have been published only since independence. At a local market, farmers sell cheese or produce from their own farms. This, too, only became possible after independence.

LINKS ACROSS THE WORLD

The Spread of Poison Winds blew Chernobyl's poisonous gases across Europe. In England, Germany, and Spain the gases poisoned milk, meat, and leafy vegetables. In Belarus, one fifth of the farmland was poisoned. And in Norway, Sweden, and Finland, the reindeer herds of the Sami ate poisoned grasses. Almost the whole herd—about 180,000 animals—had to be killed.

◀ To symbolize the deadly nature of the Chernobyl accident, a protester plants crosses near a nuclear power station.

Folk Museum in Ukraine

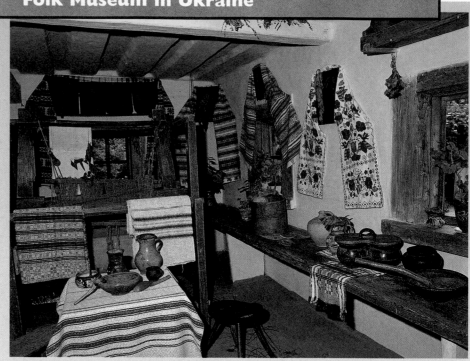

Near Kiev, Ukraine, the Museum of Folk Architecture features a traditional farmhouse. A loom, used to weave cloth, sits in the middle of the room shown here. It reminds visitors of a time when people made cloth, furniture, and tools for themselves. People on farms also grew the vegetables and grains that they ate, collected eggs from the chickens they raised, and raised cows and goats for milk and meat. **Critical Thinking** Life in Ukraine and elsewhere has changed in many ways since the days when this traditional farmhouse was used. Name some aspects of life that have not changed.

Other Ukrainian cities are also alive with the new spirit of freedom. Not far from Kiev is the city of Kharkov. Located near huge reserves of iron ore and coal, it is the busiest industrial center in the nation. But Kharkov is not all work. While you are there, you can listen to fine music or watch a play.

As you travel through Ukraine, you can see that it is in the early stages of a new time in its history. The people have always wanted freedom, and now they have it in their grasp. They know that independence is not easy. But with the land's great resources and the people's ability to work together, the Ukrainians have a good chance to make independence work.

SECTION 3 REVIEW

1. **Define** (a) chernozem, (b) collective.

2. **Identify** (a) Kiev, (b) Chernobyl, (c) Kharkov.

3. How has Ukraine's location affected its history?

4. Why do many Ukrainians want to make Ukrainian the official national language?

Critical Thinking

5. **Distinguishing Cause and Effect** In recent years, some Russian leaders have declared that they want Ukraine to become a part of Russia. Why would they want this to happen?

Activity

6. **Writing to Learn** Write a letter to one of the people who was forced to leave his or her home because of the Chernobyl explosion. You can offer comfort or advice and/or ask questions about the accident.

Russia

A LARGE AND DIVERSE COUNTRY

Reach Into Your Background

What other states in the United States have you visited? What other towns or cities have you seen? Were they very different from where you live? In Russia, as you will see, there are great differences from one region of the nation to another.

Questions to Explore

1. How do ways of life differ in a land as large as Russia?
2. What problems do Russians have today in unifying their country?

Key Terms
investor

Key Places
Kemerovo
Moscow

▼ After the collapse of communism, Russia's people joyfully used their right to speak freely about politics.

Inessa Krichevskaya (in ES uh kree CHEV sky uh) has surprising feelings about change in Russia. "You know," she says, "it's a very difficult period in our country right now, but we will just have to live through it, because this is the right direction. . . . We can never go back to what was before."

Why are Inessa's feelings so surprising? For more than 30 years, she was a loyal Communist. She lived and worked in the city of Moscow as an engineer. Like all other Russians, she always expected that the government would send her monthly checks when she grew too old to work. That was part of the communist system. But then Russia switched to the free enterprise system. Now Inessa is in her 60s and is retired. The amount she receives from the government is much less than she expected. Inessa gets about 1,300 rubles a month—only about $8.

The fall of communism caused other hardships for Inessa. During a march for democracy, her son was killed by soldiers. Still, Inessa believes that the changes are moving her country in the right direction, toward freedom. "My son, and the others who turned out that night, just wanted some sort of free life," she explains.

What kind of life have the people of Russia found as their country has turned toward a new system? To answer that question, let's look at two parts of Russia: Siberia and Moscow.

161

Russia: Energy and the Economy

Sources of Electricity

- Hydro 21%
- Combustion 68%
- Nuclear 11%

% of total generation by type

Source: Dorling Kindersley
World Desk Reference

Russia: Energy Resources KEY
- Coal
- Oil
- Natural Gas
- Hydroelectricity

Two-Point Equidistant Projection

Unemployment in Russia, 1992–1999

Source: International Labour Organization Bureau of Statistics

New restaurant workers undergo job training

Economics The map and charts above present information about energy supplies and employment in Russia. **Map and Chart Study** (a) What do you notice about the location of coal, oil, and natural gas reserves in Russia? (b) Describe how unemployment levels in Russia have changed since 1992. (c) What type of energy is generated the most in Russia?

Take It to the NET Data Update For the most recent data on Russia, visit **www.phschool.com**.

Life in Siberia

During the Soviet years, the government tried to change Siberia, the huge region of eastern Russia. It built factories to take advantage of the region's rich reserves of coal, gold, iron, oil, and natural gas. The government built the Trans-Siberian Railroad to transport materials to and from Siberia. But today, many of the factories are outdated. In the Siberian city of Kemerovo (KEM uh roh voh), factories still release black smoke into the air. Other buildings in the town are crumbling. Rusty cars move slowly down the muddy streets.

Siberian Industry: A Mixed Blessing

Black smoke belches into the cool air in the Siberian town of Ulan Ude (oo LAHN oo DAY) along the Trans-Siberian Railroad. The railroad, completed in 1905, helped to link Siberia's rich natural resources to more densely populated areas of Europe. When towns along the tracks of this railroad became industrial centers, the number of available jobs increased. But so did pollution.

In the Villages   As Kemerovo shows, the changes of free enterprise have come slowly to cities in this region. Change is even slower in rural areas. Life in many villages is almost like life on the American frontier more than 100 years ago. Many homes have no running water, so water has to be hauled from wells once a week. Sometimes the wells freeze in the winter. Then people have to drink and cook with melted snow.

Despite problems like these, Siberians know how to survive and enjoy life in their frigid climate. They follow a strict timetable so they can take advantage of changes in the seasons. Before winter comes they start collecting nuts and honey. Tractors work overtime to harvest crops before the frost. In winter, some families hang huge pieces of meat from their porches. Temperatures in winter are so cold that the meat freezes solid and does not spoil.

During winter, women wearing many layers of clothing leave their log cabins to fetch firewood. Inside the log cabins, it is warm and cozy. That is because many cabins have large stoves used both for cooking and for heating. When the nights become really cold, the family may spread a straw mat on top of the stove and sleep there to stay warm.

During the winter, the meals are hearty. To catch fresh fish, men cut holes through the ice that covers the rivers. At home, the women may also cook homemade goose soup or dumplings stuffed with meat. Or perhaps the family will make a meal of some of the meat they have frozen.

READ ACTIVELY

Visualize Visualize life in a Siberian village.

Believe it or not, some Siberians start their day by bathing in a pitcher of ice-cold water! They believe that it strengthens their body against the cold. Sometimes, they pour water to make a huge puddle in front of their houses. The water freezes quickly, and the children then play ice hockey.

While the children are playing, the adults might decide to have a Siberian-style sauna (SAW nuh), or steam bath. They crowd into a shack filled with hot steam scented with pine. There they sit until they can stand the heat no longer. Then they rush out of the sauna dripping with sweat and roll in the snow to cool down.

Changing Ways   Traditional ways still continue in Siberia. But the fall of communism and the arrival of free enterprise are starting to affect life in the region. Under the communist system, everyone was guaranteed a job. Now Siberians who work in factories and coal mines must worry about losing their jobs. On the other hand, for the first time in more than 70 years, Siberians are able to buy their own homes. Before, they had to live in houses that belonged to the state. People can also now buy stock in the companies in which they work.

Life in Moscow

Moscow, where Inessa lives, has gone through many changes since the fall of communism. At first, business took off. Investors from everywhere, including the United States, came to Moscow to make money. An **investor** is someone who spends money on improving a business in the hope of getting more money when the business succeeds. Some investors become very wealthy. When the first American fast-food chain in Russia opened in Moscow, people lined up in the streets to try it out. The restaurant served 30,000 people on the first day. Within a few years, however, things had changed.

Ask Questions What do you want to know about how the fall of the Soviet Union affected life in Siberia?

▼During the long Siberian winter, a horse-drawn sleigh hauls supplies (right) and a red-cheeked Siberian child plays on his toboggan (below).

164

Since the fall of communism, people in Moscow, Russia's capital, have started over. They have constructed new buildings and started many new businesses. Russians still face many challenges, but they have made great progress over the past few years. The number of cars in Russia has tripled, and the streets of the capital, once empty, are always busy. **Critical Thinking** How does starting a new business create jobs?

Challenges for Ordinary Russians Moscow is the capital of Russia. It has a population of more than 9 million people. In big cities like Moscow, new wealth has brought big changes. Just outside the city, a new skyscraper reaches the sky. At its top is a fine restaurant, enclosed in stone and glass. The building is the world headquarters of Gazprom (GAHS prahm), Russia's only natural gas company. Started by a former Communist official, and mostly owned by the state, it makes a huge amount of money.

The head of Gazprom is one of Russia's richest people. Many other former government leaders have become wealthy in the new Russia. Another group of newly rich Russians leads criminal gangs. Criminal gangs often force people who own businesses to pay them money. The ordinary Russians who own or work in these businesses suffer. Laws meant to protect people are often not enforced.

Ordinary Russians have been working hard since the collapse of communism in Russia. For the first time, they have been able to fulfill their dreams of starting their own new business or opening a small factory. They have been studying Western ways of doing business and gaining knowledge from the Internet, which has become popular in Russia. Unlike during Soviet times, ordinary Russians can own appliances and can sometimes afford to travel.

Yet ordinary Russians are at a disadvantage in the new Russia, especially when the economy does not thrive. In 1998, the value of the ruble fell, causing prices of goods to skyrocket and bringing heavy

READ ACTIVELY

Connect What things make a business in your neighborhood a success?

inflation. In addition, Russia faced a severe food shortage, forcing Russians to change their diets and to seek food aid from the United States.

The economy continued to struggle at the start of the 21st century but still, most Russians try to face the future with optimism. Vlad Olkhovski (vlad ohl HAWV skee) is starting a new travel agency. There used to be only one travel agency for all of Russia. But Vlad hopes that he can attract customers to his new agency. Vlad explains his approach this way:

> "We have learned that the only way you can prosper is to be the best in your market, be professional and be reliable. In America, of course, these are old lessons. But it's an entirely new [way of thinking] for people here."

Tradition and Change The collapse of communism has changed Moscow. But old Russian ways survive alongside the new. After all, Russia is a huge country with many different ways of life. On Moscow's streets you will see poor people who have come from the countryside to buy things, just as they have always done. You will see people from Mongolia wearing the traditional padded silk jackets of their region. And you will see young Russians wearing blue jeans, with haircuts in the latest American style.

On very cold winter days, some people in Moscow go to the parks to celebrate an old tradition: picnicking in the snow. At these picnics they make shish ke-bab by piercing pieces of meat with a sharp stick. Then they roast the meat over an open fire.

Moscow's art, theater, and dance also show great variety. On one evening, people might attend the Bolshoi (BOHL shoy) Ballet. Dancers

▶ GUM, Moscow's biggest department store, stands at the city's center. Its shelves are now stocked with goods rarely seen by ordinary Russians in communist times. On weekends, when the economy is doing well, up to 25,000 people a day shop here.

Russian Art

The collapse of communism has freed artists to experiment with bold modern styles in painting (left) and sculpture (above).

from this famous Russian school of ballet have performed around the world. On another evening, people might go to see a group of folk dancers from northern Russia. Wearing jeweled caps and robes with laced sleeves, the dancers twirl and stamp their feet to traditional folk songs.

The differences between Siberia and Moscow show us the challenges that Russia must meet in the future. Can a country with many different ethnic groups and an area of more than 6 million square miles (9 million sq km) hold itself together? Will the old ways and new ways become one common way for everyone? The answers to these questions are not yet clear. But Russians are united in the hope for a better future for all.

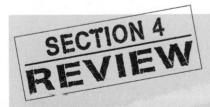
SECTION 4 REVIEW

1. **Define** investor.

2. **Identify** (a) Kemerovo, (b) Moscow.

3. What do Siberians do to survive in their very cold climate?

4. How does Moscow show the variety of Russian life?

Critical Thinking

5. **Recognizing Cause and Effect** What problems might a country have if it includes many ethnic groups that speak many different languages?

Activity

6. **Writing to Learn** Choose and conduct research on one of Russia's 100 ethnic groups. Find answers to these questions: Where do the people live? What language do they speak? What is their religion? What is their relationship to the rest of the country? Then write a brief report on the group.

Review and Activities

Reviewing Main Ideas

1. What parts of Polish life have not changed?
2. What forces are changing some basic parts of Polish town life and country life?
3. What conflicts led to the breakup of Yugoslavia?
4. (a) Name some things that Serbs, Croats, Slovenes, Montenegrins, and Macedonians have in common. (b) Name some differences.
5. (a) What are the natural resources of Ukraine? (b) How have they affected its history?
6. How did the explosion at Chernobyl damage Ukraine's rich soil?
7. What are some differences between the lifestyle in Siberia and that in Moscow?
8. How have recent events affected the people of Russia in different ways?

Reviewing Key Terms

Use each key term below in a sentence that shows the meaning of the term.

1. free enterprise
2. shrine
3. United Nations
4. economic sanctions
5. chernozem
6. collective
7. investor

Critical Thinking

1. **Making Comparisons** Compare life in a Polish village to life in Siberia. How are they alike? How are they different?
2. **Expressing Problems Clearly** What do you think would help bring lasting peace to the former Yugoslavian nations?

Graphic Organizer

Copy the chart onto a separate sheet of paper. Then fill in the empty boxes to complete the chart.

	Country	Recent Challenges	Possible Solutions
Warsaw			
Sarajevo			
Chernobyl			
Moscow			

Map Activity

Eastern Europe

For each place listed below, write the letter from the map that shows its location.

1. Ukraine

2. Kiev

3. Sarajevo

4. Bosnia-Herzegovina

5. Yugoslavia

Writing Activity

Writing an Advertisement

Write an advertisement for Janusz Rajtar's shop in Warsaw. In the advertisement, explain why people should buy from Rajtar instead of from older stores that used to be run by the government.

Take It to the NET

Activity Learn more about Poland's history, culture, economy, geography, and demographics. For help in completing this activity, visit www.phschool.com.

Chapter 5 Self-Test To review what you have learned, take the Chapter 5 Self-Test and get instant feedback on your answers. Go to www.phschool.com to take the test.

Skills Review

Turn to the Skills Activity. Review the steps for recognizing cause and effect. Then, list three unrelated events of your own life history. For each event, name at least one cause and one effect.

How Am I Doing?

Answer these questions to help you check your progress.

1. Do I understand the clash between tradition and change in both Poland and Russia?

2. Do I understand some of the causes of the breakup of Yugoslavia?

3. Do I understand how Ukraine's natural resources have helped and hurt that country?

4. Do I know some of the changes talking place in Russia?

5. What information from this chapter can I include in my journal?

Plan a New Railroad Line

Siberia, the vast Asian region of Russia, has many natural resources, but it has few transportation routes. The region's major rail line, the Trans-Siberian Railroad, was completed in 1905. The route is thousands of miles long, but it covers only a part of Siberia. An addition to the rail line would make it easier for people to move throughout the region.

Purpose

In this activity, you will plan a new branch of the Trans-Siberian Railroad. As you work on the activity, you will learn about Siberia's resources.

Draw a Resource Map

A new rail line in Siberia would transport some of the region's many natural resources to other parts of Russia. Look in an encyclopedia for Siberia and for Russia. Make a list of Siberian mineral resources. Next to each item on the list, note its uses. Draw a small symbol, or picture, to represent each resource. Then draw a map of Siberia. Put the symbols on the map to show where these resources can be found.

Make a Circle Graph

Money to build a new rail line will come from cities and towns located along the line, from the Siberian regional government, and from the Russian national government. Using the figures below, draw a circle graph to show the percentages of the total money each source would contribute.

- Cities and towns   15%
- Regional government   32%
- National government   53%

Decide on a Route

Look at some maps of Siberia, including your mineral resources map. Then decide where you think a new rail line should run.

▶ A Trans-Siberian Railroad station

Trans-Siberian Railroad

KEY

— Trans-Siberian Railroad

— National boundary

⊛ National capital

• Other city

Two-Point Equidistant Projection

Write down a list of cities and towns the route might pass through. On your list, write the distances between the cities and towns. Figure out the total distance of the route. Finally, circle the places where the line will start and end.

Write a Proposal

Write a proposal to persuade the national government to build a new rail line in Siberia. Start with a brief history of the Trans-Siberian Railroad. Then tell where the new rail line will run, what purpose it will serve, and how the project will be paid for.

Write a Railroad Song

Once a new rail line is built, people need to hear about it. Write a song that will advertise the new railroad. In your song lyrics, describe the features of the new train. Tell about the resources and wildlife of Siberia. Try to use the rhythm and sounds of a train in your own rhythm and melody.

Links to Other Subjects

Making a mineral resource chart	**Earth Science**
Making a circle graph	**Math**
Determining routes and distances	**Math**
Writing a proposal	**Language Arts**
Writing a song	**Language Arts & Music**

ANALYSIS AND CONCLUSION

Write a summary explaining what you've learned from planning and proposing the railroad extension. Be sure to answer the following questions in your summary:

1. What have you learned about the geography of Siberia and its mineral resources?

2. What did you learn about writing an effective proposal and song?

FROM
Zlata's Diary
A Child's Life in Sarajevo

BY ZLATA FILIPOVIĆ

Reach Into Your Background

To whom do you tell your secret thoughts? Many people write in a diary or journal what they would tell no other person. Diaries can give people hope and courage, especially during hard times.

Zlata Filipović (ZLAH tah FIL uh POH vich) kept a diary from 1991 through 1993, during the civil war in the country of Bosnia. She was eleven years old when she began her diary, which she called Mimmy. At that time, life in the city of Sarajevo (sar uh YEH voh) was normal for Zlata and her parents. In the spring of 1992, however, their lives changed when war broke out around them. Schools closed. Zlata's family, like many others, spent their days in the basement to avoid gunfire. Food and water became scarce. In December of 1993, Zlata and her parents were able to leave Bosnia safely.

Questions to Explore

1. What do these diary entries tell you about war?
2. How do you think the experience of living through a war affected Zlata?

shrapnel *n.:* fragments of a bomb, mine, or shell

Thursday, May 7, 1992

Dear Mimmy,

I was almost positive the war would stop, but today . . . Today a shell fell on the park in front of my house, the park where I used to play and sit with my girlfriends. A lot of people were hurt. From what I hear Jaca, Jaca's mother, Selma, Nina, our neighbor Dado and who knows how many other people who happened to be there were wounded. Dado, Jaca and her mother have come home from the hospital, Selma lost a kidney but I don't know how she is, because she's still in the hospital. AND NINA IS DEAD. A piece of shrapnel lodged in her brain and she died. She was such a sweet, nice little girl. We went to kindergarten together, and we used to play together in the park. Is it possible I'll never see Nina again? Nina, an innocent eleven-year-old little girl—the victim of a stupid war. I feel sad. I cry and wonder why? She didn't do anything. A disgusting war has destroyed a young child's life. Nina, I'll always remember you as a wonderful little girl.

Love, Mimmy,
Zlata

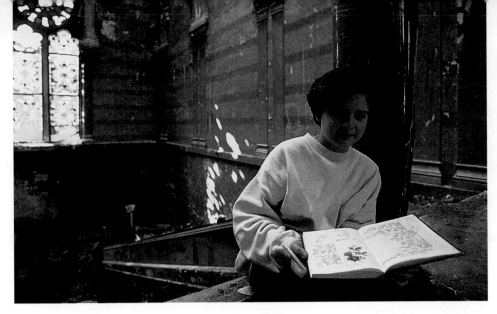

Thursday, December 3, 1992

Dear Mimmy,

Today is my birthday. My first wartime birthday. Twelve years old. Congratulations. Happy birthday to me!

The day started off with kisses and congratulations. First Mommy and Daddy, then everyone else. Mommy and Daddy gave me three Chinese vanity cases—with flowers on them!

As usual there was no electricity. Auntie Melica came with her family (Kenan, Naida, Nihad) and gave me a book. And Braco Lajtner came, of course. The whole neighborhood got together in the evening. I got chocolate, vitamins, a heart shaped soap (small, orange), a key chain with a picture of Maja and Bojana, a pendant made of a stone from Cyprus, a ring (silver) and earrings (bingo!).

The table was nicely laid, with little rolls, fish and rice salad, cream cheese (with Feta), canned corned beef, a pie, and, of course—a birthday cake. Not how it used to be, but there's a war on. Luckily there was no shooting, so we could celebrate.

It was nice, but something was missing. It's called peace!

Your Zlata

READ ACTIVELY

Connect How can people celebrate one thing while being sad about another? Explain why you think people do this.

Melica (MEE lit zuh)
Kenan (KEN ahn)
Naida (NY duh)
Nihad (NEE hahd)
Braco Lajtner (BRAHT zoh LYT nur)
Maja (MY uh)
Bojana (BOY ah nuh)

EXPLORING YOUR READING

Look Back

1. What bad experiences does Zlata record in her entries? What good experiences does she write about?

Think It Over

2. How would you describe Zlata's outlook on her world?

3. Why do you think Zlata treats her diary as a friend?

Go Beyond

4. How do you think the war has changed Zlata?

Ideas for Writing: Diary

5. Keep a diary for a week, writing one entry each day. Write about what makes you happy as well as things that bother or upset you. At the end of the week, write an entry telling what you think about keeping a diary.

EUROPE AND RUSSIA
PROJECT POSSIBILITIES

The following questions will help you direct your reading about Europe and Russia:

☛ **GEOGRAPHY** How has physical geography affected the environment and cultures of Europe and Russia?

☛ **HISTORY** How have the people of Europe and Russia been shaped by historical experiences?

☛ **CULTURE** What values and traditions do the people of Europe and Russia have in common?

☛ **GOVERNMENT** How have changes in government affected Russia and some European nations?

☛ **ECONOMICS** How have Russian and European economies developed into what they are today?

These projects will give you the chance to show what you know about Europe and Russia!

GEO LEO

Project Menu

The chapters in this book have some answers to these questions. Now it's time for you to find your own answers by doing projects on your own or with a group. You can make your own discoveries about Europe and Russia.

Changing Climates It's not always easy to get used to life in a new climate. Someone who moved from Norway to Greece, for example, might be surprised about the way the climate affects how the Greek people live. Choose a European country near the Arctic or one near the Mediterranean. Find out about ways of life that have to do with the climate. Look for details about housing, clothing, food, and recreation.

Based on what you find, write a guide for someone moving to that region from the other end of the continent. Include special tips for things like very hot or cold days, comfortable sleeping, or special snacks.

From Questions to Careers

INTERNATIONAL TRADE

The United States trades many goods and services with Europe and Russia. This trade is important to people in both places. Many international businesspeople work to make this trade happen. Some Americans work in Europe, and some stay here.

There are many careers in international trade. People with careers in international marketing and sales sell products and services to customers in other countries. Shipping companies transport products by boat or by plane. Sailors, pilots, shippers, and handlers make shipping possible.

When people work in other countries, they often need translators. English is the most common language for international business, so some Americans can work in Europe without knowing other languages. However, all who work with other countries must know something about those countries. International managers train workers in the cultures of their trade partners.

▼ Many people have careers in international shipping, as this man does.

Olympic Cities Plan an Olympic season in a European city. As you read this book, keep track of cities that you find interesting. Research them at the library or on the Internet.

After you have gathered your information, choose a city that you think would do a good job of hosting either the summer or winter Olympics. Write a proposal to Olympic officials, explaining what the city has to offer to the Olympics. Include maps or pictures of your city with your proposal.

Tourism in Eastern Europe Many former communist countries would like to have more tourists, who bring money to their economies. Choose a country in Eastern Europe. Read about parts of the culture and landscape that might interest visitors—for example, ski slopes in Slovakia.

Create a travel advertisement for that country. Write your own text and use pictures that you draw or cut out from magazines.

Folklore Corner Create a library of folk and fairy tales from countries throughout Europe. As you read about a country in this book, find a traditional tale from that country. Think about how the stories reflect the country's culture.

With your classmates, build a Folklore Corner in your classroom. Create a display of books of folk tales. Include objects, drawings, and photographs that represent the culture in these tales. Label each tale with its country of origin.

Reference

TABLE OF CONTENTS

This Map and Globe Handbook is designed to help you develop some of the skills you need to be a world explorer. These can help you whether you explore from the top of an elephant in India or from a computer at school.

You can use the information in this handbook to improve your map and globe skills. But the best way to sharpen your skills is to practice. The more you practice the better you'll get.

GEO CLEO and GEO LEO

Table of Contents

Five Themes of Geography

Studying the geography of the entire world can be a huge task. You can make that task easier by using the five themes of geography: location, place, human-environment interaction, movement, and regions. The themes are tools you can use to organize information and to answer the where, why, and how of geography.

1 **Location** answers the question, "Where is it?" You can think of the location of a continent or a country as its address. You might give an absolute location such as "22 South Lake Street" or "40° N and 80° W." You might also use a relative address, telling where one place is by referring to another place. "Between school and the mall" and "eight miles east of Pleasant City" are examples of relative locations.

2 **Place** identifies the natural and human features that make one place different from every other place. You can identify a specific place by its landforms, climate, plants, animals, people, or cultures. You might even think of place as a geographic signature. Use the signature to help you understand the natural and human features that make one place different from every other place.

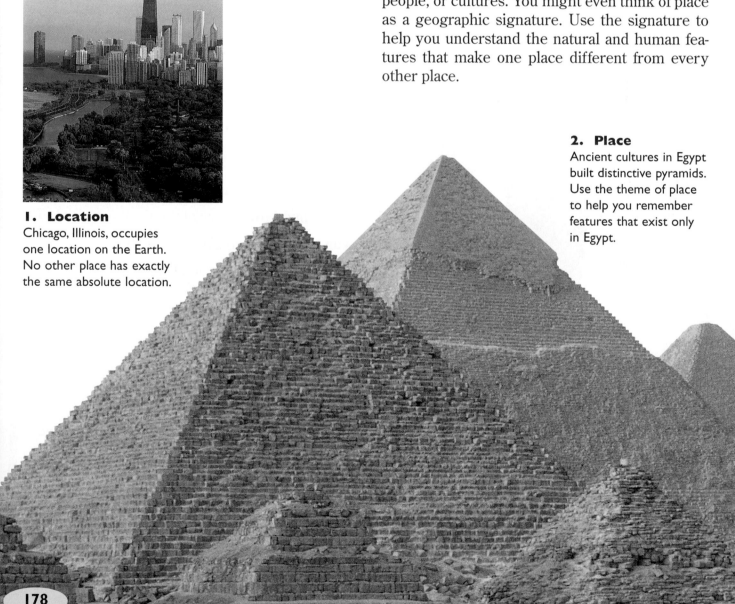

I. Location
Chicago, Illinois, occupies one location on the Earth. No other place has exactly the same absolute location.

2. Place
Ancient cultures in Egypt built distinctive pyramids. Use the theme of place to help you remember features that exist only in Egypt.

3 **Human-Environment Interaction** focuses on the relationship between people and the environment. As people live in an area, they often begin to make changes to it, usually to make their lives easier. For example, they might build a dam to control flooding during rainy seasons. Also, the environment can affect how people live, work, dress, travel, and communicate.

4 **Movement** answers the question "How do people, goods, and ideas move from place to place?" Remember that, often, what happens in one place can affect what happens in another. Use the theme of movement to help you trace the spread of goods, people, and ideas from one location to the next.

5 **Regions** is the last geographic theme. A region is a group of places that share common features. Geographers divide the world into many types of regions. For example, countries, states, and cities are political regions. The people in these places live under the same type of government. Other features can be used to define regions. Places that have the same climate belong to a particular climate region. Places that share the same culture belong to a cultural region. The same place can be found in more than one region. The state of Hawaii is in the political region of the United States. Because it has a tropical climate, Hawaii is also part of a tropical climate region.

3. Human-Environment Interaction
Peruvians have changed steep mountain slopes into terraces suitable for farming. Think how this environment looked before people made changes.

PRACTICE YOUR WORLD EXPLORER SKILLS

1 What is the absolute location of your school? What is one way to describe its relative location?

2 What might be a "geographic signature" of the town or city you live in?

3 Give an example of human-environment interaction where you live.

4 Name at least one thing that comes into your town or city and one that goes out. How is each moved? Where does it come from? Where does it go?

5 What are several regions you think your town or city belongs in?

4. Movement
Arab traders brought not only goods to Kuala Lumpur, Malaysia, but also Arab building styles and the Islamic religion.

5. Regions
Wheat farming is an important activity in Kansas. This means that Kansas is part of a farming region.

Understanding Movements of the Earth

lanet Earth is part of our solar system. The Earth revolves around the sun in a nearly circular path called an orbit. A revolution, or one complete orbit around the sun, takes 365 1/4 days, or a year. As the Earth revolves around the sun, it is also spinning around in space. This movement is called a rotation. The Earth rotates on its axis—an invisible line through the center of the Earth from the North Pole to the South Pole. The Earth makes one full rotation about every 24 hours. As the Earth rotates, it is daytime on the side facing the sun. It is night on the side away from the sun.

The Earth's axis is tilted at an angle. Because of this tilt, sunlight strikes different parts of the Earth at certain points in the year, creating different seasons.

Earth's Revolution and the Seasons

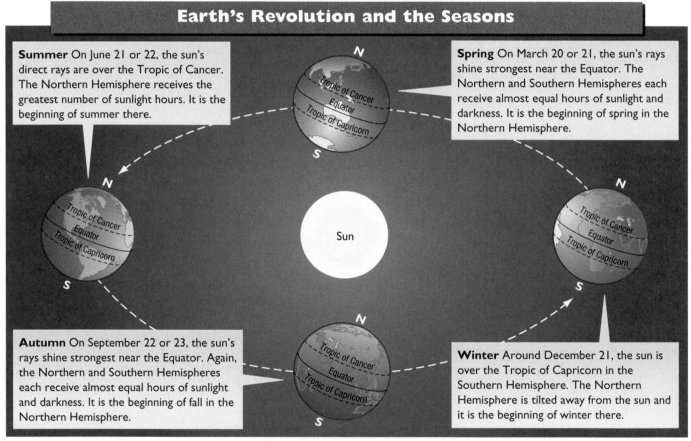

Summer On June 21 or 22, the sun's direct rays are over the Tropic of Cancer. The Northern Hemisphere receives the greatest number of sunlight hours. It is the beginning of summer there.

Spring On March 20 or 21, the sun's rays shine strongest near the Equator. The Northern and Southern Hemispheres each receive almost equal hours of sunlight and darkness. It is the beginning of spring in the Northern Hemisphere.

Autumn On September 22 or 23, the sun's rays shine strongest near the Equator. Again, the Northern and Southern Hemispheres each receive almost equal hours of sunlight and darkness. It is the beginning of fall in the Northern Hemisphere.

Winter Around December 21, the sun is over the Tropic of Capricorn in the Southern Hemisphere. The Northern Hemisphere is tilted away from the sun and it is the beginning of winter there.

▲ **Location** This diagram shows how the Earth's tilt and orbit around the sun combine to create the seasons. Remember, in the Southern Hemisphere the seasons are reversed.

PRACTICE YOUR WORLD EXPLORER SKILLS

1 What causes the seasons in the Northern Hemisphere to be the opposite of those in the Southern Hemisphere?

2 During which two months of the year do the Northern and Southern Hemispheres have about equal hours of daylight and darkness?

Maps and Globes Represent the Earth

Globes

A globe is a scale model of the Earth. It shows the actual shapes, sizes, and locations of all the Earth's landmasses and bodies of water. Features on the surface of the Earth are drawn to scale on a globe. This means a smaller unit of measure on the globe stands for a larger unit of measure on the Earth.

Because a globe is made in the true shape of the Earth, it offers these advantages for studying the Earth.

- The shape of all land and water bodies are accurate.
- Compass directions from one point to any other point are correct.
- The distance from one location to another is always accurately represented.

However, a globe presents some disadvantages for studying the Earth. Because a globe shows the entire Earth, it cannot show small areas in great detail. Also, a globe is not easily folded and carried from one place to another. For these reasons, geographers often use maps to learn about the Earth.

Maps

A map is a drawing or representation, on a flat surface, of a region. A map can show details too small to be seen on a globe. Floor plans, mall directories, and road maps are among the maps we use most often.

While maps solve some of the problems posed by globes, they have some disadvantages of their own. Maps flatten the real round world. Mapmakers cut, stretch, push, and pull some parts of the Earth to get it all flat on paper. As a result, some locations may be distorted. That is, their size, shape, and relative location may not be accurate. For example, on most maps of the entire world, the size and shape of the Antarctic and Arctic regions are not accurate.

PRACTICE YOUR WORLD EXPLORER SKILLS

1. What is the main difference between a globe and a map?

2. What is one advantage of using a globe instead of a map?

Global Gores

◀ **Location**
When mapmakers flatten the surface of the Earth, curves become straight lines. As a result, size, shape, and distance are distorted.

Locating Places on a Map or a Globe

The Hemispheres

Another name for a round ball like a globe is a sphere. The Equator, an imaginary line halfway between the North and South Poles, divides the globe into two hemispheres. (The prefix *hemi* means "half.") Land and water south of the Equator are in the Southern Hemisphere. Land and water north of the Equator are in the Northern Hemisphere.

Mapmakers sometimes divide the globe along an imaginary line that runs from North Pole to South Pole. This line, called the Prime Meridian, divides the globe into the Eastern and Western Hemispheres.

Northern Hemisphere

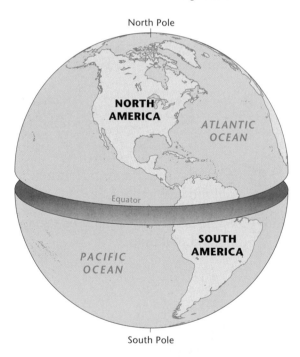

Southern Hemisphere

▲ The Equator divides the Northern Hemisphere from the Southern Hemisphere.

Western Hemisphere   **Eastern Hemisphere**

▲ The Prime Meridian divides the Eastern Hemisphere from the Western Hemisphere.

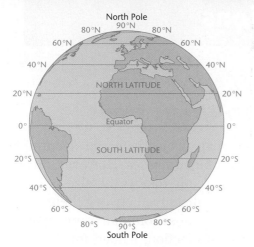

Parallels of Latitude

The Equator, at 0° latitude, is the starting place for measuring latitude or distances north and south. Most globes do not show every parallel of latitude. They may show every 10, 20, or even 30 degrees.

Meridians of Longitude

The Prime Meridian, at 0° longitude, runs from pole to pole through Greenwich, England. It is the starting place for measuring longitude or distances east and west. Each meridian of longitude meets its opposite longitude at the North and South Poles.

The Global Grid

Two sets of lines cover most globes. One set of lines runs parallel to the Equator. These lines, including the Equator, are called *parallels of latitude.* They are measured in degrees (°). One degree of latitude represents a distance of about 70 miles (112 km). The Equator has a location of 0°. The other parallels of latitude tell the direction and distance from the Equator to another location.

The second set of lines runs north and south. These lines are called *meridians of longitude.* Meridians show the degrees of longitude east or west of the Prime Meridian, which is located at 0°. A meridian of longitude tells the direction and distance from the Prime Meridian to another location. Unlike parallels, meridians are not the same distance apart everywhere on the globe.

Together the pattern of parallels of latitude and meridians of longitude is called the global grid. Using the lines of latitude and longitude, you can locate any place on Earth. For example, the location of 30° north latitude and 90° west longitude is usually written as 30°N, 90°W. Only one place on Earth has these coordinates—the city of New Orleans, in the state of Louisiana.

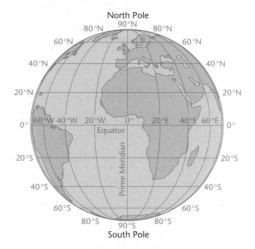

The Global Grid

By using lines of latitude and longitude, you can give the absolute location of any place on the Earth.

1 Which continents lie completely in the Northern Hemisphere? The Western Hemisphere?

2 Is there land or water at 20°S latitude and the Prime Meridian? At the Equator and 60°W longitude?

Map Projections

*I*magine *trying to flatten out a complete orange peel. The peel would split. The shape would change. You would have to cut the peel to get it to lie flat. In much the same way, maps cannot show the correct size and shape of every landmass or body of water on the Earth's curved surface. Maps shrink some places and stretch others. This shrinking and stretching is called* distortion—*a change made to a shape.*

To make up for this disadvantage, mapmakers use different map projections. Each map projection is a way of showing the round Earth on flat paper. Each type of projection has some distortion. No one projection can accurately show the correct area, shape, distance, and direction for the Earth's surface. Mapmakers use the projection that has the least distortion for the information they are studying.

Same-Shape Maps

Some map projections can accurately show the shapes of landmasses. However, these projections often greatly distort the size of landmasses as well as the distance between them.

One of the most common same-shape maps is a Mercator projection, named for the mapmaker who invented it. The Mercator projection accurately shows shape and direction, but it distorts distance and size. In this projection, the northern and southern areas of the globe appear stretched more than areas near the Equator. Because the projection shows true directions, ships' navigators use it to chart a straight line course between two ports.

Mercator Projection

Equal-Area Maps

Some map projections can show the correct size of landmasses. Maps that use these projections are called equal-area maps. In order to show the correct size of landmasses, these maps usually distort shapes. The distortion is usually greater at the edges of the map and less at the center.

Robinson Maps

Many of the maps in this book use the Robinson projection. This is a compromise between the Mercator and equal-area projections. It gives a useful overall picture of the world. The Robinson projection keeps the size and shape relationships of most continents and oceans but does distort size of the polar regions.

Azimuthal Maps

Another kind of projection shows true compass direction. Maps that use this projection are called azimuthal maps. Such maps are easy to recognize—they are usually circular. Azimuthal maps are often used to show the areas of the North and South Poles. However, azimuthal maps distort scale, area, and shape.

Equal-Area Projection

Robinson Projection

Azimuthal Projection

1. What feature is distorted on an equal-area map?

2. Would you use a Mercator projection to find the exact distance between two locations? Tell why or why not.

3. Which would be a better choice for studying the Antarctic—an azimuthal projection or a Robinson projection? Explain.

Parts of a Map

Mapmakers provide several clues to help you understand the information on a map. As an explorer, it is your job to read and interpret these clues.

Compass

Many maps show north at the top of the map. One way to show direction on a map is to use an arrow that points north. There may be an N shown with the arrow. Many maps give more information about direction by displaying a compass showing the directions, north, east, south, and west. The letters N, E, S, and W are placed to indicate these directions.

Title

The title of a map is the most basic clue. It signals what kinds of information you are likely to find on the map. A map titled *West Africa: Population Density* will be most useful for locating information about where people live in West Africa.

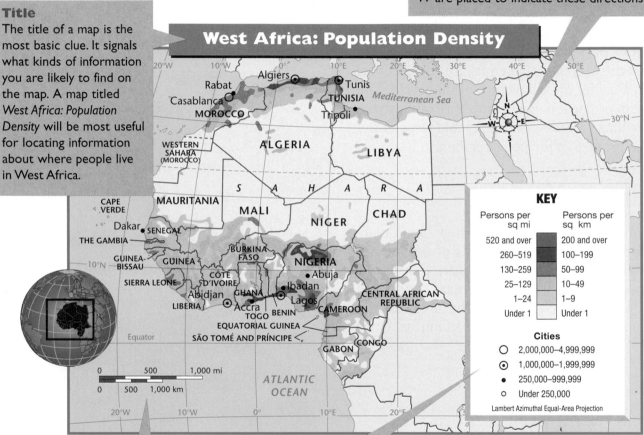

West Africa: Population Density

KEY

Persons per sq mi	Persons per sq km
520 and over	200 and over
260–519	100–199
130–259	50–99
25–129	10–49
1–24	1–9
Under 1	Under 1

Cities

○ 2,000,000–4,999,999
◉ 1,000,000–1,999,999
● 250,000–999,999
○ Under 250,000

Lambert Azimuthal Equal-Area Projection

Scale

A map scale helps you find the actual distances between points shown on the map. You can measure the distance between any two points on the map, compare them to the scale, and find out the actual distance between the points. Most map scales show distances in both miles and kilometers.

Key

Often a map has a key, or legend, that shows the symbols used on the map and what each one means. On some maps, color is used as a symbol. On those maps, the key also tells the meaning of each color.

PRACTICE YOUR WORLD EXPLORER SKILLS

1. What part of a map tells you what the map is about?

2. Where on the map should you look to find out the meaning of this symbol? ●

3. What part of the map can you use to find the distance between two cities?

Comparing Maps of Different Scale

ere are three maps drawn to three different scales. The first map shows Moscow's location in the northeastern portion of Russia. This map shows the greatest area—a large section of northern Europe. It has the smallest scale (1 inch = about 900 miles) and shows the fewest details. This map can tell you what direction to travel to reach Moscow from Finland.

Find the red box on Map 1. It shows the whole area covered by Map 2. Study Map 2. It gives a closer look at the city of Moscow. It shows the features around the city, the city's boundary, and the general shape of the city. This map can help you find your way from the airport to the center of town.

Now find the red box on Map 2. This box shows the area shown on Map 3. This map moves you closer into the city. Like the zoom on a computer or camera, Map 3 shows the smallest area but has the greatest detail. This map has the largest scale (1 inch = about 0.8 miles). This is the map to use to explore downtown Moscow.

Map 1

KEY

—— National boundary

0   500   1,000 mi

0   500   1,000 km

One inch = about 900 miles

Map 2

KEY

▢ Built-up area

══ Road or street

0   5   10 mi

0   5   10 km

One inch = about 12.5 miles

Map 3

KEY

══ Road or street

■ Point of interest

0   .5   1 mi

0   .5   1 km

One inch = about 0.8 miles

PRACTICE YOUR WORLD EXPLORER SKILLS

1. Which map would be best for finding the location of Red Square? Why?

2. Which map best shows Moscow's location relative to Poland? Explain.

3. Which map best shows the area immediately surrounding the city?

Political Maps

Mapmakers create maps to show all kinds of information. The kind of information presented affects the way a map looks. One type of map is called a political map. Its main purpose is to show continents, countries, and divisions within countries such as states or provinces. Usually different colors are used to show different countries or divisions within a country. The colors do not have any special meaning. They are used only to make the map easier to read.

Political maps also show where people have built towns and cities. Symbols can help you tell capital cities from other cities and towns. Even though political maps do not give information that shows what the land looks like, they often include some physical features such as oceans, lakes, and rivers.

Political maps usually have many labels. They give country names, and the names of capital and major cities. Bodies of water such as lakes, rivers, oceans, seas, gulfs, and bays are also labeled.

PRACTICE YOUR WORLD EXPLORER SKILLS

1. What symbol shows the continental boundary?

2. What symbol is used to indicate a capital city? A major city?

3. What kinds of landforms are shown on this map?

Russia: Political

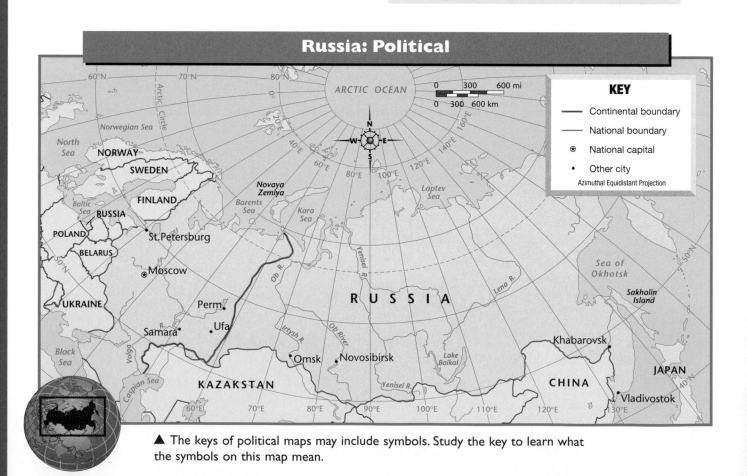

KEY
— Continental boundary
— National boundary
⊛ National capital
• Other city
Azimuthal Equidistant Projection

▲ The keys of political maps may include symbols. Study the key to learn what the symbols on this map mean.

Physical Maps

Like political maps, physical maps show country labels and labels for capital cities. However, physical maps also show what the land of a region looks like by showing the major physical features such as plains, hills, plateaus, or mountains. Labels give the names of features such as mountain peaks, mountains, plateaus, and river basins.

In order to tell one landform from another, physical maps often show elevation and relief.

Elevation is the height of the land above sea level. Physical maps in this book use color to show elevation. Browns and oranges show higher lands while blues and greens show lands that are at or below sea level.

Relief shows how quickly the land rises or falls. Hills, mountains, and plateaus are shown on relief maps using shades of gray. Level or nearly level land is shown without shading. Darkly shaded areas indicate steeper lands.

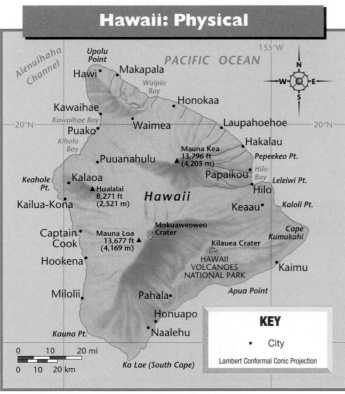

Hawaii: Physical

▲ On a physical map, shading is sometimes used to show relief. Use the shading to locate the mountains in Hawaii.

PRACTICE YOUR WORLD EXPLORER SKILLS

1. How is relief shown on the map to the left?

2. How can you use relief to decide which areas will be the most difficult to climb?

3. What information is given with the name of a mountain peak?

▼ Mauna Kea, an extinct volcano, is the highest peak in the state of Hawaii. Find Mauna Kea on the map.

Special Purpose Maps

As you explore the world, you will encounter many different kinds of special purpose maps. For example, a road map is a special purpose map. The title of each special purpose map tells the purpose and content of the map. Usually a special purpose map highlights only one kind of information. Examples of special purpose maps include land use, population distribution, recreation, transportation, natural resources, or weather.

The key on a special purpose map is very important. Even though a special purpose map shows only one kind of information, it may present many different pieces of data. This data can be shown in symbols, colors, or arrows. In this way, the key acts like a dictionary for the map.

Reading a special purpose map is a skill in itself. Look at the map below. First, try to get an overall sense of what it shows. Then, study the map to identify its main ideas. For example, one main idea of this map is that much of the petroleum production in the region takes place around the Persian Gulf.

1. What part of a special purpose map tells what information is contained on the map?

2. What part of a special purpose map acts like a dictionary for the map?

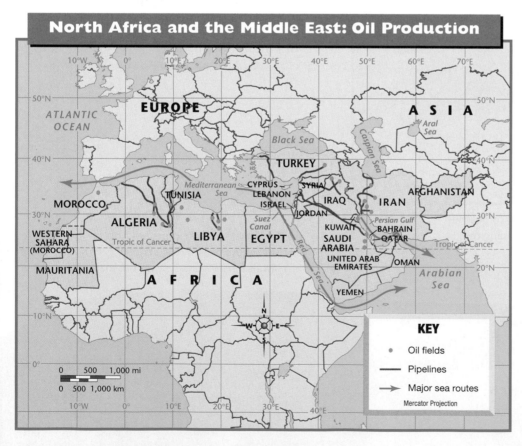

North Africa and the Middle East: Oil Production

◀ The title on a special purpose map indicates what information can be found on the map. The symbols used on the map are explained in the map's key.

KEY
- Oil fields
— Pipelines
→ Major sea routes

Mercator Projection

Landforms, Climate Regions, and Natural Vegetation Regions

Maps that show landforms, climate, and vegetation regions are special purpose maps. Unlike the boundary lines on a political map, the boundary lines on these maps do not separate the land into exact divisions. A tropical wet climate gradually changes to a tropical wet and dry climate. A tundra gradually changes to an ice cap. Even though the boundaries between regions may not be exact, the information on these maps can help you understand the region and the lives of people in it.

Landforms

Understanding how people use the land requires an understanding of the shape of the land itself. The four most important landforms are mountains, hills, plateaus, and plains. Human activity in every region in the world is influenced by these landforms.

- **Mountains** are high and steep. Most are wide at the bottom and rise to a narrow peak or ridge. Most geographers classify a mountain as land that rises at least 2,000 feet (610 m) above sea level. A series of mountains is called a mountain range.

- **Hills** rise above surrounding land and have rounded tops. Hills are lower and usually less steep than mountains. The elevation of surrounding land determines whether a landform is called a mountain or a hill.

- A **plateau** is a large, mostly flat area of land that rises above the surrounding land. At least one side of a plateau has a steep slope.

- **Plains** are large areas of flat or gently rolling land. Plains have few changes in elevation. Many plains areas are located along coasts. Others are located in the interior regions of some continents.

▶ A satellite view of the Earth showing North and South America. What landforms are visible in the photograph?

Climate Regions

Another important influence in the ways people live their lives is the climate of their region. Climate is the weather of a given location over a long period of time. Use the descriptions in the table below to help you visualize the climate regions shown on maps.

Climate	Temperatures	Precipitation
Tropical		
Tropical wet	Hot all year round	Heavy all year round
Tropical wet and dry	Hot all year round	Heavy when sun is overhead, dry other times
Dry		
Semiarid	Hot summers, mild to cold winters	Light
Arid	Hot days, cold nights	Very light
Mild		
Mediterranean	Hot summers, cool winters	Dry summers, wet winters
Humid subtropical	Hot summers, cool winters	Year round, heavier in summer than in winter
Marine west coast	Warm summers, cool winters	Year round, heavier in winter than in summer
Continental		
Humid continental	Hot summers, cold winters	Year round, heavier in summer than in winter
Subarctic	Cool summers, cold winters	Light
Polar		
Tundra	Cool summers, very cold winters	Light
Ice cap	Cold all year round	Light
Highlands	Varies, depending on altitude and direction of prevailing winds	Varies, depending on altitude and direction of prevailing winds

Natural Vegetation Regions

Natural vegetation is the plant life that grows wild without the help of humans. A world vegetation map tells what the vegetation in a place would be if people had not cut down forests or cleared grasslands. The table below provides descriptions of natural vegetation regions shown on maps. Comparing climate and vegetation regions can help you see the close relationship between climate and vegetation.

Vegetation	Description
Tropical rain forest	Tall, close-growing trees forming a canopy over smaller trees, dense growth in general
Deciduous forest	Trees and plants that regularly lose their leaves after each growing season
Mixed forest	Both leaf-losing and cone-bearing trees, no type of tree dominant
Coniferous forest	Cone-bearing trees, evergreen trees and plants
Mediterranean vegetation	Evergreen shrubs and small plants
Tropical savanna	Tall grasses with occasional trees and shrubs
Temperate grassland	Tall grasses with occasional stands of trees
Desert scrub	Low shrubs and bushes, hardy plants
Desert	Little or no vegetation
Tundra	Low shrubs, mosses, lichens; no trees
Ice cap	Little or no vegetation
Highlands	Varies, depending on altitude and direction of prevailing winds

PRACTICE YOUR **WORLD EXPLORER** SKILLS

1 How are mountains and hills similar? How are they different?

2 What is the difference between a plateau and a plain?

Europe

North Pole

ARCTIC OCEAN

Arctic Circle

Bering Sea

East Siberian Sea

Barents Sea

IRELAND
Dublin ⊛
UNITED KINGDOM
London
Lisbon ⊛
PORTUGAL
BELGIUM
NETHERLANDS
NORWAY
Oslo ⊛
SPAIN
Paris ⊛
FRANCE
Brussels ⊛
The Hague
DENMARK
SWEDEN
FINLAND
Madrid ⊛
Luxembourg ⊛
LUX.
Copenhagen ⊛
Stockholm ⊛
Bern ⊛
GERMANY
Berlin ⊛
Helsinki ⊛
SWITZERLAND
(RUSSIA)
AFRICA
AUSTRIA
Vienna ⊛
St. Petersburg •
Rome ⊛
ITALY
See Inset Below
Moscow •

RUSSIA

Black Sea

Caspian

Mediterranean Sea

Tropic of Cancer

Sea of Okhotsk

Kuril Islands (Russia)

Sakhalin Island

Irkutsk •
Lake Baikal

Vladivostok •
Sea of Japan

ASIA

Yellow Sea

East China Sea

Inset map

Baltic Sea
Tallinn ⊛
ESTONIA
Riga ⊛
LATVIA
RUSSIA
LITHUANIA
RUSSIA
Vilnius ⊛
Minsk ⊛
BELARUS
POLAND
Warsaw ⊛
Kiev ⊛
CZECH REP.
Prague •
UKRAINE
SLOVAKIA
MOLDOVA
Bratislava •
Budapest ⊛
Chişinău ⊛
HUNGARY
ROMANIA
Ljubljana •
SLOVENIA
Zagreb ⊛
Bucharest ⊛
CROATIA
Belgrade ⊛
Black Sea
BULGARIA
Sarajevo ⊛
YUGOSLAVIA
BOSNIA-HERZEGOVINA
Skopje ⊛
Sofia ⊛
MACEDONIA
Tiranë ⊛
ALBANIA
GREECE
Athens ⊛

Mediterranean Sea

0   200 mi
0   200 km

Arabian Sea

Bay of Bengal

Philippine Sea

INDIAN   OCEAN

0   500   1,000 mi
0   500   1,000 km

Java Sea

Europe and Russia: Political
KEY

—— National boundary
⊛ National capital
• Other city

Two-Point Equidistant Projection

GEOFACTS

Europe

Population: 728,646,000

Most Populated City: Moscow, Russia (11.8 million)

Largest Country: Ukraine (223,090 sq mi/ 603,700 sq km)

Smallest Country: Vatican City (0.17 sq mi/ 0.44 sq km)

Highest Point: Mt. Elbrus (18,481 ft/5,633 m)

Lowest Point: Caspian Sea (-92 ft/-28 m)

Longest River: Volga River (2,291mi/3,687 km)

Arc de Triomphe, France

Ben Lomond, Scotland

Northern Europe

ICELAND
Reykjavik

Arctic Circle

30°W 20°W 10°W 0° 10°E 20°E 70°N

Narvik Kiruna

Oulu

FINLAND

Trondheim SWEDEN Vaasa

NORWAY Tampere

Lillehammer Helsinki

Faeroe Is.
(Denmark)

60°N

Shetland Is.
(U.K.) Bergen

Oslo L. Vänern Stockholm

ATLANTIC
OCEAN Norrköping

L. Vättern Göteborg

NORTHERN
IRELAND
(U.K.) SCOTLAND

North
Sea DENMARK

Copenhagen Malmö

Glasgow

Belfast UNITED
Dublin KINGDOM

Baltic Sea

IRELAND Liverpool

Birmingham

WALES

London

Gulf of Bothnia

Gulf of Finland

0 250 500 mi

0 250 500 km

50°N

10°W 0° 10°E 20°E 50°N

Capital: Copenhagen

Area: 16,629 sq mi/43,070 sq km

Population: 5.3 million

Ethnic Groups: Danish, Faeroe, Inuit,
Scandinavian

Religions: Evangelical Lutheran,
Roman Catholic

Government: constitutional monarchy

Currency: Danish krone, Euro

Exports: machinery and instru-
ments, meat and meat products

Official Language: Danish

Denmark
(DEN mahrk)

Capital: Helsinki

Area: 117,610 sq mi/304,610 sq km

Population: 5.2 million

Ethnic Groups: Finnish, Sami

Religions: Evangelical Lutheran,
Finnish Orthodox, Roman Catholic

Government: republic

Currency: Markka, Euro

Exports: machinery and equipment,
chemicals, metals, timber, paper, pulp

Official Languages: Finnish and
Swedish

Finland
(FIN lund)

Background Photo: Stockholm Town Hall, Sweden

Capital: Reykjavik

Area: 38,707 sq mi/100,250 sq km

Population: 279,000

Ethnic Group: Icelanders

Religions: Evangelical Lutheran, Christian

Government: constitutional republic

Currency: Icelandic krona

Exports: fish and fish products, animal products, aluminum, diatomite, ferrosilicon

Official Language: Icelandic

Iceland
(EYES lund)

Capital: Stockholm

Area: 158,926 sq mi/411,620 sq km

Population: 8.9 million

Ethnic Groups: Swedish, Finnish, Sami

Religions: Evangelical Lutheran, Roman Catholic, Russian Orthodox, other Protestant

Government: constitutional monarchy

Currency: Swedish krona, Euro

Exports: machinery, motor vehicles, paper products, pulp, wood

Official Language: Swedish

Sweden
(SWEED un)

Capital: Dublin

Area: 26,598 sq mi/68,890 sq km

Population: 3.7 million

Ethnic Groups: Celtic, English

Religions: Roman Catholic, Anglican, Jewish

Government: republic

Currency: Punt, Euro

Exports: machinery and equipment, computers, chemicals, pharmaceuticals, live animals, animal products

Official Languages: Irish and English

Ireland
(EYER lund)

Capital: London

Area: 93,282 sq mi/241,600 sq km

Population: 58.7 million

Ethnic Groups: English, Scottish, Welsh, Northern Irish

Religions: Anglican, Roman Catholic, Presbyterian, Muslim, Methodist

Government: constitutional monarchy

Exports: manufactured goods, fuels, chemicals, food, beverages

Currency: Pound sterling, Euro

Official Languages: English and Welsh

United Kingdom
(yoo NY tid KING dum)

Capital: Oslo

Area: 118,467 sq mi/306,830 sq km

Population: 4.4 million

Ethnic Groups: Norwegian, Sami

Religions: Evangelical Lutheran, Roman Catholic

Government: constitutional monarchy

Currency: Norwegian krone

Exports: petroleum and petroleum products, machinery and equipment, metals, chemicals, ships, fish

Official Language: Norwegian

Norway
(NAWR way)

Western Europe

Capital: Andorra la Vella

Area: 181 sq mi/468 sq km

Population: 65,000

Ethnic Groups: Spanish, Andorran, Portuguese, French

Religion: Roman Catholic

Government: parliamentary democracy

Currency: French franc and Spanish peseta

Exports: tobacco products, furniture

Official Language: Catalan

Andorra
(an DAWR uh)

Background Photo: Bavaria, Germany

Capital: Vienna

Area: 32,942 sq mi/82,730 sq km

Population: 8.2 million

Ethnic Groups: German, Croat, Slovene, Hungarian

Religions: Roman Catholic, Protestant, Muslim

Government: federal republic

Currency: Austrian schilling, Euro

Exports: machinery and equipment, paper, paperboard, metal goods

Official Language: German

Austria
(AW stree uh)

Capital: Paris

Area: 212,394 sq mi/550,100 sq km

Population: 58.9 million

Ethnic Groups: French, North African, German, Breton

Religions: Roman Catholic, Muslim, Protestant, Buddhist, Jewish

Government: republic

Currency: Franc, Euro

Exports: machinery and transportation equipment, chemicals, iron and steel products

Official Language: French

France
(frans)

Capital: Brussels

Area: 12,672 sq mi/32,820 sq km

Population: 10.2 million

Ethnic Groups: Fleming, Walloon, Italian, Moroccan

Religions: Roman Catholic, Muslim

Government: federal monarchy

Currency: Belgian franc, Euro

Exports: machinery and equipment, chemicals, diamonds, metals

Official Languages: Flemish, French, German

Belgium
(BEL jum)

Capital: Berlin

Area: 134,910 sq mi/349,520 sq km

Population: 82.2 million

Ethnic Groups: German, Turkish

Religions: Protestant, Roman Catholic, Muslim

Government: federal republic

Currency: Deutsche Mark, Euro

Exports: machinery, vehicles, chemicals, metals and manufactures, foodstuffs, textiles

Official Language: German

Germany
(JUR muh nee)

Vaduz Castle, Liechtenstein

Capital: Vaduz

Area: 62 sq mi/160 sq km

Population: 31,000

Ethnic Groups: Alemmanic, Italian, Turkish

Religions: Roman Catholic, Protestant

Government: hereditary constitutional monarchy

Currency: Swiss franc

Exports: small specialty machinery, dental products, stamps, hardware

Official Language: German

Liechtenstein
(LIK tun styn)

Capital: Luxembourg

Area: 998 sq mi/2,585 sq km

Population: 426,000

Ethnic Groups: Celtic with French and German, Portuguese, Italian

Religions: Roman Catholic, Protestant, Greek Orthodox, Jewish

Government: constitutional monarchy

Currency: Luxembourg franc, Euro

Exports: finished steel products, chemicals, rubber products, glass

Official Languages: French, Letzeburgish, German

Luxembourg
(LUK sum burg)

The Matterhorn, Switzerland

Capital: Monaco

Area: 0.75 sq mi/1.95 sq km

Population: 32,000

Ethnic Groups: French, Monegasque, Italian

Religions: Roman Catholic, Protestant

Government: constitutional monarchy

Currency: French franc

Official Language: French

Monaco
(MAHN uh koh)

Monte Carlo, Monaco

Capital: Amsterdam

Area: 13,097 sq mi/33,920 sq km

Population: 15.7 million

Ethnic Groups: Dutch, Moroccan, Turkish

Religions: Roman Catholic, Protestant, Muslim

Government: constitutional monarchy

Currency: Netherlands guilder, Euro

Exports: machinery and equipment, chemicals, fuels, foodstuffs

Official Language: Dutch

Netherlands
(NETH ur lundz)

Capital: Bern

Area: 15,355 sq mi/39,770 sq km

Population: 7.3 million

Ethnic Groups: German, French, Italian, Romansh

Religions: Roman Catholic, Protestant, Muslim

Government: federal republic

Currency: Swiss franc

Exports: machinery, chemicals, vehicles, metals, watches

Official Languages: French, German, Italian

Switzerland
(SWIT sur lund)

REGIONAL · DATABASE

Southern Europe

Map of Southern Europe showing:

ATLANTIC OCEAN, Bay of Biscay, PORTUGAL, Lisbon, SPAIN, Madrid, Ebro River, Barcelona, Gulf of Lion, Valencia, Balearic Islands, Strait of Gibraltar, Gibraltar (U.K.), Mediterranean Sea, Turin, Milan, Po River, Venice, Genoa, Florence, SAN MARINO, Adriatic Sea, Tiber R., Rome, HOLY SEE, ITALY, Naples, Sardinia, Tyrrhenian Sea, Sicily, MALTA, Valletta, Corfu, Ionian Sea, GREECE, Athens, Thessaloniki, Aegean Sea, Rhodes, Crete

Scale: 0 150 300 mi / 0 150 300 km

Capital: Athens

Area: 50,521 sq mi/130,850 sq km

Population: 10.6 million

Ethnic Group: Greek

Religions: Greek Orthodox, Muslim

Government: parliamentary republic

Currency: Drachma, Euro

Exports: manufactured goods, food and beverages, fuels

Official Language: Greek

Greece
(grees)

Capital: Vatican City

Area: 0.17 sq mi/0.44 sq km

Population: 1,000

Ethnic Groups: Italian, Swiss

Religion: Roman Catholic

Government: monarchy

Currency: Lira

Exports: none

Official Languages: Italian and Latin

Holy See (Vatican City)
(HO lee see VAT i kun SI tee)

Background Photo: Florence, Italy

202

Capital: Rome

Area: 301,270 sq mi/294,060 sq km

Population: 57.3 million

Ethnic Groups: Italian, Sardinian

Religions: Roman Catholic, Protestant, Jewish, Muslim

Government: republic

Currency: Italian lira, Euro

Exports: engineering products, textiles, clothing, production machinery, motor vehicles

Official Language: Italian

Italy
(IT uh lee)

Capital: San Marino

Area: 24 sq mi/61 sq km

Population: 26,000

Ethnic Groups: Sammarinese, Italian

Religion: Roman Catholic

Government: republic

Currency: Lira

Exports: building stone, lime, wood, chestnuts, wheat, wine, baked goods, hides, ceramics

Official Language: Italian

San Marino
(san muh REE noh)

Capital: Valletta

Area: 124 sq mi/320 sq km

Population: 386,000

Ethnic Groups: Maltese

Religion: Roman Catholic

Government: parliamentary democracy

Currency: Maltese lira

Exports: machinery and transport equipment, manufactures

Official Languages: English, Maltese

Malta
(MAWL tuh)

Capital: Madrid

Area: 192,834 sq mi/499,440 sq km

Population: 39.6 million

Ethnic Groups: Castillian Spanish, Catalan, Galician, Basque, Romany

Religion: Roman Catholic

Government: parliamentary monarchy

Currency: Spanish peseta, Euro

Exports: machinery, motor vehicles, foodstuffs, other consumer goods

Official Languages: Spanish, Galician, Basque, Catalan

Spain
(spayn)

Capital: Lisbon

Area: 35,502 sq mi/91,950 sq km

Population: 9.9 million

Ethnic Groups: Portuguese, African

Religions: Roman Catholic, Protestant

Government: parliamentary democracy

Currency: Portuguese escudo, Euro

Exports: machinery, clothing, footwear, chemicals, cork and paper products, hides

Official Language: Portuguese

Portugal
(PAWR chuh gul)

Eastern Europe

KEY

— National boundary

⊛ National capital

• Other city

Lambert Azimuthal Equal-Area Projection

SWEDEN

Tallinn
ESTONIA
Lake Peipus

Riga
LATVIA

LITHUANIA
Vilnius
RUSSIA

Gdánsk

Minsk

BELARUS

RUSSIA

POLAND
Warsaw
Brest

Łódź
Kiev

Prague
Katowice
UKRAINE

CZECH REPUBLIC

SLOVAKIA

Bratislava
Budapest
MOLDOVA
Chişinău
Sea of Azov

AUSTRIA
HUNGARY
Cluj
Odessa

Ljubljana
ROMANIA

SLOVENIA
Zagreb

CROATIA
BOSNIA-HERZ.
Belgrade
Bucharest
Black Sea

Sarajevo
YUGOSLAVIA
BULGARIA

Podgorica
Sofia
TURKEY

ITALY
Skopje

Tiranë
MACEDONIA

ALBANIA
GREECE

0   150   300 mi
0   150   300 km

Capital: Tirana

Area: 10,579 sq mi/27,400 sq km

Population: 3.1 million

Ethnic Groups: Albanian, Greek, Vlach, Gypsy, Serb, Bulgarian

Religions: Sunni Muslim, Orthodox, Roman Catholic

Government: parliamentary republic

Currency: Lek

Exports: textiles, footwear, asphalt, metals and metallic ores, crude oil

Official Language: Albanian

Albania
(al BAY nee uh)

Capital: Minsk

Area: 80,154 sq mi/207,600 sq km

Population: 10.3 million

Ethnic Groups: Belorussian, Russian, Polish, Ukrainian

Religions: Russian Orthodox, Roman Catholic, Muslim, Jewish, Protestant

Government: republic

Currency: Belorussian ruble

Exports: machinery and equipment, chemicals, metals, textiles, foodstuffs

Official Languages: Belorussian, Russian

Belarus
(bel uh ROOS)

Background Photo: Prague, Czech Republic

Capital: Sarajevo

Area: 19,741 sq mi/51,130 sq km

Population: 3.8 million

Ethnic Groups: Bosniak, Serb, Croat, Yugoslav

Religions: Muslim, Serbian Orthodox, Roman Catholic, Protestant

Government: emerging democracy

Currency: Maraka

Exports: none of significance

Official Language: Serbo-Croat

Bosnia–Herzegovina
(BOZ nee uh hurt suh goh VEE nuh)

Capital: Zagreb

Area: 21,829 sq mi/56,538 sq km

Population: 4.5 million

Ethnic Groups: Croat, Serb, Yugoslav

Religions: Roman Catholic, Orthodox, Muslim

Government: presidential/parliamentary democracy

Currency: Kuna

Exports: textiles, chemicals, foodstuffs, fuels

Official Language: Croatian

Croatia
(kroh AY shuh)

Capital: Sofia

Area: 42,683 sq mi/110,550 sq km

Population: 8.3 million

Ethnic Groups: Bulgarian, Turkish, Macedonian, Romany

Religions: Bulgarian Orthodox, Muslim, Roman Catholic, Jewish

Government: parliamentary democracy

Currency: Lev

Exports: machinery and equipment, metals, minerals, fuels, chemicals

Official Language: Bulgarian

Bulgaria
(bul GAYR ee uh)

Capital: Prague

Area: 30,449 sq mi/78,864 sq km

Population: 10.3 million

Ethnic Groups: Czech, Moravian, Slovak

Religions: Roman Catholic, Hossites, Protestant

Government: parliamentary democracy

Currency: Czech koruna

Exports: machinery and transport equipment, manufactured goods

Official Language: Czech

Czech Republic
(chek ri PUB lik)

Capital: Tallinn

Area: 17,423 sq mi/45,125 sq km

Population: 1.4 million

Ethnic Groups: Russian, Estonian

Religions: Evangelical Lutheran, Russian Orthodox, Estonian Orthodox

Government: parliamentary democracy

Currency: Kroon

Exports: machinery and appliances, wood products, textiles, food

Official Language: Estonian

Estonia
(e STOH nee uh)

Capital: Budapest

Area: 35,652 sq mi/92,340 sq km

Population: 10.1 million

Ethnic Groups: Magyar, German, Romany, Slovak

Religions: Roman Catholic, Calvinist, Lutheran, Greek Orthodox

Government: parliamentary democracy

Currency: Forint

Exports: machinery and equipment, other manufactures, agriculture

Official Language: Hungarian

Hungary
(HUNG guh ree)

Capital: Skopje

Area: 9,929 sq mi/25,715 sq km

Population: 2 million

Ethnic Groups: Macedonian, Albanian, Turkish, Serb, Romany

Religions: Macedonian Orthodox, Muslim

Government: republic

Currency: Macedonian denar

Exports: food, beverages, tobacco, miscellaneous manufactures, iron, steel

Official Language: Macedonian

Macedonia
(mas i DOH nee uh)

Capital: Riga

Area: 24,938 sq mi/ 64,589 sq km

Population: 2.4 million

Ethnic Groups: Latvian, Russian, Belorussian, Ukrainian

Religions: Lutheran, Roman Catholic, Russian Orthodox

Government: parliamentary democracy

Currency: Lat

Exports: wood and wood products, machinery and equipment, metals

Official Language: Latvian

Latvia
(LAT vee uh)

Capital: Chisinau

Area: 13,000 sq mi/33,700 sq km

Population: 4.4 million

Ethnic Groups: Moldovan, Ukrainian, Russian, Gagauz

Religions: Eastern Orthodox, Jewish, Baptist

Government: republic

Currency: Leu

Exports: foodstuffs, wine, tobacco, textiles, footwear, machinery

Official Language: Romanian

Moldova
(mawl DOH vuh)

Capital: Vilnius

Area: 25,174 sq mi/65,200 sq km

Population: 3.7 million

Ethnic Groups: Lithuanian, Russian, Polish, Belorussian

Religions: Roman Catholic, Lutheran, Russian Orthodox

Government: parliamentary democracy

Currency: Litas

Exports: machinery and equipment, mineral products, textiles

Official Language: Lithuanian

Lithuania
(lith oo AY nee uh)

Capital: Warsaw

Area: 117,552 sq mi/304,460 sq km

Population: 38.7 million

Ethnic Groups: Polish, German

Religions: Roman Catholic, Eastern Orthodox

Government: republic

Currency: Zloty

Exports: manufactured goods, chemicals, machinery and equipment, food, live animals, mineral fuels

Official Language: Polish

Poland
(POH lund)

Capital: Ljubljana

Area: 7,820 sq mi/20,250 sq km

Population: 2 million

Ethnic Groups: Slovene, Croat, Serb, Bosniak

Religions: Roman Catholic, Orthodox Catholic, Muslim

Government: parliamentary democratic republic

Currency: Tolar

Exports: manufactured goods, machinery, transport equipment

Official Language: Slovene

Slovenia
(sloh VEE nee uh)

Capital: Bucharest

Area: 88,934 sq mi/230,340 sq km

Population: 22.4 million

Ethnic Groups: Romanian, Magyar, Romany

Religions: Romanian Orthodox, Roman Catholic, Protestant

Government: republic

Currency: Leu

Exports: textiles, footwear, metals and metal products, machinery and equipment, minerals, fuels

Official Language: Romanian

Romania
(roh MAY nee uh)

Capital: Kiev

Area: 223,090 sq mi/603,700 sq km

Population: 50.7 million

Ethnic Groups: Ukrainian, Russian, Jewish

Religions: Ukrainian Orthodox, Catholic, Protestant, Jewish

Government: republic

Currency: Hryvna

Exports: metals, fuel and petroleum products, machinery

Official Language: Ukrainian

Ukraine
(yoo KRAYN)

Capital: Bratislava

Area: 18,933 sq mi/49,036 sq km

Population: 5.4 million

Ethnic Groups: Slovak, Hungarian, Gypsy

Religions: Roman Catholic, Protestant, Orthodox

Government: parliamentary democracy

Currency: Koruna

Exports: machinery and transport equipment, manufactured goods

Official Language: Slovak

Slovakia
(sloh VAH kee uh)

Capital: Belgrade

Area: 39,449 sq mi/102,173 sq km

Population: 10.6 million

Ethnic Groups: Serb, Albanian, Montenegrin, Bosniak, Magyar

Religions: Eastern Orthodox, Muslim, Roman Catholic, Protestant

Government: republic

Currency: Yugoslav dinar

Exports: manufactured goods, food, live animals, raw materials

Official Language: Serbo-Croat

Yugoslavia
(yoo goh SLAH vee uh)

Russia

North Pole

ARCTIC OCEAN

0   500   1,000 mi
0   500   1,000 km

North Sea

Barents Sea

Novaya Zemlya

Kara Sea

White Sea

Laptev Sea

Bering Strait

Bering Sea

RUSSIA

St. Petersburg

Verkhoyansk

Lena River

Arctic Circle

Sea of Okhotsk

Moscow

Nizhniy Novgorod

Ob River

Yenisel R.

RUSSIA

Sakhalin Island

Nizhniy Tagil

Samara

Yekaterinburg

Lena River

Magnitogorsk

Volga River

Ob River

Dnieper R.

Black Sea

Omsk

Novosibirsk

Bratsk

Irkutsk

Lake Baikal

Vladivostok

Caspian Sea

Yenisel R.

N
W   E
S

Peterhof Grand Palace, St. Petersburg

Background Photo: St. Basil's Cathedral, Moscow, Russia

Tchesme Church, St. Petersburg

Capital: Moscow

Area: 6,592,812 sq mi/17,075,400 sq km

Population: 147.2 million

Ethnic Groups: Russian, Tatar, Ukrainian, Chuvash

Religions: Russian Orthodox, Muslim

Government: federation

Currency: Ruble

Exports: petroleum and petroleum products, natural gas, wood and wood products, metals, chemicals, civilian and military manufactures

Official Language: Russian

Russian Federation

Lake Onega, Russia

Atlas

The World: Political

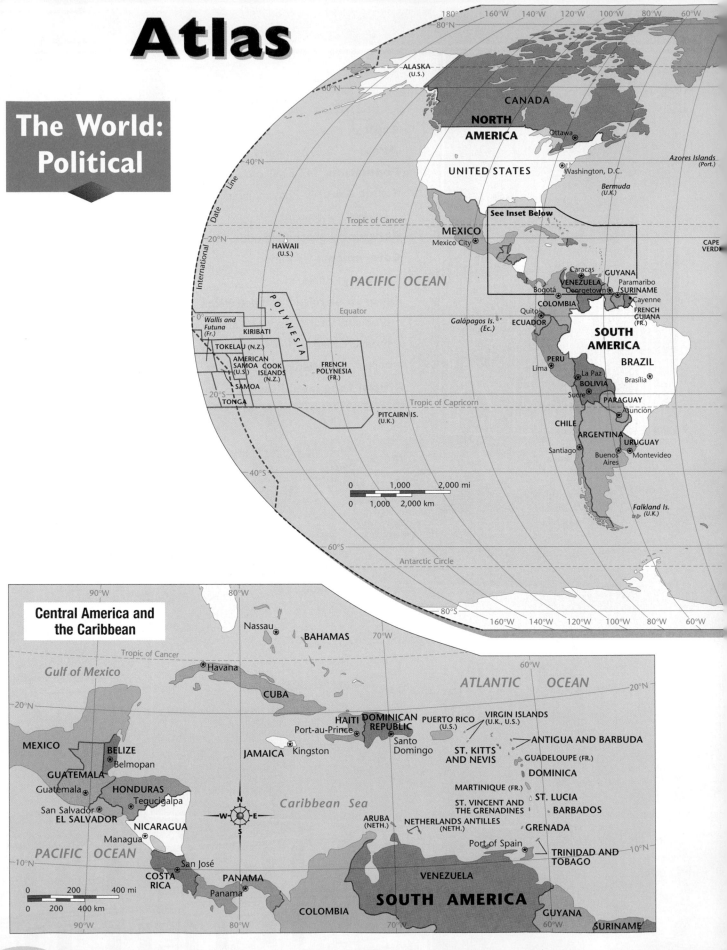

Central America and the Caribbean

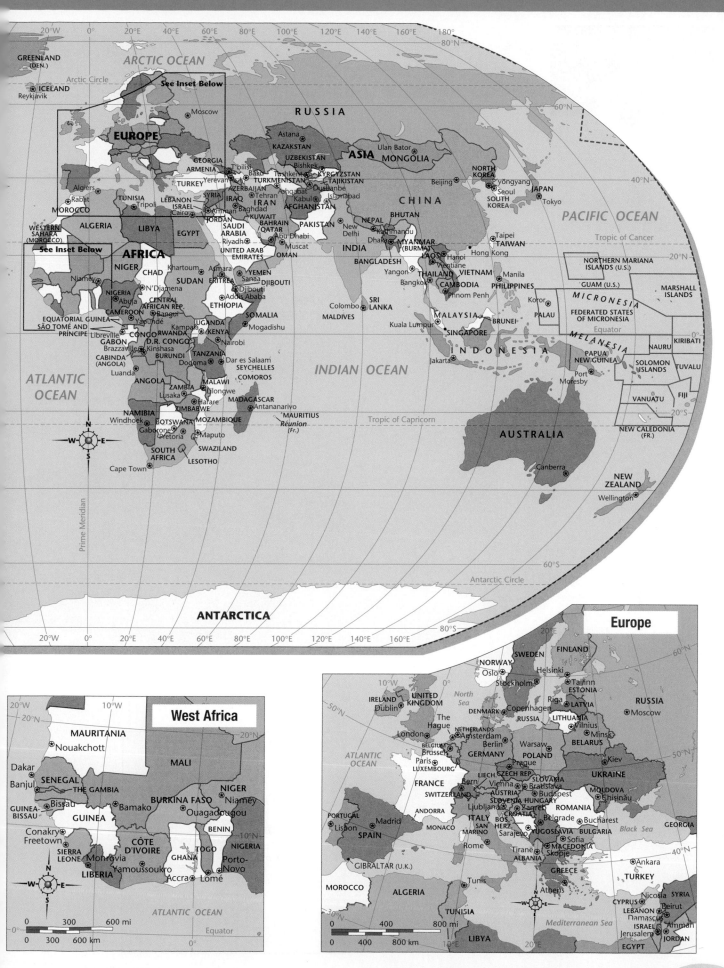

GREENLAND
(DEN.)

ARCTIC OCEAN

Arctic Circle

ICELAND
Reykjavik

RUSSIA

See Inset Below

EUROPE

Moscow

80°N

60°N

KAZAKSTAN
Astana

ASIA

Ulan Bator
MONGOLIA

UZBEKISTAN
Bishkek
KYRGYZSTAN

NORTH
KOREA
Beijing
P'yŏngyang
Seoul
SOUTH
KOREA

JAPAN
Tokyo

PACIFIC OCEAN

GEORGIA
ARMENIA
T'bilisi
Baku
TURKEY
Yerevan
AZERBAIJAN
Tashkent
TURKMENISTAN
TAJIKISTAN
Dushanbe
Ashgabat

CHINA

40°N

Algiers
Rabat
TUNISIA
Tripoli
MOROCCO

SYRIA
LEBANON
ISRAEL
Amman
Cairo
IRAN
Tehran
Baghdad
IRAQ
Kabul
Islamabad
AFGHANISTAN

Kathmandu
NEPAL
BHUTAN

New
Delhi
Dhaka
MYANMAR
(BURMA)

Taipei
TAIWAN
Hong Kong

NORTHERN MARIANA
ISLANDS (U.S.)

Tropic of Cancer

20°N

ALGERIA
LIBYA
EGYPT
JORDAN
KUWAIT
BAHRAIN
SAUDI
ARABIA
QATAR
Riyadh
Abu Dhabi
Muscat
UNITED ARAB
EMIRATES
OMAN

PAKISTAN

INDIA

BANGLADESH

LAOS
Hanoi
Vientiane
THAILAND
Bangkok
VIETNAM
CAMBODIA
Phnom Penh

Manila
PHILIPPINES

GUAM (U.S.)

MICRONESIA

MARSHALL
ISLANDS

WESTERN
SAHARA
(MOROCCO)

See Inset Below

AFRICA

NIGER
CHAD
Khartoum
SUDAN
Asmara
ERITREA
Sanaa
YEMEN
DJIBOUTI
Djibouti
Addis Ababa
ETHIOPIA

FEDERATED STATES
OF MICRONESIA
PALAU

KIRIBATI

Niamey

N'Djamena

NIGERIA
Abuja
CENTRAL
AFRICAN REP.
CAMEROON
Bangui
Yaoundé

Colombo
MALDIVES
SRI
LANKA

SOMALIA
Mogadishu

MALAYSIA
Kuala Lumpur

BRUNEI

Koror

NAURU

0°

EQUATORIAL GUINEA
SÃO TOMÉ AND
PRÍNCIPE
Libreville
CONGO
GABON
Brazzaville
D.R. CONGO
Kinshasa

UGANDA
Kampala
RWANDA
BURUNDI
KENYA
Nairobi
TANZANIA
Dodoma
Dar es Salaam
SEYCHELLES
COMOROS

INDONESIA

Jakarta

SINGAPORE

Equator

MELANESIA

PAPUA
NEW GUINEA
Port
Moresby

SOLOMON
ISLANDS

TUVALU

ATLANTIC
OCEAN

CABINDA
(ANGOLA)
Luanda

ANGOLA
ZAMBIA
Lusaka
MALAWI
Lilongwe
ZIMBABWE
Harare
MOZAMBIQUE
MADAGASCAR
Antananarivo
MAURITIUS
Réunion
(Fr.)

INDIAN OCEAN

VANUATU

FIJI

NEW CALEDONIA
(Fr.)

20°S

NAMIBIA
Windhoek
BOTSWANA
Gaborone
Pretoria
SOUTH
AFRICA
Maputo
SWAZILAND
LESOTHO

Tropic of Capricorn

AUSTRALIA

Cape Town

Canberra

NEW
ZEALAND

Wellington

60°S

Antarctic Circle

ANTARCTICA

80°S

20°W   0°   20°E   40°E   60°E   80°E   100°E   120°E   140°E   160°E

West Africa

20°W   10°W

20°N

MAURITANIA
Nouakchott

MALI

Dakar
SENEGAL
Banjul
THE GAMBIA
GUINEA-
BISSAU
Bissau
GUINEA
Conakry
Freetown
SIERRA
LEONE
Monrovia
LIBERIA
Bamako
BURKINA FASO
Ouagadougou
NIGER
Niamey

BENIN
CÔTE
D'IVOIRE
Yamoussoukro
GHANA
Accra
TOGO
Lomé
NIGERIA
Porto-
Novo

10°N

N
W   E
S

0   300   600 mi
0   300   600 km

ATLANTIC OCEAN

Equator   0°

Europe

10°W   0°

NORWAY
Oslo
SWEDEN
FINLAND
Helsinki
60°N

IRELAND
Dublin
UNITED
KINGDOM
North
Sea
DENMARK
Copenhagen
Stockholm
Tallinn
ESTONIA
Riga
LATVIA
RUSSIA
Moscow

50°N

ATLANTIC
OCEAN

The
Hague
London
NETHERLANDS
Amsterdam
BELGIUM
Brussels
Paris
LUXEMBOURG
GERMANY
Berlin
RUSSIA
LITHUANIA
Vilnius
Minsk
BELARUS
Warsaw
POLAND
Prague
Kiev
UKRAINE

50°N

FRANCE
SWITZERLAND
Bern
LIECH.
CZECH REP.
Vienna
AUSTRIA
SLOVAKIA
Bratislava
Budapest
HUNGARY
MOLDOVA
Chişinău
ROMANIA

PORTUGAL
Lisbon
ANDORRA
Madrid
SPAIN
MONACO
ITALY
SLOVENIA
Ljubljana
Zagreb
CROATIA
SAN
MARINO
BOS.
HERZ.
Sarajevo
Belgrade
YUGOSLAVIA
Sofia
BULGARIA
Bucharest
GEORGIA
Black Sea

40°N

GIBRALTAR (U.K.)

Rome
Tiranë
MACEDONIA
Skopje
ALBANIA
GREECE
Ankara
TURKEY

MOROCCO
ALGERIA
Tunis
TUNISIA
Athens
Mediterranean Sea

CYPRUS
Nicosia
SYRIA
LEBANON
Beirut
Damascus
ISRAEL
Jerusalem
Amman
JORDAN

0   400   800 mi
0   400   800 km

LIBYA
EGYPT

N
W   E
S

10°E   20°E

The World: Physical

ARCTIC OCEAN
180° 160°W 140°W 120°W 100°W 80°W 60°W
80°N
Beaufort
Sea
Greer
Baffin
Island
Yukon R.
Bering
60°N
Sea
Hudson
Bay
ROCKY MOUNTAINS
NORTH
AMERICA
CANADIAN SHIELD
Aleutian Islands
St. Lawrence R.
Great
Lakes
40°N
Missouri R.
APPALACHIAN MTS.
Mississippi R.
GREAT PLAINS
ATLANTIC
OCEAN
SIERRA MADRE OCCIDENTAL
SIERRA MADRE ORIENTAL
Hawaiian Islands
Tropic of Cancer
Gulf of
Mexico
West Indies
20°N
Caribbean Sea
PACIFIC OCEAN
Orinoco R.
GUIANA HIGHLANDS
P O L Y N E S I A
0°
Equator
AMAZON
Amazon R.
BASIN
SOUTH
AMERICA
ANDES
BRAZILIAN
HIGHLANDS
20°S
Tropic of Capricorn
PAMPAS
Rio de
la Plata
40°S
PATAGONIA
Cape Horn
Drake Passage
60°S
Antarctic Circle
ANTARCTIC
PENINSULA
80°S
160°W 140°W 120°W 100°W 80°W 60°W

KEY

Elevation

Feet		Meters
14,000		4,270
7,000		2,135
1,500		457
700		213
(sea level) 0		0 (sea level)

Ice pack

Ice shelf

Orthographic Projection

South Pole

SOUTHERN OCEAN
QUEEN MAUD LAND
COATS
LAND
ENDERBY
LAND
Antarctic Weddell
Peninsula Sea
Prime Meridian
Amery Ice Shelf
Ronne
Ice Shelf
TRANSANTARCTIC MTS.
ANTARCTICA
90° E
QUEEN MAUD MTS.
South Pole
0   800 mi
Ross
Ice Shelf
0   800 km
WILKES LAND
Roosevelt I.
Ross
Sea
VICTORIA
LAND
South
Magnetic
+ Pole
International Date Line

North Pole

United States: Political

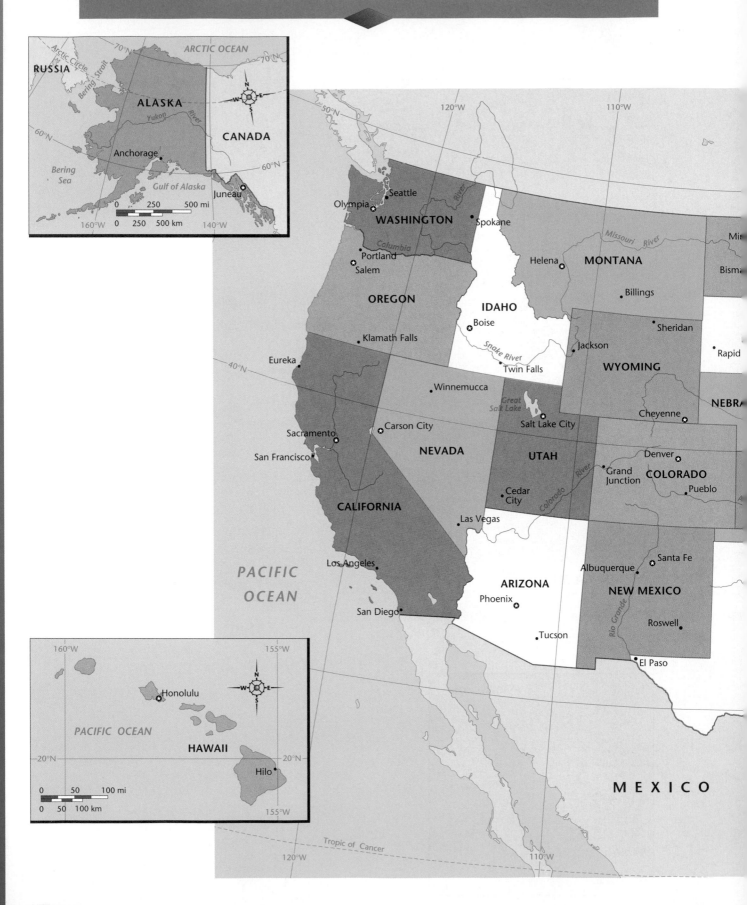

RUSSIA

ARCTIC OCEAN

ALASKA

CANADA

Anchorage

Bering Sea

Gulf of Alaska

Juneau

| 0 | 250 | 500 mi |
| 0 | 250 | 500 km |

CANADA

WASHINGTON
Seattle
Olympia
Spokane
Portland
Salem
OREGON
Klamath Falls
Eureka

IDAHO
Boise
Snake River
Twin Falls

Helena
MONTANA
Billings

WYOMING
Jackson
Sheridan
Rapid

Winnemucca
Great Salt Lake
Salt Lake City
Carson City
Sacramento
San Francisco
NEVADA
UTAH
Cheyenne
NEBR
Denver
COLORADO
Grand Junction
Pueblo

CALIFORNIA
Cedar City
Las Vegas

Los Angeles
San Diego

ARIZONA
Phoenix
Tucson

Santa Fe
Albuquerque
NEW MEXICO
Roswell
El Paso

PACIFIC OCEAN

MEXICO

Missouri River
Bisma
Mir

Columbia
River

Colorado

Rio Grande

Tropic of Cancer

120°W
110°W

50°N
120°W
110°W
40°N

PACIFIC OCEAN

160°W
155°W
Honolulu
HAWAII
Hilo
20°N
20°N
155°W

| 0 | 50 | 100 mi |
| 0 | 50 | 100 km |

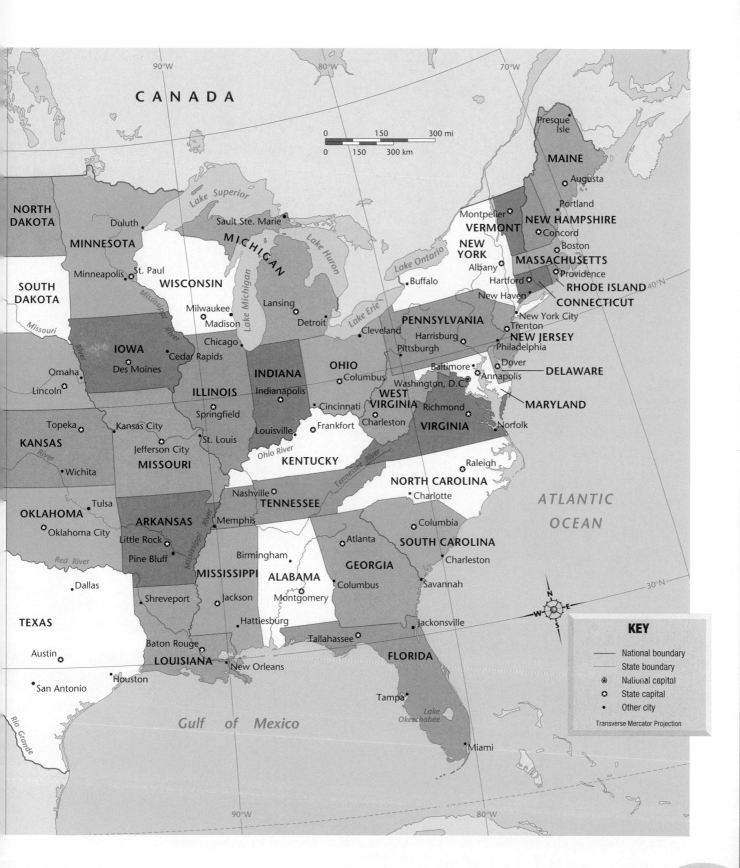

CANADA

NORTH DAKOTA

Duluth

MINNESOTA

Sault Ste. Marie

MICHIGAN

Lake Superior

Lake Huron

Presque Isle

MAINE

Augusta

Portland

Montpelier

NEW HAMPSHIRE

Concord

VERMONT

NEW YORK

Boston

Albany

MASSACHUSETTS

Providence

Hartford

RHODE ISLAND

New Haven

CONNECTICUT

Minneapolis St. Paul

WISCONSIN

Lake Michigan

Milwaukee

Madison

Lansing

Lake Ontario

Lake Erie

Buffalo

SOUTH DAKOTA

Mississippi River

Missouri

Chicago

IOWA

Cedar Rapids

Des Moines

Omaha

Lincoln

ILLINOIS

Springfield

INDIANA

Indianapolis

Detroit

OHIO

Columbus

Cleveland

PENNSYLVANIA

Harrisburg

Pittsburgh

New York City

Trenton

NEW JERSEY

Philadelphia

Dover

DELAWARE

Baltimore

Annapolis

MARYLAND

Cincinnati

WEST VIRGINIA

Charleston

Louisville

Frankfort

Richmond

VIRGINIA

Norfolk

Topeka

Kansas City

KANSAS

Wichita

Jefferson City

MISSOURI

St. Louis

KENTUCKY

Tennessee River

Raleigh

NORTH CAROLINA

Washington, D.C.

River

Ohio River

Oklahoma

Tulsa

OKLAHOMA

Oklahoma City

Red River

ARKANSAS

Little Rock

Pine Bluff

Nashville

TENNESSEE

Memphis

Mississippi River

Charlotte

Columbia

SOUTH CAROLINA

Charleston

Atlanta

GEORGIA

Savannah

ATLANTIC OCEAN

TEXAS

Dallas

Austin

San Antonio

Shreveport

MISSISSIPPI

Jackson

Hattiesburg

Baton Rouge

LOUISIANA

Houston

New Orleans

Birmingham

ALABAMA

Montgomery

Columbus

Tallahassee

Jacksonville

FLORIDA

Tampa

Lake Okeechobee

Miami

Gulf of Mexico

Rio Grande

KEY

National boundary

State boundary

National capital

State capital

Other city

Transverse Mercator Projection

90°W   80°W   70°W

40°N

30°N

0   150   300 mi
0   150   300 km

North and South America: Political

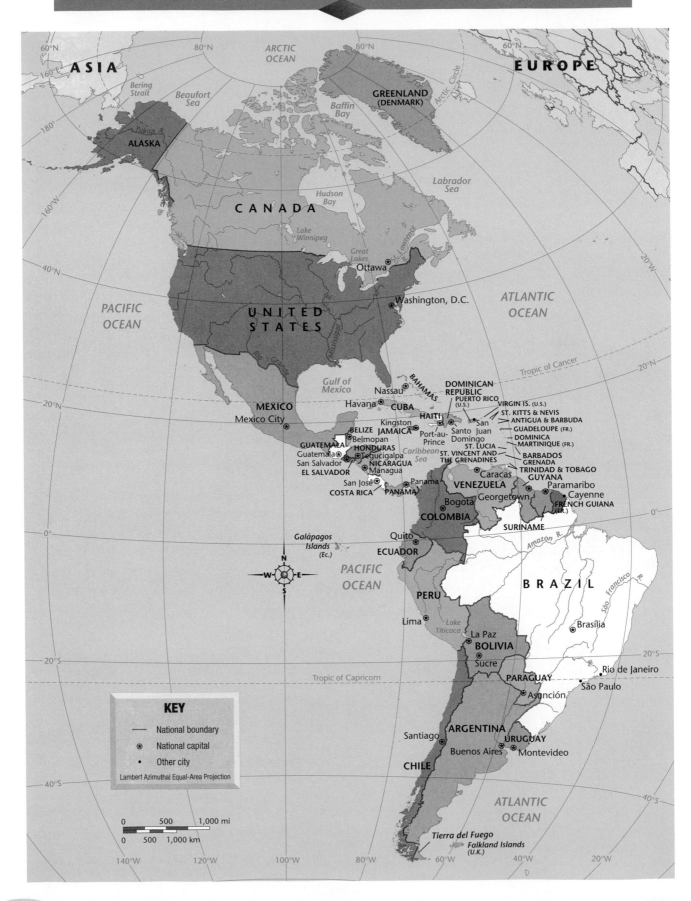

ASIA

ARCTIC OCEAN

EUROPE

Bering Strait

Beaufort Sea

Baffin Bay

GREENLAND (DENMARK)

ALASKA

Yukon R.

Labrador Sea

Hudson Bay

CANADA

Lake Winnipeg

Great Lakes

St. Lawrence R.

Ottawa

PACIFIC OCEAN

40°N

UNITED STATES

Washington, D.C.

ATLANTIC OCEAN

Mississippi

Rio Grande

Tropic of Cancer

20°N

Gulf of Mexico

BAHAMAS

Nassau

DOMINICAN REPUBLIC

PUERTO RICO (U.S.)

VIRGIN IS. (U.S.)

MEXICO

Havana

CUBA

ST. KITTS & NEVIS

ANTIGUA & BARBUDA

Mexico City

HAITI

San Juan

GUADELOUPE (FR.)

Kingston

Santo Domingo

DOMINICA

BELIZE

JAMAICA

Port-au-Prince

MARTINIQUE (FR.)

Belmopan

ST. LUCIA

GUATEMALA

HONDURAS

Caribbean Sea

ST. VINCENT AND THE GRENADINES

BARBADOS

Guatemala

Tegucigalpa

GRENADA

San Salvador

NICARAGUA

TRINIDAD & TOBAGO

EL SALVADOR

Managua

GUYANA

Caracas

San José

Panama

VENEZUELA

Paramaribo

COSTA RICA

PANAMA

Georgetown

Cayenne

Bogota

FRENCH GUIANA (FR.)

COLOMBIA

SURINAME

Galápagos Islands (Ec.)

Quito

0°

ECUADOR

Amazon R.

PACIFIC OCEAN

BRAZIL

São Francisco R.

PERU

Lima

Lake Titicaca

Brasília

La Paz

BOLIVIA

20°S

Sucre

Rio de Janeiro

Tropic of Capricorn

PARAGUAY

São Paulo

Asunción

KEY

— National boundary

⊛ National capital

• Other city

Lambert Azimuthal Equal-Area Projection

ARGENTINA

Santiago

URUGUAY

Buenos Aires

Montevideo

CHILE

0   500   1,000 mi

0   500   1,000 km

ATLANTIC OCEAN

Tierra del Fuego

Falkland Islands (U.K.)

60°N   80°N   80°N   60°N

160°E

180°

160°W

40°N

PACIFIC OCEAN

20°N

20°N

0°

20°S

20°S

40°S

40°S

140°W   120°W   100°W   80°W   60°W   40°W   20°W

North and South America: Physical

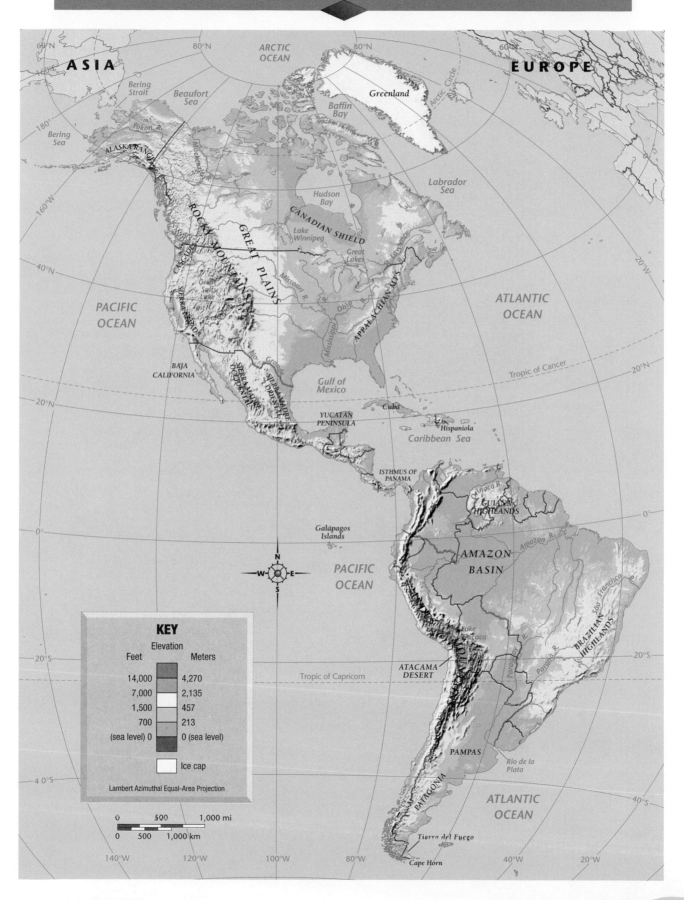

ASIA

ARCTIC OCEAN

EUROPE

Bering Strait
Beaufort Sea
Greenland
Baffin Bay
Bering Sea
Yukon R.
ALASKA RANGE
Mackenzie R.
Labrador Sea
Hudson Bay
CANADIAN SHIELD
ROCKY MOUNTAINS
GREAT PLAINS
Lake Winnipeg
Great Lakes
St. Lawrence R.
CASCADES
SIERRA NEVADA
Great Salt Lake
Missouri R.
Ohio R.
APPALACHIAN MTS.
PACIFIC OCEAN
ATLANTIC OCEAN
BAJA CALIFORNIA
SIERRA MADRE OCCIDENTAL
SIERRA MADRE ORIENTAL
Rio Grande
Mississippi R.
Tropic of Cancer
Gulf of Mexico
Cuba
YUCATÁN PENINSULA
Hispaniola
Caribbean Sea
ISTHMUS OF PANAMA
Orinoco R.
GUIANA HIGHLANDS
Galápagos Islands
AMAZON BASIN
Amazon R.
ANDES
Lake Titicaca
São Francisco R.
BRAZILIAN HIGHLANDS
ATACAMA DESERT
Tropic of Capricorn
Paraguay R.
Paraná R.
PAMPAS
Rio de la Plata
PATAGONIA
Tierra del Fuego
Cape Horn
ATLANTIC OCEAN

N W E S

KEY

Elevation

Feet		Meters
14,000		4,270
7,000		2,135
1,500		457
700		213
(sea level) 0		0 (sea level)
	Ice cap	

Lambert Azimuthal Equal-Area Projection

0   500   1,000 mi

0   500   1,000 km

Europe: Political

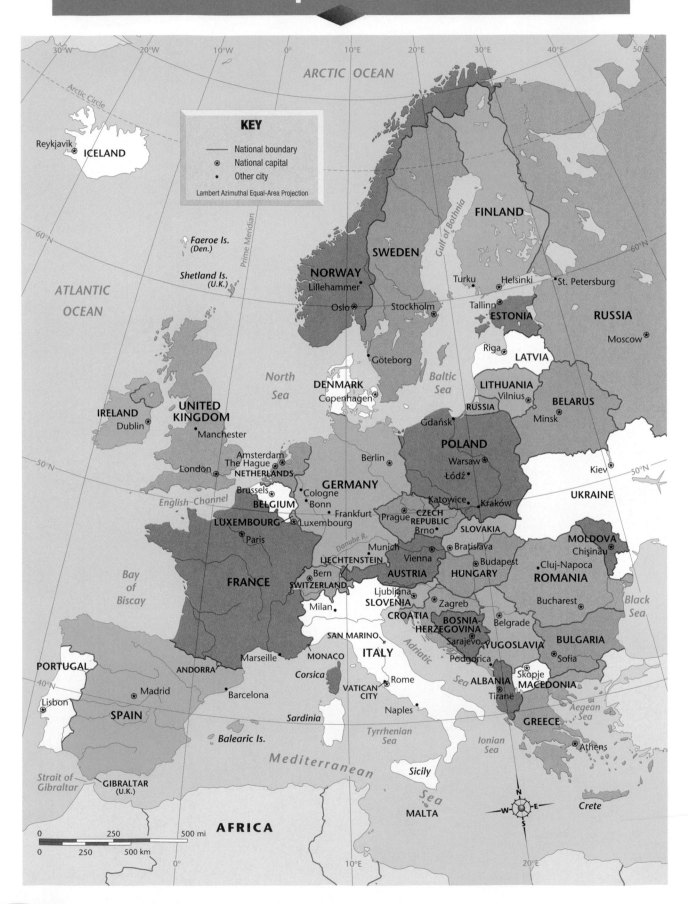

KEY

—— National boundary

✲ National capital

• Other city

Lambert Azimuthal Equal-Area Projection

ARCTIC OCEAN

Arctic Circle

Reykjavik ✲ ICELAND

Faeroe Is.
(Den.)

Shetland Is.
(U.K.)

ATLANTIC
OCEAN

FINLAND

Gulf of Bothnia

SWEDEN

NORWAY

Lillehammer •

Turku •   Helsinki ✲   • St. Petersburg

Oslo ✲

Stockholm ✲

Tallinn ✲

ESTONIA

RUSSIA

Moscow ✲

Göteborg •

Riga ✲

LATVIA

North
Sea

DENMARK

Copenhagen ✲

Baltic
Sea

LITHUANIA

Vilnius ✲

BELARUS

RUSSIA

Minsk ✲

IRELAND

Dublin ✲

UNITED
KINGDOM

• Manchester

Gdańsk •

POLAND

Warsaw ✲

Łódź •

Berlin ✲

Kiev ✲

Amsterdam ✲
The Hague ✲
NETHERLANDS

London ✲

Brussels ✲

BELGIUM

Cologne •

GERMANY

Katowice •

Kraków •

UKRAINE

Bonn •

• Frankfurt

Prague ✲

CZECH
REPUBLIC

English Channel

LUXEMBOURG

Luxembourg ✲

Brno •

SLOVAKIA

MOLDOVA

Chişinău ✲

• Paris

Danube R.

• Munich

Vienna ✲

✲ Bratislava

Cluj-Napoca •

Bay
of
Biscay

FRANCE

LIECHTENSTEIN

Bern ✲

SWITZERLAND

AUSTRIA

HUNGARY

Budapest ✲

ROMANIA

Ljubljana ✲

SLOVENIA

✲ Zagreb

Bucharest ✲

Black
Sea

Milan •

CROATIA

Belgrade ✲

BULGARIA

SAN MARINO

BOSNIA-
HERZEGOVINA

Sarajevo ✲

YUGOSLAVIA

Adriatic

PORTUGAL

ANDORRA

Marseille •

MONACO

ITALY

Sofia ✲

Podgorica •

Sea

Corsica

Rome ✲

ALBANIA

Skopje ✲

MACEDONIA

Madrid •

VATICAN
CITY

Tiranë ✲

Aegean
Sea

Lisbon ✲

• Barcelona

Naples •

GREECE

SPAIN

Sardinia

Balearic Is.

Tyrrhenian
Sea

Ionian
Sea

Athens ✲

Strait of
Gibraltar

GIBRALTAR
(U.K.)

Mediterranean

Sicily

Crete

Sea

AFRICA

MALTA

N
W · E
S

| 0 | 250 | 500 mi |
| 0 | 250 | 500 km |

Africa: Political

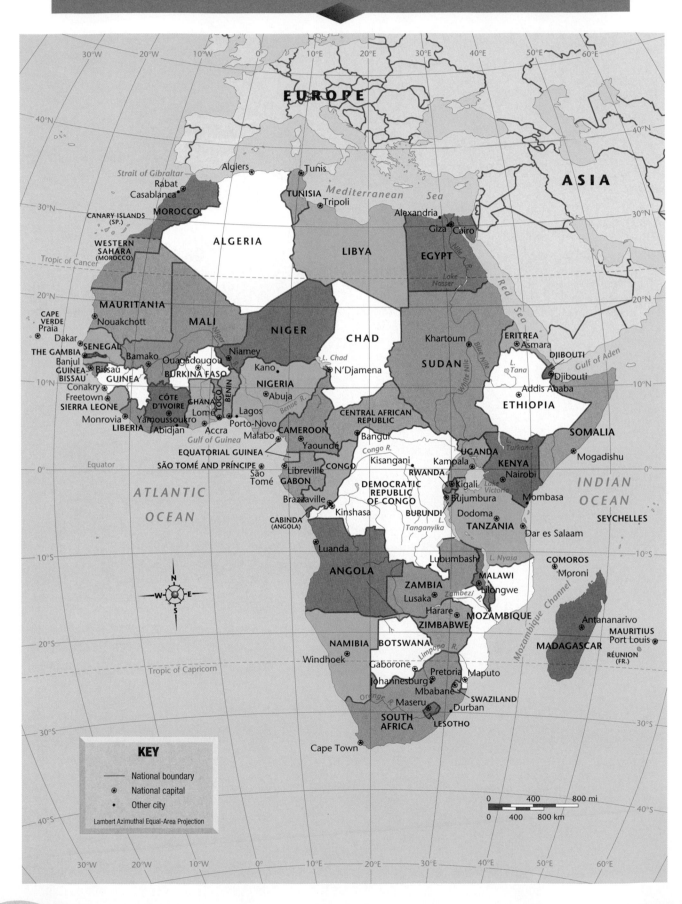

30°W 20°W 10°W 0° 10°E 20°E 30°E 40°E 50°E 60°E

EUROPE

ASIA

40°N

Strait of Gibraltar
Algiers
Rabat
Casablanca
CANARY ISLANDS
(SP.)
MOROCCO
30°N

Tunis
TUNISIA
Tripoli

Mediterranean Sea
Alexandria
Giza Cairo
EGYPT

WESTERN
SAHARA
(MOROCCO)
Tropic of Cancer
ALGERIA
LIBYA
Nile R.
Lake
Nasser

Red Sea

20°N

MAURITANIA
CAPE
VERDE
Praia
Nouakchott
MALI
NIGER
CHAD
Khartoum
ERITREA
Asmara
DJIBOUTI
Gulf of Aden

Dakar
SENEGAL
Niger R.
Niamey
SUDAN
L.
Tana
Djibouti
THE GAMBIA
Banjul
GUINEA
BISSAU
Bissau
Bamako
Ouagadougou
BURKINA FASO
Kano
N'Djamena
Blue Nile
Addis Ababa
10°N

GUINEA
Conakry
Freetown
SIERRA LEONE
Monrovia
LIBERIA
CÔTE
D'IVOIRE
Yamoussoukro
Abidjan
GHANA
Lomé
Accra
TOGO
BENIN
Porto-Novo
NIGERIA
Abuja
Lagos
Malabo
CAMEROON
Yaoundé
Benue R.
CENTRAL AFRICAN
REPUBLIC
Bangui
White Nile
ETHIOPIA
SOMALIA

Equator
Gulf of Guinea
EQUATORIAL GUINEA
SÃO TOMÉ AND PRÍNCIPE
São
Tomé
Libreville
GABON
CONGO
Kisangani
Congo R.
DEMOCRATIC
REPUBLIC
OF CONGO
RWANDA
Kigali
BURUNDI
Bujumbura
Kampala
UGANDA
Lake
Victoria
KENYA
Nairobi
Mombasa
Mogadishu
INDIAN
OCEAN
0°
L.
Turkana

ATLANTIC
OCEAN
Brazzaville
Kinshasa
CABINDA
(ANGOLA)
L.
Tanganyika
Dodoma
TANZANIA
Dar es Salaam
SEYCHELLES
10°S

Luanda
Lubumbashi
L. Nyasa
COMOROS
Moroni

ANGOLA
ZAMBIA
Lusaka
Zambezi R.
MALAWI
Lilongwe
MOZAMBIQUE
Antananarivo
MAURITIUS
Port Louis
MADAGASCAR
RÉUNION
(FR.)
20°S

Harare
ZIMBABWE
Mozambique Channel

NAMIBIA
BOTSWANA
Limpopo R.
Windhoek
Gaborone
Pretoria
Maputo
Johannesburg
Mbabane
SWAZILAND
Orange R.
Maseru
Durban
30°S

SOUTH
AFRICA
LESOTHO

Cape Town

KEY

— National boundary
⊛ National capital
• Other city

Lambert Azimuthal Equal-Area Projection

| 0 | 400 | 800 mi |
| 0 | 400 | 800 km |

30°W 20°W 10°W 0° 10°E 20°E 30°E 40°E 50°E 60°E

Africa: Physical

EUROPE

ASIA

Strait of Gibraltar

ATLAS MOUNTAINS

Mediterranean Sea

Canary Islands

QATTARA DEPRESSION

Suez Canal

ARABIAN DESERT

Tropic of Cancer

S A H A R A

AHAGGAR MOUNTAINS

LIBYAN DESERT

Nile R.

Lake Nasser

Red Sea

Cape Verde Islands

Senegal R.

S A H E L

Niger R.

L. Chad

Gulf of Aden

Benue R.

MANDARY

ETHIOPIAN PLATEAU

Blue Nile

FOUTA DJALLON

SUDD

White Nile

Gulf of Guinea

Ubangi R.

Congo R.

L. Albert

L. Turkana

Equator

ATLANTIC OCEAN

C O N G O B A S I N

L. Edward

GREAT RIFT VALLEY

Kilimanjaro 19,341 ft (5,895 m)

INDIAN OCEAN

L. Mai-Ndombe

Lake Victoria

SERENGETI PLAIN

Kasai R.

Zanzibar

Tanganyika

Lake Nyasa

Comoros Islands

Zambezi R.

Mauritius

Réunion

Okavango Basin

Mozambique Channel

Tropic of Capricorn

NAMIB DESERT

KALAHARI DESERT

Limpopo R.

Orange R.

Cape of Good Hope

Cape Agulhas

KEY

Elevation

Feet		Meters
Over 13,000		Over 3,960
6,500–13,000		1,980–3,960
1,600–6,500		480–1,980
650–1,600		200–480
0–650		0–200
Below sea level		Below sea level

Lambert Azimuthal Equal-Area Projection

0   400   800 mi

0   400   800 km

Asia: Political

KEY
- European Russia
- National boundary
- ⊛ National capital
- • Other city
- Two-Point Equidistant Projection

ARCTIC OCEAN
+ North Pole

EUROPE

PACIFIC OCEAN

Bering Sea

Kuril Islands (Russia)

Sakhalin Island

Sea of Okhotsk

East Siberian Sea

Tokyo
Vladivostok
Sea of Japan
JAPAN
N. KOREA
Seoul
S. KOREA
Pyongyang
Yellow Sea
East China Sea
Ryukyu Islands
Taipei
TAIWAN
Hong Kong
Macau

Philippine Sea
PHILIPPINES
Manila

PALAU
Koror

PAPUA NEW GUINEA
New Guinea
Port Moresby

Equator

Verkhoyansk

Harbin
Beijing
Fuzhou

RUSSIA

Lena R.
Yenisei R.
Ob R.
Irtysh R.

Lake Baikal
Bratsk
Irkutsk
Ulan Bator
MONGOLIA

CHINA
Xi'an
Huang He
Yangzi R.

Hanoi
VIETNAM
LAOS
Vientiane
THAILAND
Bangkok
CAMBODIA
Phnom Penh
MYANMAR (BURMA)
Yangon

MALAYSIA
BRUNEI
Bandar Seri Begawan
Borneo
Kuala Lumpur
SINGAPORE
Singapore
Sumatra
Jakarta
Java
Java Sea
Celebes
INDONESIA
Tanimbar
Timor

Yekaterinburg
Omsk

Astana
Qaraghandy
KAZAKSTAN
Lake Balkhash
Almaty
Bishkek
KYRGYZSTAN
Tashkent
UZBEKISTAN
Dushanbe
TAJIKISTAN
Aral Sea

St. Petersburg
Moscow
Samara
Volga R.

BHUTAN
Thimphu
NEPAL
Kathmandu
Islamabad
AFGHANISTAN
Kabul
PAKISTAN
New Delhi
INDIA
Ganges R.
BANGLADESH
Dhaka
Bay of Bengal
Chennai (Madras)
SRI LANKA
Colombo
Male
MALDIVES

Mumbai (Bombay)

Arabian Sea

INDIAN OCEAN

(RUSSIA)
GEORGIA
Caspian Sea
Baku
AZERBAIJAN
TURKMENISTAN
Ashgabat
IRAN
Tehran
Shiraz
TURKEY
Ankara
Nicosia
CYPRUS
ARMENIA
Yerevan
Tbilisi
LEBANON
Beirut
SYRIA
Damascus
Amman
IRAQ
Baghdad
JORDAN
Jerusalem
ISRAEL
Kuwait
KUWAIT
BAHRAIN
QATAR
UNITED ARAB EMIRATES
Abu Dhabi
Persian Gulf
Gulf of Oman
Muscat
OMAN
SAUDI ARABIA
Riyadh
Mecca
Sanaa
YEMEN
Socotra (Yemen)
Gulf of Aden
Red Sea
Black Sea
Mediterranean Sea

AFRICA

Tropic of Cancer
Arctic Circle
Barents Sea

Equator

1,000 mi
500
1,000 km
0   500

Asia: Physical

KEY

Feet	Elevation	Meters
14,000		4,270
7,000		2,135
1,500		457
700		213
(sea level) 0		0 (sea level)

Two-Point Equidistant Projection

ARCTIC OCEAN

North Pole

EUROPE

URAL MOUNTAINS

NORTH SIBERIAN LOWLAND

CENTRAL SIBERIAN PLATEAU

Yenisei R.

Ob R.

Irtysh R.

KOLYMA MTS.

STANOVOY RANGE

KAMCHATKA PENINSULA

Bering Sea

East Siberian Sea

Barents Sea

Arctic Circle

Amur R.

Lake Baikal

Sea of Okhotsk

Sakhalin Island

Kuril Islands

Hokkaido

Honshu

Shikoku

Kyushu

Sea of Japan

MONGOLIAN PLATEAU

GOBI DESERT

TIEN SHAN

PLATEAU OF TIBET

Lake Balkhash

Aral Sea

Caspian Sea

CAUCASUS MTS.

Black Sea

PLATEAU OF ANATOLIA

Mediterranean Sea

Red Sea

ARABIAN PENINSULA

ZAGROS MTS.

Persian Gulf

Gulf of Aden

Socotra

Arabian Sea

Yellow Sea

East China Sea

Ryukyu Islands

Tropic of Cancer

South China Sea

INDOCHINA PENINSULA

MALAY PENINSULA

Bay of Bengal

INDIAN PENINSULA

DECCAN PLATEAU

WESTERN GHATS

EASTERN GHATS

Ganges R.

INDIAN OCEAN

PACIFIC OCEAN

Philippine Sea

Luzon

Mindanao

Celebes

Borneo

Sumatra

Java Sea

Java

Tanimbar

Timor

New Guinea

AUSTRALIA

Equator

AFRICA

Tropic of Cancer

North Pole

1,000 mi

500   1,000 km

0   500

Australia, New Zealand, and the Pacific Islands: Physical–Political

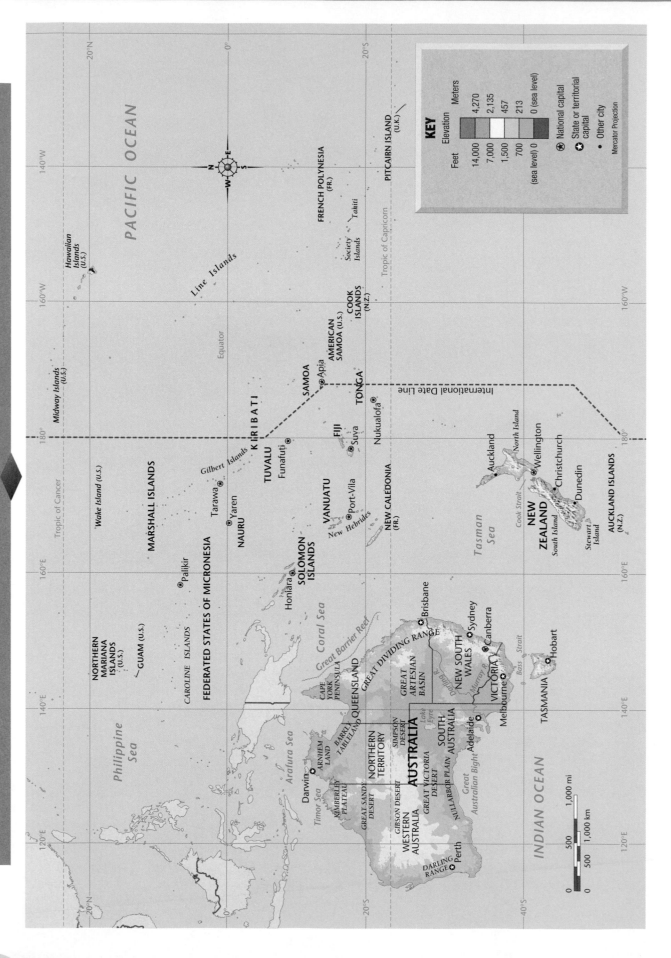

KEY

Feet	Elevation	Meters
14,000		4,270
7,000		2,135
1,500		457
700		213
(sea level) 0		0 (sea level)

⊛ National capital
✪ State or territorial capital
• Other city

Mercator Projection

PACIFIC OCEAN

PITCAIRN ISLAND (U.K.)

FRENCH POLYNESIA (FR.)

Tahiti

Society Islands

Tropic of Capricorn

Hawaiian Islands (U.S.)

Line Islands

Equator

Midway Islands (U.S.)

COOK ISLANDS (N.Z.)

AMERICAN SAMOA (U.S.)

SAMOA
⊛ Apia

TONGA
⊛ Nukualofa

International Date Line

Wake Island (U.S.)

KIRIBATI

MARSHALL ISLANDS

Tarawa

Gilbert Islands

TUVALU
⊛ Funafuti

FIJI
• Suva

VANUATU
• Port-Vila

NEW CALEDONIA (FR.)

New Hebrides

Tropic of Cancer

Yaren
⊛ NAURU

NORTHERN MARIANA ISLANDS (U.S.)

GUAM (U.S.)

CAROLINE ISLANDS

FEDERATED STATES OF MICRONESIA
⊛ Palikir

SOLOMON ISLANDS
⊛ Honiara

Coral Sea

Philippine Sea

Auckland

North Island

Wellington ⊛
• Christchurch
• Dunedin

NEW ZEALAND
South Island

Stewart Island

Cook Strait

AUCKLAND ISLANDS (N.Z.)

Tasman Sea

Great Barrier Reef

Brisbane
• Sydney
⊛ Canberra
NEW SOUTH WALES

CAPE YORK PENINSULA

GREAT DIVIDING RANGE

QUEENSLAND

GREAT ARTESIAN BASIN

VICTORIA ✪
Melbourne ✪

Bass Strait

TASMANIA
✪ Hobart

Arafura Sea

Darwin ✪

Timor Sea

ARNHEM LAND

BARKLY TABLELAND

NORTHERN TERRITORY

SIMPSON DESERT

Lake Eyre

AUSTRALIA

SOUTH AUSTRALIA
✪ Adelaide

Murray R.

Darling R.

KIMBERLEY PLATEAU

GREAT SANDY DESERT

GIBSON DESERT

WESTERN AUSTRALIA

GREAT VICTORIA DESERT

NULLARBOR PLAIN

Great Australian Bight

DARLING RANGE
• Perth

INDIAN OCEAN

0 500 1,000 mi
0 500 1,000 km

20°N
0°
20°S
40°S

120°E 140°E 160°E 180° 160°W 140°W

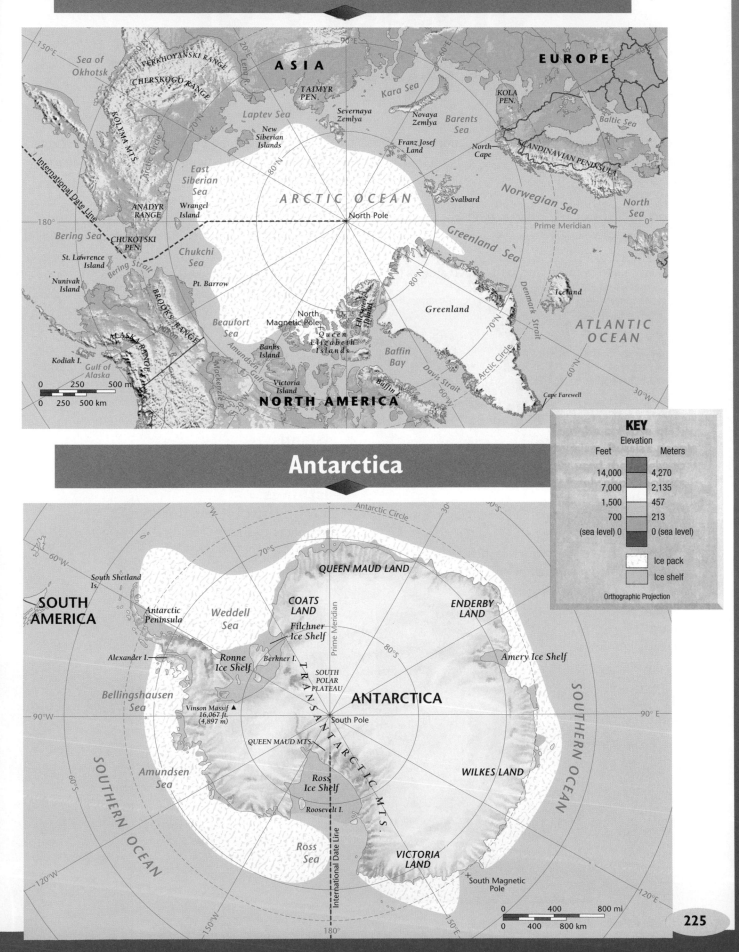

The Arctic

Asia / Europe / North America (Arctic map)

Sea of Okhotsk
VERKHOYANSKI RANGE
CHERSKOGO RANGE
KOLYMA MTS.
Arctic Circle
ANADYR RANGE
International Date Line
180°
Bering Sea
CHUKOTSKI PEN.
St. Lawrence Island
Nunivak Island
Kodiak I.
Gulf of Alaska
BROOKS RANGE
ALASKA RANGE
Yukon R.

ASIA
TAIMYR PEN.
Laptev Sea
Severnaya Zemlya
New Siberian Islands
East Siberian Sea
Wrangel Island
Chukchi Sea
Pt. Barrow
Beaufort Sea
North Magnetic Pole
Banks Island
Amundsen Gulf
Mackenzie R.
Victoria Island
Kara Sea
Novaya Zemlya
Franz Josef Land
North Cape
KOLA PEN.
Barents Sea
Svalbard
SCANDINAVIAN PENINSULA
Baltic Sea
Norwegian Sea
North Sea

ARCTIC OCEAN
North Pole
80°N
Prime Meridian
Greenland Sea
80°N
Greenland
70°N
Denmark Strait
Iceland
ATLANTIC OCEAN
60°N
Davis Strait
Arctic Circle
Cape Farewell
30°W

EUROPE

Queen Elizabeth Islands
Ellesmere Island
Baffin Bay
Baffin I.
Victoria Island
NORTH AMERICA

150°E
20°E
Lena R.
90°E
30°E
70°N
60°N

0   250   500 mi
0   250   500 km

Antarctica

SOUTH AMERICA
South Shetland Is.
Antarctic Peninsula
Alexander I.
Bellingshausen Sea
SOUTHERN OCEAN
Amundsen Sea
Ross Sea

Antarctic Circle
QUEEN MAUD LAND
COATS LAND
Filchner Ice Shelf
Weddell Sea
Ronne Ice Shelf
Berkner I.
SOUTH POLAR PLATEAU
Vinson Massif ▲ 16,067 ft. (4,897 m)
TRANSANTARCTIC MTS.
QUEEN MAUD MTS.
Ross Ice Shelf
Roosevelt I.
ANTARCTICA
South Pole
ENDERBY LAND
Amery Ice Shelf
SOUTHERN OCEAN
WILKES LAND
VICTORIA LAND
South Magnetic Pole

Prime Meridian
60°W
70°S
80°S
90°W
90°E
60°S
International Date Line
150°W
180°
150°E
120°W
30°W
30°E
120°E

0   400   800 mi
0   400   800 km

KEY

Elevation

Feet		Meters
14,000		4,270
7,000		2,135
1,500		457
700		213
(sea level) 0		0 (sea level)

Ice pack
Ice shelf

Orthographic Projection

225

Glossary of Geographic Terms

basin
a depression in the surface of the land; some basins are filled with water

bay
a part of a sea or lake that extends into the land

butte
a small raised area of land with steep sides

▲ butte

canyon
a deep, narrow valley with steep sides; often has a stream flowing through it

cataract
a large waterfall; any strong flood or rush of water

◀ cataract

delta
a triangular-shaped plain at the mouth of a river, formed when sediment is deposited by flowing water

flood plain
a broad plain on either side of a river, formed when sediment settles on the riverbanks

glacier
a huge, slow-moving mass of snow and ice

hill
an area that rises above surrounding land and has a rounded top; lower and usually less steep than a mountain

island
an area of land completely surrounded by water

isthmus
a narrow strip of land that connects two larger areas of land

mesa
a high, flat-topped landform with cliff-like sides; larger than a butte

mountain
an area that rises steeply at least 2,000 feet (610 m) above surrounding land; usually wide at the bottom and rising to a narrow peak or ridge

▶ glacier

◀ delta

mountain pass
a gap between mountains

peninsula
an area of land almost completely surrounded by water and connected to the mainland by an isthmus

plain
a large area of flat or gently rolling land

plateau
a large, flat area that rises above the surrounding land; at least one side has a steep slope

river mouth
the point where a river enters a lake or sea

strait
a narrow stretch of water that connects two larger bodies of water

tributary
a river or stream that flows into a larger river

volcano
an opening in the Earth's surface through which molten rock, ashes, and gasses from the Earth's interior escape

▶ volcano

Gazetteer

A

Aix-en-Provence (43.32°N, 5.27°E) a city in southern France, p. 104

Alpine Mountain System a range of mountains extending through south central Europe; a popular vacation and ski area, includes Mont Blanc, p. 11

Alps (46.18°N, 8.42°E) the major south-central European mountain system; the range includes Mont Blanc and the Matterhorn, p. 13

Asia (50°N, 100°E) the world's largest continent, surrounded by the Arctic Ocean, the Pacific Ocean, the Indian Ocean, and Europe, p. 10

Athens (38°N, 23.38°E) the capital city of modern Greece; the world's most powerful cultural center in the 400s B.C., p. 33

B

Barcelona (41.25°N, 2.08°E) a city and seaport in northeastern Spain, p. 16

Belgrade (44.48°N, 20.32°E) the capital city of Yugoslavia, p. 148

Berlin (51.31°N, 13.28°E) the capital city of Germany; divided into East Berlin and West Berlin between 1949 and 1989, p. 74

Buckingham Palace (51.3°N, .08°W) the palace in London, England, where the British king or queen resides, p. 100

C

Caspian Sea (40°N, 52°E) a salt lake that is below sea level, located between Europe and Asia, p. 14

Central Uplands an area of mountains and plateaus in the center of southern Europe; region of pastureland and mining, p. 11

Chernobyl (51.17°N, 30.14°E) the city in northern Ukraine where a nuclear power station accident occurred in 1986, p. 158

Czech Republic (50°N, 15°E) a country in Eastern Europe, p. 84

E

Eurasia the landmass that includes the European and Asian continents, p. 10

Europe (50°N, 15°E) the world's second-smallest continent; a peninsula of the Eurasian landmass bounded by the Arctic Ocean, the Atlantic Ocean, the Mediterranean Sea, and Asia, p. 10

I

Irkutsk (52.16°N, 104°E) a city in east-central Russia, on the Central Siberian Plateau, p. 16

K

Kemerovo (55.31°N, 86.05°E) a city in south-central Russia, p. 162

Kharkov (49.33°N, 35.55°E) a province in eastern Ukraine, p. 160

Kiev (50.27°N, 30.3°E) the capital city of Ukraine, p. 154

L

Locorotondo (40.45°N, 17.20°E) a city in the "heel" of southern Italy, p. 125

London (51.3°N, .07°W) the capital city of the United Kingdom, p. 74

M

Madrid (40.26°N, 3.42°W) the capital city of Spain, p. 74

Mediterranean Sea (36.22°N, 13.25°E) the large sea that separates Europe and Africa, p. 16

Milan (45.29°N, 9.12°E) a city in northwestern Italy, p. 124

Moscow (55.45°N, 37.37°E) the capital city of modern Russia; the home of the czars, p. 161

N

North European Plain a plain extending from the European part of Russia all the way to France, p. 11

North Sea (56.09°N, 3.16°E) an arm of the Atlantic Ocean between Great Britain and the European mainland, p. 24

Northwestern Highlands a mountainous timberland in the far north of Europe, p. 11

P

Paris (48.51°N, 2.2°E) the capital city of France, p. 74

R

Rhine River (50.34°N, 7.21°E) a river flowing from Switzerland north through Germany, then west through the Netherlands, and into the North Sea in Holland, p. 14

Rome (41.52°N, 12.37°E) the capital of modern Italy; one of the world's greatest ancient empires (753 B.C.–A.D. 476), p. 36

Ruhr (51.18°N, 8.17°E) a river along the major industrial region in western Germany, p. 26

Russia (61°N, 60°E) a country in northern Eurasia, p. 10

S

St. Petersburg (59.57°N, 30.2°E) the second-largest city in Russia (previous names: Petrograd, Leningrad), located on the Baltic Sea; founded by Peter the Great, p. 91

Sarajevo (43.5°N, 18.26°E) the capital city of Bosnia-Herzegovina, p. 146

Siberia (57°N, 97°E) a resource-rich region of Russia, extending east across northern Asia from the Ural Mountains to the Pacific Coast, p. 13

Silesia (50.58°N, 16.53°E) a historic region located in today's southwestern Poland, p. 27

Slovakia (48.5°N, 20°E) a country in Eastern Europe, p. 83

U

Ural Mountains (56.28°N, 58.13°E) a mountain system in northern Eurasia forming part of the border between Europe and Asia, p. 10

V

Vatican (41.54°N, 12.22°E) an independent state situated in Rome; the seat of the Roman Catholic Church and residence of the pope, p. 121

Volga River (47.30°N, 46.20°E) the longest river in Europe, flowing from Russia through Europe to the Caspian Sea, p. 14

Y

Yugoslavia an eastern European nation which broke up in 1991; the official name of Serbia and Montenegro; the former Yugoslavia is now the nations of Yugoslavia, Bosnia-Herzegovina, Croatia, Slovenia, and Macedonia, p. 87

Glossary

This glossary lists key terms and other useful terms from the book.

A

absolute monarch a ruler who has complete power over his or her subjects, for example, Louis XIV of France, p. 43

alliance a mutual agreement between countries to protect and defend each other, p. 52

B

benefit a free service or payment, p. 115

C

ceremony a formal, set activity usually carried out by a group of people, p. 100

chernozem a rich, black soil found in Ukraine, p. 156

city-state a city that is also an independent nation; many existed in ancient Greece, p. 34

civil war a war between groups within a country, p. 62

civilian a person who is not serving in the armed forces, p. 52

cobblestone a round stone used with others to make streets before modern paving was invented, p. 74

Cold War a time of tension between the United States and the former Soviet Union without actual war; it lasted from about 1945 to 1991, p. 63

collective a huge government-owned farm, p. 156

colony a territory ruled by another nation, p. 43

Colosseum a stadium built in Rome about A.D. 80, p. 32

communism a theory of government in which property such as farms and factories is owned by the government for the benefit of all citizens; a political system in which the central government controls all aspects of citizens' lives, p. 61

constitutional monarchy a government in which a king or queen is the head of state but has limited powers, for example, the present government of Great Britain, p. 100

consumer goods the goods that ordinary people buy, such as food, clothing, and cars, p. 64

culture language, religious beliefs, values, customs, and other ways of life shared by a group of people, p. 77

custom usual way of doing something, p. 84

czar title of Russian emperors before the formation of the Soviet Union, p. 56

D

debate argument; discussion with people arguing opposite sides of a question, p. 110

democracy a type of government in which people rule themselves through elected representatives, p. 34

dialect a version of a language found only in a certain region, p. 83

dictator a leader who has absolute power, for example, Josef Stalin in Russia, p. 62

E

economic sanctions actions to limit trade with nations that have violated international laws, p. 151

elegant graceful and beautiful, p. 91

emigrate to move away, or to leave one country to resettle in another, p. 110

empire a large collection of people and lands ruled by a single government, p. 35

ethnic group a group of people who share the same ancestors, culture, language, or religion, p. 83

F

fate final outcome; what happens, p. 86

feudalism a kind of society in which people worked and sometimes fought for a local lord in return for protection and the use of land, p. 38

fossil fuel fuel developed from the remains of ancient plants and animals; includes coal, oil, and natural gas, p. 26

free enterprise an economic system in which individuals can start and run their own businesses, p. 140

G

goods things and products that people can buy and sell, p. 49

H

heritage the customs and practices passed from one generation to the next, p. 88

Holocaust the execution of 6 million Jews by German Nazis during World War II, p. 129

humanism an approach to knowledge that focused on worldly rather than religious values, p. 41

hydroelectric power the power generated by water-driven turbines, p. 25

I

identity a sense of belonging to a certain group or place, p. 126

immigrant a person who moves from one country to another, p. 76

imperialism the control by one country of the political and economic life of another country or region, p. 50

Industrial Revolution a period in European history during the early 1800s when products once made by hand in homes began to be made by machines in factories, p. 48

intricate fancy; complicated; detailed, p. 90

investor a person who spends money on improving a business in hopes of making more money, p. 164

L

loess a type of rich, dustlike soil found on the North European Plain, p. 25

M

manor a piece of land owned by a lord in the feudal system, p. 38

manufacturing the process of turning raw materials into finished products, p. 124

Middle Ages the period in European history between ancient and modern times; approximately A.D. 500–1500, p. 34

middle class a group of people that included traders, merchants, and others who were economically between the poor and the very rich, p. 42

migration a movement from place to place, p. 82

monarch the ruler of a kingdom or empire, such as a king or queen, p. 42

multicultural influenced by many cultures, p. 77

N

NATO (North Atlantic Treaty Organization) an alliance between the United States, Canada, and other western nations; founded in 1949 to protect the interests of the member nations and to promote international cooperation, p. 87

national debt the amount of money a government owes, p. 118

nationalism pride in one's country; an elevation of one's own nation above others, p. 51

navigable wide enough and deep enough for ships to travel through, p. 15

P

Parliament a group of elected officials in Great Britain who help govern by deciding about taxes and other laws, p. 99

Pax Romana Roman peace; a 200-year period of peace that began when Augustus, the first emperor of Rome, took power in 27 B.C., p. 36

peninsula land area nearly surrounded by water, p. 11

permafrost soil that is permanently frozen, p. 21

plateau a large, raised area of mostly level land, p. 12

polder a new piece of land reclaimed from the sea; in the Netherlands, land created by building dikes and draining water, p. 9

policy one of the methods and plans a government uses to do its work, p. 34

population density the average number of people living in an area, p. 10

prairie an area of grassland, p. 20

propaganda the spread of ideas designed to promote a specific cause, p. 90

province a political division within a country, similar to a state in the United States, p. 149

R

rain shadow an area on the sheltered side of a mountain that receives little rainfall, p. 18

Renaissance a period of European history that included a rebirth of interest in learning and art, peaking in the 1500s, p. 41

representative a person who represents, or stands for, a group of people, usually in government, p. 99

repress to put down, keep from acting, p. 89

reserves the available supplies of something, such as oil or coal, p. 28

reunification the process of becoming unified again, p. 132

revolution a complete change in government, often achieved through violent means, p. 43

revolutionary relating to or causing the overthrow of a government or other great change, p. 60

S

Scandinavia a historical term for a region of northern Europe that includes Norway, Sweden, and Denmark, p. 136

Scientific Revolution a movement that took place during the 1600s and 1700s, when scientists began to base their study of the world on observable facts rather than on beliefs, p. 44

security safety; freedom from needing or wanting something important, p. 116

serf a person who lived on and farmed a lord's land in feudal times; he or she did not own land and depended on the lord for protection, p. 38

shrine a holy place, p. 142

Slavs a major ethnic group in Eastern Europe whose members share a similar cultural background though not the same religion; there are several subgroups of Slavs, each with their own language, p. 83

steppe a mostly treeless plain; in Russia the steppes are grasslands of fertile soil suitable for farming, p. 21

T

taiga an enormous Russian forest, covering more than three million acres, p. 21

tariff a fee or tax that a government charges for goods entering the country, p. 79

textile a cloth product, p. 49

tradition a practice or way of doing something passed from one generation to the next, p. 99

tributary a river or stream that flows into a larger river, p. 14

tundra a treeless plain in arctic areas with permanently frozen ground; during the brief season when the topsoil thaws, grasses and mosses grow, p. 21

U

unified brought together as one; united, p. 43

unique one of a kind; having no equal, p. 110

United Nations an organization of countries established in 1945 that works for peace and cooperation around the world, p. 151

urbanization the movement of populations toward cities and the resulting city growth, p. 76

W

welfare government help to people in need, p. 117

welfare state a country in which many services are paid for by the government, p. 115

westernization the adoption of Western culture, as is taking place in Russia and many Eastern European countries, p. 55

Index

The *italicized* page numbers refer to illustrations. The *m, c,* or *p* preceding the number refers to maps (*m*), charts, tables and graphs (*c*), or pictures (*p*).

in Sweden, 118–119
See also communism, democracy
Grabarka, 142
grasslands, of Europe, 20, *m 20*
Great Britain, 97–103, *m 98,* 197
Chunnel and, *p 53*
Country Profile of, *m 98, c 98*
empire building in, 101–102
government of, 43–44, 99, *p 99*
imperialism in, 51
Industrial Revolution in, 49–50
monarchy and, 99–100
natural resources of, 26, 101, *p 102*
resources and the economy, *m 98, c 98*
trains in, 73
in World War I, 52
in World War II, 52, 101
See also United Kingdom
"Great Charter." *See* Magna Carta
Great Plains, of the United States, 21
Greece, 174, 202
Boston Marathon and, 33
major accomplishments of, 34–35, *c 34*
Gulf of Mexico, 17, *m 18*
Gulf Stream, 17, *m 18*

H

Hall of Mirrors, *p 43*
Hammerfest, Norway, 136, 137
Hargreaves, James, *c 50*
Havel, Vaclav, 85–86
health care, Swedish system of, 118
hemispheres, 182
heritage, defined, 88, 231
Hermitage, *p 92*
highlands
Northwestern, 11, 12, *m 12*
Scottish, *p 10*
hill, 226
history, *c 34*
Hitler, Adolf, 128–129
Holocaust, 129, 231
Holy See. *See also* Vatican City

House of Commons, 99, *p 99*
Huang He Valley, 25
Hudson Bay (Canada), 10
humanism, 41, 231
Hungary, 154, 206
ethnic groups of, 84
standard of living in, *c 143*
hydroelectric power, 25, *m 25, m 28, m 155,* 221
Hylten-Cavallius, Olof, 114

I

Iceland, 197
Loki Volcano, 19
identity, 231
illustrations, interpretation of, 46–47
immigrants, 231
in Western Europe, 76–77
immigration, to France, 110–111, *p 110*
imperialism, 50, *m 50–51,* 231
Age of, 51
Indian Ocean, *m 3,* 76
industrialization. *See* Industrial Revolution
Industrial Revolution, 45, 48, 75, 76, 231
changes in production during, 49
governmental changes during, 50–52
inventions of, *p 50, c 50*
population of London during, 49
population of Paris during, 49
societal changes during, 49
intricate, 90, 231
investment, 231
in Moscow, 164–165
Ireland, *m 98,* 101, 197
Irkutsk, Siberia, 16, *g 17,* 19, *p 65,* 228
iron, *m 25, m 155*
Iron Curtain, 64
iron ore, 28, *m 28*
Islam, *p 110,* 147, 148, 150
island, 226

isthmus, 226
Italy, 121–126, 203
Country Profile of, *m 122, c 123*
imperialism in, 51
land use and the economy, *m 122, c 122*
manufacturing in, 124
nationalism and, 52
population of, *c 122*
religion in, *c 122,* 123
the Vatican and, 121
in World War II, 52
Ivan I, 56
Ivan III, 56
Ivan IV, 56–57
Ivan the Moneybag. *See* Ivan I
Ivan the Terrible. *See* Ivan IV

J

Japan, 52, 58
Jesus, 38, 125
John Paul II, Pope, *p 123, 142*

K

Kandinsky, Vasily, 90
Kay, John, *c 50*
Kazan, Russia, *p 58*
Kemerovo, Siberia, 162, 228
Kennedy, John F., *p 130*
Khan, Kublai, 40
Kharkov, Ukraine, 160, 228
Khrushchev, Nikita, *p 130*
Kiev, Muscovy, 55, 230
Kiev, Ukraine, 159, 160
knights, *c 39*
Korea, 58
Kosovo, 87
Kostunica, Vojislav *p 151*
Krichevskaya, Inessa, 161

L

labor force, *c 76*
Lake Baikal, *p 14*

Munich, Germany, *p 75*
Muscovy, 55, 56
Museum of Folk Architecture (Ukraine), *p 160*
music, *p 125*
Muslims, 89, 147
Bosnian, 150

N

Naples, Italy, 126
national alliances, 52
national debt, 232
of Sweden, 118
nationalism, 232
creative, 53
destructive, 51–52
Italian, 123
NATO. *See* North Atlantic Treaty Organization
natural gas, *m 25, 28, m 28, p 102, m 155*
natural resources
of Eastern Europe, 27
of Russia, 27–29, *m 28*
of Siberia, 162, *c 162, p 163*
of Ukraine, *m 155*
of Western Europe, 24–26
navigation, 15, 224
Nentsy, *p 89*
Netherlands, the, 9, *p 9,* 152, 201
labor force in, *c 76*
population density of, 10
service industries and, *c 76*
size and location of, 10
trade and, 42
Neva River, 91, 92
Nicholas II, 58–59, *p 59, p 91*
nickel, *m 28*
Non–Indo-European languages, *m 83*
Nordic, 234
North Africa, 76
North African immigrants, in France, *p 110*
North America, *m 184–185, m 216, m 217*
North Atlantic Current, 17, 18, *m 18,* 19

North Atlantic Treaty Organization (NATO), 87, 151, 232
North China Plain, 25
Northern Europe, *m 196*
Northern Hemisphere, 136
Northern Ireland, *m 98, c 98,* 101
Northern League, 126, *p 126*
North European Plain, 12, *m 12,* 25, 82, 229
North Pole, 117, 136–137
North Sea, 9, 24, *p 24,* 102, 229
natural gas deposits in, *p 102*
Northwestern Highlands, *p 10,* 11, *m 12*
population density of, 12
Norway, 17, 26, 174, 197
labor force in, *c 76*
natural resources in, 26
service industries and, *c 76*
Notre Dame Cathedral, *p 38*
nuclear accident. *See* Chernobyl
nuclear power, 158–159
nuclear waste, in Siberian rivers, 29. *See also* Chernobyl
nuclear weapons, 64

O

oceans
Arctic, *m 3,* 11, 14, 15
Atlantic, *m 3,* 11, 17
effect of, on climate, 17–18
Indian, *m 3,* 76
Pacific, *m 3*
Odessa, Ukraine, *p 157*
oil, 24, *c 26,* 29
oil rigs, in the North Sea, 24, *p 24*
Oktoberfest, *p 75*
Olkhovski, Vlad, 166
Olympic Games, 175
Opera House (Paris, France), *p 109*
Orlov, Aleksei, 54
Oslobodjenje, 148
Ottoman Turks, 148

P

Pacific Ocean, *m 3*
Padania, *p 126*
Paine, Thomas, 43
Paley, Grace, 63
Parc Astérix, 111
Paris, France, *p 38,* 49, 74, *p 110,* 229
Opera House in, *p 109*
parliament, British, 43, 99, *p 99,* 232
Pax Romana, 36, *p 36,* 37, 232
pelmeny, 16
peninsula, 11, *p 11,* 227, 232
"peninsula of peninsulas"
See Western Europe
permafrost, 21, *m 28,* 232
Peter the Great, 57–58
petroleum, *p 24, m 25, m 28, m 155*
Pheidippides, 33
phosphates, *m 25, m 28*
Picabia, Jeannine, 52
Pius, Antoninus, *p 36*
plain, 227
plankton, 26, *m 26*
plateaus, 12, 227, 232
Plato, *c 34*
Pobrezova, Slovakia, *p 27*
Podolak, Janusz, 139, 144
Poland, 27, 82, 138–145, 154
capitalism in, 140
collapse of communism in, 139, 141, 153
Country Profile of, *m 140, c 140*
economy of, 143–144, *c 143*
farming in, *m 140, c 140,* 141
land use and the economy, *m 140, c 140*
language of, 142–143
natural resources of, 27
Regional Database, 207
Roman Catholicism in, 141–142
Solidarity movement in, *p 141*
standard of living in, *c 143*
polders, 9, *p 9, m 12,* 232
policy, 232

vegetation of, 20–21, *m 21*
and World War I, 52, 61
and World War II, 52
See also Soviet Union
Russian Orthodox Church, 88, 89, 147, *c 162*

S

Sahlin, Mona, 117
St. Edward's crown, *p 97*
St. Petersburg, Russia, 13, 91, 92, 229
See also Winter Palace
Saint Peter's Church, *p 121*
Sakharov, Andrei, 64
sales tax, in Sweden, 116
Sami people, in Sweden, 115
San Marino, 203
Sarajevo, Bosnia-Herzegovina, 146, *p 146*, 150, *p 150*, 172–173, 229
Scandinavia, 136, 232
Schumann, Conrad, 127, *p 127*, 130, 131
science, *c 34*
scientific method, 44, *c 45*
Scientific Revolution, 43–45, 232
Scotland, *p 1*, *p 10*, *m 98*, *c 98*, 101
Scottish Highlands, *p 10*
security, 232
Senegal, 110
Serbia, 87, 149
Serbo-Croatian language, 147
serfs, 38–39, *c 39*, 68–71, 233
Russian, 62
service industries, *c 76*
Sheffield, England, *p 48*
shipping industry, in Ukraine, 157
shrine, 233
Siberia, 13, *p 13*, 229
air pollution in, 29
exile of Andrei Sakharov to, 64
families in, *p 89*
farming in, *p 13*
industry in, 162, *p 163*
modern-day, 162–164
natural resources of, 28–29,

162, *c 162*, *p 163*
prison camps in, 62
skiing, *p 16*
Trans-Siberian Railroad and, 162, 170–171, *m 171*
Silesia, 27, 229
silver, *m 28*, 42
Sistine Chapel, 122
skiing, in Siberia, *p 16*
Slavic cultures, 83–84, 89
Slavs, 83, 146–147, 233
Slovakia, 83, 154, 175, 207, 229
iron ore and, *p 27*
Slovenes, 146
Slovenia, 84, 87, 150, 207
Social Democrats, in Sweden, 116, 117
socialist realism, *p 90*
Social Studies Skills Activities
interpreting diagrams and illustrations, 46–47
recognizing cause and effect, 152–153
summarizing information, 80–81
using regional maps, 22–23
using the writing process, 112–113
soil, 25
Solidarity movement, *p 141*
South America, *m 184–185*, *m 210–211*, *m 212–213*, *m 216*, *m 217*
South Asia, 76
South Pole, 117, 136–137
Southern Europe, *m 202*
Soviet Union
blockade of West Berlin by, *m 129*
Cold War and, 63–64
collapse of, 64–65, 88, 90
Czechoslovakia and, 85
German invasion of, during World War II, 63, *p 63*
public education in, 92–93
religion in, 88–89, *p 88*
See also Russia, Union of Soviet Socialist Republics
Spain, 203
imperialism in, 51

labor force in, *c 76*
natural resources of, 26
trade and, 42
spices, importance to trade of, 42
spinning mule, *p 49*
spinning wheel, *p 49*
Stalin, Josef, 62–63, 149
Stalingrad, Russia, *p 63*
steam engine, Industrial Revolution and, *c 50*
steelworks, in Podbrezova, Slovakia, *p 27*
steppes, 21, 233
Stockholm, Sweden, *p 119*
strait, 227
superpowers, 63
Sweden, 26, 114–120
business in, 118–119, *p 118*
Country Profile of, *m 115*, *c 115*
emigration from, in the 1800s, 116
government of, 116–117
health care system in, 118
history of, 116–117
national debt in, 118
natural resources in, 119, *p 119*
people and the environment, *m 115*, *c 115*
population of, *c 115*
Regional Database, 197
social problems in, 118–119
as welfare state, 114–120
Swiss Alps, *p 11*, 13
Switzerland, 14, 26
Syracuse, Italy, 126

T

taiga forest, 21, 233
Tang, Yang-Mee, 76–77
tarantella, *p 125*
tariffs, 79, 233
taxes, in Sweden, 116–118
Tchaikovsky, Peter, 90
textiles, 49, 233
Thourslund, Mats, 120

Acknowledgments

Cover Design
Bruce Bond, Suzanne Schineller, and Olena Serbyn

Cover Photo
Jon Chomitz

Maps
MapQuest.com, Inc.
Map information sources: Columbia Encyclopedia, Encyclopaedia Britannica, Microsoft® Encarta®, National Geographic Atlas of the World, Rand McNally Commercial Atlas, The Times Atlas of the World.

Staff Credits
The people who made up the *World Explorer* team—representing editorial, editorial services, design services, on-line services/multimedia development, product marketing, production services, project office, and publishing processes—are listed below. Bold type denotes core team members.

Joyce Barisano, Margaret Broucek, Ed DeLeon, **Paul Gagnon, Mary Hanisco, Dotti Marshall,** Kirsten Reichert, Susan Swan, and Carol Signorino.

Additional Credits
Art and Design: Emily Soltanoff. Editorial: Debra Reardon, Nancy Rogier. Market Research: Marilyn Leitao. Publishing Processes: Wendy Bohannan.

Program Development and Production
Editorial and Project Management: Summer Street Press
Production: Pronk&Associates

Text
68, From *Pearl in the Egg* by Dorothy Van Woerkom. Copyright © 1980 by Dorothy Van Woerkom. Reprinted by permission of HarperCollins Publishers. **161, 166,** Excerpt from "New Face of Russia a Year After Coup, Ordinary Citizens Adapt to Change," by Howard Witt, *Chicago Tribune*, August 16, 1992. Copyrighted, Chicago Tribune Company. All rights reserved. Used with permission. **172,** From *Zlata's Diary* by Zlata Filipović, Translation copyright © 1994 Editions Robert Laffont/Fixot. Used by permission of Viking Penguin, a division of Penguin Books USA Inc.

Photo Research
Feldman & Associates, Inc.

Photos
iv bottom left, © SuperStock International, **iv–v bottom center,** Michael Rosenfeld/Tony Stone Images, **iv center left,** © Steve Vidler/Tony Stone Images, **v top left,** © John Drysdale/Woodfin Camp & Associates, **v top right,** © Chad Ehlers/Tony Stone Images, **v bottom right,** © Corbis-Bettmann, **1 top left,** ©Robert Wallis/Sipa Press, **1 top right,** © Superstock International, **1 center,** © Superstock International, **1 center left,** © Superstock International, **1 center right,** © George Steinmetz, **1 background,** Artbase Inc., **5 center,** © Mark Thayer, Boston, **8 center right,** © Julian Calder/Tony Stone Images, **9 bottom right,** © B. & C. Alexander/Bryan & Cherry Alexander Photography, **10 bottom left,** © M. Feeney/Trip Photographic, **11 bottom,** © W. Jacobs/Trip Photographic, **13 top right,** © James Balog/Tony Stone Images, **14 center right,** © Robert Wallis/Sipa Press, **15 top left,** © Adam Woolfitt/Woodfin Camp & Associates, **16 bottom left,** © D. MacDonald/Trip Photographic, **19 bottom left,** My Family in Winter, by Helin Tikerpuu, age 12, Estonia. Courtesy of the International Children's Art Museum, **24 bottom left,** ©

Arnulf Husmo/Tony Stone Images, **27 center right,** © Eastcott/Momatiuk/Woodfin Camp & Associates, **29 top left,** © Wolfgang Kaehler/Wolfgang Kaehler Photography, **29 top right,** © Wolfgang Kaehler/Wolfgang Kaehler Photography, **32 center right,** © N. Ray/Trip Photographic, **33 bottom right,** © Matthew Stockman/AllSport USA, **35 top right,** © SuperStock International, **36 top right,** © Scala/Art Resource, **37 center,** © Erich Lessing/Art Resource, **38 bottom left,** © Marie Ueda/Tony Stone Images, **40 bottom left,** © The Granger Collection, **41 top right,** © Biblioteca Reale, Turin, Italy/SuperStock International, **41 top left,** © Erich Lessing/Art Resource, **42 bottom right,** The Granger Collection, **42 bottom left,** The Granger Collection, **43 top right,** © SuperStock International, **44 center left,** © Explorer, Paris/SuperStock International, **44 top right,** © SuperStock International, **46 bottom,** © Michael Newman/PhotoEdit, **48 bottom left,** © North Wind Picture Archives, **49 top left,** © The Granger Collection, **49 top center,** © The Bettmann Archive/Corbis-Bettmann, **50 top right,** © The Bettmann Archive/Corbis-Bettmann, **50 top left,** © Stock Montage, **52 bottom,** © The Granger Collection, **53 top left,** © AP/Wide World Photos, **54 bottom left,** © Historical Museum, Moscow, Russia/SuperStock International, **55 bottom right,** © Bridgeman/Art Resource, **57 bottom left,** © Charles Lenars/CORBIS/MAGMA, **58 bottom right,** © Stock Montage, **59 top left,** © SuperStock International, **60 bottom left,** © Novosti/Corbis-Bettmann, **61 top center,** © SuperStock International, **62 bottom left,** © The Granger Collection, **63 top center,** © UPI/Corbis-Bettmann, **64 bottom,** © Reuters/Corbis-Bettmann, **65 top left,** © SuperStock International, **69 bottom right,** © Giraudon/Art Resource, **70 top right,** © Erich Lessing/Art Resource, **72 center right,** © SuperStock International, **73 bottom right,** © David Barnes/Stock Market, **74 bottom,** © Stephen Johnson/Tony Stone Images, **74 center left,** © SuperStock International, **75 top right,** © SuperStock International, **77 bottom left,** © Joseph Okwesa/Trip Photographic, **78 center right,** © UPI/Corbis-Bettmann, **79 top left,** © Michael Rosenfeld/Tony Stone Images, **81 top left,** © Michael Newman/PhotoEdit, **82 bottom left,** © North Wind Picture Archives, **84 top right,** © Alain Le Garsmeur/Tony Stone Images, **84 top left,** © Ibrahim/Trip Photographic, **85 bottom left,** Prague Castle, by Darina Vassova, age 10, Czech Republic. Courtesy of the International Children's Art Museum, **87 top left,** © AP/Wide World Photos, **88 bottom left,** © SuperStock International, **89 bottom right,** SuperStock International, **89 bottom left,** © A. Kuznetsov/Trip Photographic, **90 top right,** © Alexandra Avakian/Woodfin Camp & Associates, **91 center left,** © Joseph Coscia, Jr., Metropolitan Museum of Art, The FORBES Magazine Collection, New York. All rights reserved/Forbes, **92 bottom,** © Wolfgang Kaehler/Wolfgang Kaehler Photography, **92 center left,** © J. Wiseman/Trip Photographic, **93 top right,** © Sichuv/Sipa Press, **97 bottom center,** © John Drysdale/Woodfin Camp & Associates, **99 bottom left,** © AP/Wide World Photos, **99 bottom right,** © The Bettmann Archive/Corbis-Bettmann, **100 top right,** © SuperStock International, **100 center left,** © Stuart Westmorland/Tony Stone Images, **102 bottom right,** © John Madere/Stock Market, **104 bottom left,** © Chad Ehlers/Tony Stone Images, **105 bottom left,** © Miles Ertman/Masterfile, **106 bottom right,** © SuperStock International, **108 bottom right,** © Corbis-Bettmann, **109 top left,** © George Hunter/Tony Stone Images, **109 center right,** © Chad Ehlers/Tony Stone Images, **110 bottom right,** © AP/Wide World Photos, **110 bottom left,** © SuperStock International, **111 top right,** © A. M. Bazalik/Trip Photographic, **112 bottom,** © Michael Newman/PhotoEdit, **114 bottom left,** © Joseph Nettis/Tony Stone Images, **115 center left,** © Trip/C. Gibson, **116 top right,** © Gary A. Conner, **117 bottom,** © SuperStock International, **118 top right,** © Raymond Reuter/Sygma, **119 bottom left,** © Chad Ehlers/Tony Stone Images, **119 bottom right,** © Lorentz Gullachsen/Tony Stone Images, **120 top right,** © J. Merryweather/Trip Photographic, **121 bottom right,** © Jean Pragen/Tony Stone Images, **122 center left,** © John Heseltine/Dorling Kindersley, **123 bottom left,** © Mary Altier/Mary Altier Photography, **124 bottom left,** © George Steinmetz, **124 bottom right,** © The Granger Collection, **125 top center,** © SuperStock International, **126 top center,** © Archive Photos, **127 bottom right,** © AP/Wide World Photos, **128 center left,** © Helga Lade/Peter Arnold, **130 bottom right,** © AP/Wide World Photos, **130 bottom left,** © UPI/Corbis-Bettmann, **131 top left,** © AP/Wide World Photos, **132 top left,** © SuperStock International, **132 top right,** © Corbis-Bettmann, **133 top,** © Owen Franken/Corbis, **136 center right,** © Michael Newman/PhotoEdit, **137**